The Idea Magazine For Teachers®
PRESCHOOL

2002 – 2003
YEARBOOK

Michele Dare de Miranda, Managing Editor, *The Mailbox* Magazine
Kelly Coder, Managing Editor, *The Mailbox* Yearbook

The Education Center, Inc.
Greensboro, North Carolina

The Mailbox® 2002–2003 Preschool Yearbook

MANAGING EDITOR: Michele Dare de Miranda
EDITOR AT LARGE: Diane Badden
COPY EDITORS: Tazmen Carlisle, Karen Brewer Grossman, Amy Kirtley-Hill, Karen L. Mayworth, Kristy Parton, Debbie Shoffner, Cathy Edwards Simrell
ART DEPARTMENT: Pam Crane, Nick Greenwood, Clevell Harris, Rebecca Saunders (SENIOR ARTISTS); Theresa Lewis Goode, Ivy L. Koonce, Sheila Krill, Clint Moore, Greg D. Rieves, Barry Slate, Donna K. Teal
THE MAILBOX® COMPANION.COM: Jennifer Tipton Bennett (DESIGNER/ARTIST); Stuart Smith (PRODUCTION ARTIST); Karen White (INTERNET COORDINATOR); Paul Fleetwood, Xiaoyun Wu (SYSTEMS)
COVER ARTIST: Lois Axeman
FOUNDING EDITOR IN CHIEF: Margaret Michel
PUBLISHER: The Education Center, Inc.
CHAIRMAN, CEO: Stephen Knight Pond
EXECUTIVE DIRECTORS: Katharine P. S. Brower (MAGAZINE PUBLISHING); Joseph C. Bucci (PRESIDENT, THE MAILBOX BOOK COMPANY™); James R. Martin (FINANCE AND OPERATIONS)
CURRICULUM DIRECTOR: Karen P. Shelton
EDITORIAL PLANNING: Kimberley Bruck (MANAGER); Debra Liverman, Sharon Murphy, Susan Walker (TEAM LEADERS)
EDITORIAL AND FREELANCE MANAGEMENT: Karen A. Brudnak; Hope Rodgers (EDITORIAL ASSISTANT)
EDITORIAL PRODUCTION: Lisa K. Pitts (TRAFFIC MANAGER); Lynette Dickerson (TYPE SYSTEMS); Mark Rainey (TYPESETTER)
LIBRARIAN: Dorothy C. McKinney
PREPRESS: Rhonda Ramsey (MANAGER)
MARKETING: Stephen Levy
MARKETING SERVICES: Lori Z. Henry (MANAGER); Vickie Corbett (ASSISTANT MANAGER); Georgia B. Davis, Troy Lawrence, Leslie Miller

ISBN 1-56234-563-X
ISSN 1088-5536

The Education Center, Inc.
P.O. Box 9753
Greensboro, NC 27429-0753

Look for *The Mailbox*® 2003–2004 Preschool Yearbook in the summer of 2004. The Education Center, Inc., is the publisher of *The Mailbox*®, *Teacher's Helper*®, *The Mailbox*® BOOKBAG®, and *Learning*® magazines, as well as other fine products. Look for these wherever quality teacher materials are sold, or call 1-800-714-7991.

Contents

BOOK FEATURES

Bill Martin Jr / Eric Carle

Brown Bear, Brown Bear, What Do You See?

Brown Bear, Brown Bear, What Do You See?

Teacher, teacher, what will you see? You'll see emerging literacy! Open your youngsters' eyes to some growlin' good literature fun with these extensions to Bill Martin Jr.'s book *Brown Bear, Brown Bear, What Do You See?*

ideas contributed by Dena Warner—PreK
Kendall-Whittier Elementary School, Tulsa, OK

Say Cheese!

Before your initial reading, familiarize youngsters with the catchy and predictable chant in the book. Seat students in a circle; then hold up a picture frame without glass or a backing. As you hold the frame to your face, say, "Children, children, guess what I see!" Then use the name of the child sitting beside you and recite the first line of the rhyme shown. Pass the frame to the named child and have her look through it. Recite the second and third lines of the rhyme and repeat the activity in a similar manner. Continue chanting and passing the frame until each child has had a turn. Begin reading the book, and your preschoolers will quickly chime in! *language development, literature experience*

I see [child's name] looking
 at me!
[Child's name], [child's name],
What do you see?

Quack!

Quack!

Brown Bear, Brown Bear, What Do You *Say?*

After the initial reading, your preschoolers will most likely say, "Read it again!" So get youngsters actively involved in a second reading with this idea. Show students each animal in the book and have them imitate the sound the animal makes. Then invite your preschoolers to add animal sound effects during a second reading. For example, encourage youngsters to say, "Quack! Quack!" after you read "I see a yellow duck looking at me." As you read the last two pages of the book, have students make a sound after each animal is mentioned. "We see a brown bear (Grr!), a red bird (Cheep! Cheep!), a yellow duck (Quack! Quack!)...." *listener participation, dramatic expression*

Story in a Sack

What's the best thing about this story-extension idea? It's predictable *and* unpredictable at the same time! Use a photocopier to enlarge the patterns on page 8 for each child. Cut out the patterns and then have the child color them. (For a more personalized activity, also provide each child with a photocopied picture of the class and of you.) Program a paper lunch bag similar to the one shown; then have the child place the patterns in it.

To use the storytelling sack, a child pulls a pattern out of the bag and begins the chant. For example, if he pulls out a green frog, he begins the story by saying, "Green Frog, Green Frog, what do you see?" He removes another pattern from the bag and continues the predictable chanting from the book. The activity continues in this manner until all of the patterns have been used. What's the unpredictable aspect of this activity? You never know which character will show up next! *color identification, story adaptation, language development*

Brown Bear, Brown Bear, What do you see?

Animal Recall

"I see a pair of purple cats looking at me!" That's what your preschoolers might say when you set up a Brown Bear memory game. To prepare, make two photocopies of page 8. Color the patterns. Cut them out and then glue each one onto a tagboard card. Place the cards at your games area and invite students to use them to play the game. For younger students, remove some of the pairs or divide the cards to create two separate memory games. *memory process, visual discrimination, color matching*

What Do You See?

Develop youngsters' eye for art with this idea. Provide each child with a large sheet of white fingerpainting paper. Fold the paper in half and then unfold it to create a crease in the middle. Invite the child to choose a color of liquid tempera paint. Then help her squirt a small amount of paint in the crease. Have the child refold the paper and then press on it to spread the paint. Unfold the paper and encourage the child to dictate what she thinks the paint looks like. Provide her with craft items to use to add features to her creation. Display each child's masterpiece on a bulletin board and then add captions similar to the ones shown. "I see wonderful artwork looking at me!" *creative development*

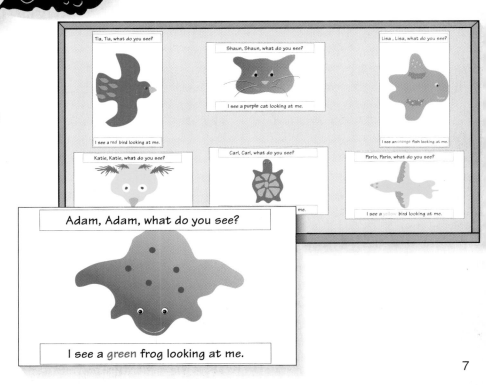

Tia, Tia, what do you see?

I see a red bird looking at me.

Shaun, Shaun, what do you see?

I see a purple cat looking at me.

Lisa, Lisa, what do you see?

I see an orange fish looking at me.

Katie, Katie, what do you see?

Carl, Carl, what do you see?

Paris, Paris, what do you see?

I see a yellow bird looking at me.

Adam, Adam, what do you see?

I see a green frog looking at me.

Patterns
Use with "Story in a Sack" and "Animal Recall" on page 7.

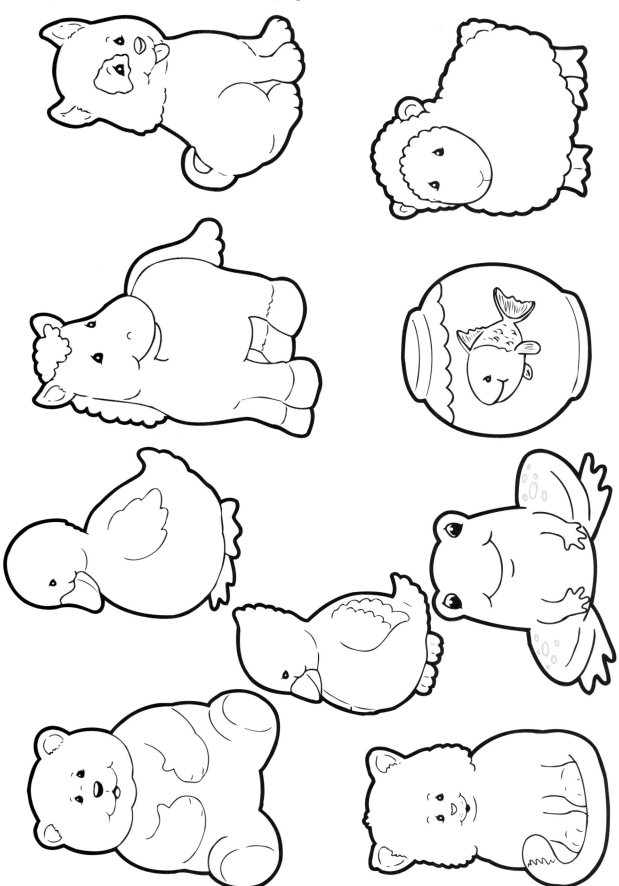

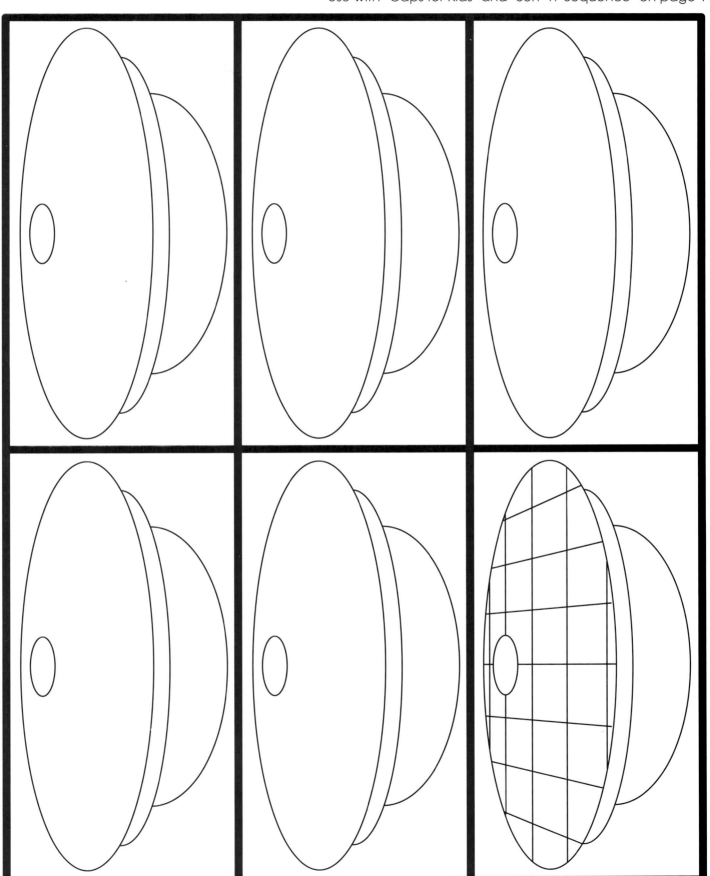

Caps for Sale: A Tale of a Peddler, Some Monkeys and Their Monkey Business

Written and illustrated by Esphyr Slobodkina

Monkey business abounds in this timeless tale of a cap peddler who loses his caps. Share the story with your preschoolers; then invite them to monkey around with these follow-up activities!

by Ada Goren, Winston-Salem, NC

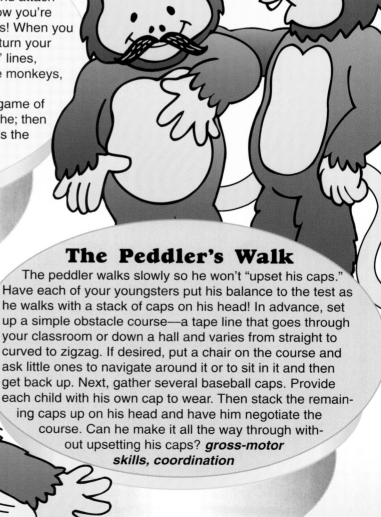

Monkeys See, Monkeys Do

After the initial reading of the story, add some drama to a second reading. Cut a mustache shape from black paper and attach it above your upper lip with a bit of Sticky-Tac adhesive. Now you're set to play the peddler, and your little ones are the monkeys! When you shake your finger at the monkeys and demand that they return your caps, have them imitate your actions and say the monkeys' lines, "Tsz, tsz, tsz!" Have them continue to act out the part of the monkeys, including pretending to throw their caps to the ground.

Afterward, expand on this idea of imitation by playing a game of Follow the Peddler. Provide each child with a paper mustache; then have her take a turn wearing the mustache as she leads the group in various actions. *dramatic play*

The Peddler's Walk

The peddler walks slowly so he won't "upset his caps." Have each of your youngsters put his balance to the test as he walks with a stack of caps on his head! In advance, set up a simple obstacle course—a tape line that goes through your classroom or down a hall and varies from straight to curved to zigzag. If desired, put a chair on the course and ask little ones to navigate around it or to sit in it and then get back up. Next, gather several baseball caps. Provide each child with his own cap to wear. Then stack the remaining caps up on his head and have him negotiate the course. Can he make it all the way through without upsetting his caps? *gross-motor skills, coordination*

Caps for Kids

Make some colorful cap headbands for use in dramatizing the story and as the springboard for a class book featuring students' names and color words. First, enlarge one of the cap patterns on page 9; then duplicate it to make a class supply. Give each child a cap pattern and invite her to color it as she wishes. Then staple the colored cap to the center of a sentence strip. Fit the strip to the child's head and staple the ends together. To make the class book, take a photo of each child wearing her cap headband. Mount the photo on a larger sheet of paper; then print a sentence below it similar to the one shown. Bind the pages together behind a cover that reads "Colorful Caps." Then watch your preschoolers' confidence soar as they "read" each page! *literacy*

Andy has a blue cap.

pam crane

Sort 'n' Sequence

The peddler has his caps grouped by color, and he always carries them in the same order on his head. Encourage your youngsters to sort and sequence the caps just as the peddler does! Copy the caps on page 9 onto gray, brown, blue, and red paper. Also make one copy of the checked cap on white paper. Cut all the caps apart and store them in a zippered plastic bag. Have a child sort the caps by color and then "stack" them (line them up vertically on the tabletop) to match the stack of caps in the book. *classification, matching*

Monkey Munchies

Cap off your story study with snacks that resemble those mischievous monkeys! To make one snack, spread peanut butter on top of a rice cake. (Or use soy-nut butter for students with peanut allergies.) Add a monkey face with two raisin eyes, two miniature chocolate chips for a nose, two halves of a banana slice for ears, and a smile drawn with black gel icing in a tube. Now that's a treat fit for a hungry peddler—or a hungry preschooler! *sensory awareness*

The Jacket I Wear in the Snow

Written by Shirley Neitzel

"This is the jacket I wear in the snow. This is the zipper that's stuck on the jacket I wear in the snow." So begins this catchy tale by Shirley Neitzel. With its repetitive text and cumulative verses, this book will have your preschoolers saying, "Read it again!" So read it again and again! Then use the following activities to bundle up the book with learning opportunities. "This is the jacket I wear in the snow." These are the ideas to use with *The Jacket I Wear in the Snow.*

ideas contributed by Eva Bareis
Cinnamon Hill Preschool, Rapid City, SD

This Is the Jacket I Wear in the Rain

Here's a great way to lead into your first reading of *The Jacket I Wear in the Snow.* In advance, collect a variety of coats and jackets, such as a raincoat, a windbreaker, a jogging-suit jacket, and a ski jacket. During your group time, introduce each jacket to students by naming its use. For example, you might say, "This is the jacket I wear in the rain" or "This is the jacket I wear when I ski." Invite your youngsters to examine the jacket and discuss its use. Repeat the activity in this manner until each jacket has been discussed. Then hold up each jacket in turn. Have students review each jacket by repeating the sentence used to describe it. Then introduce the book *The Jacket I Wear in the Snow.*

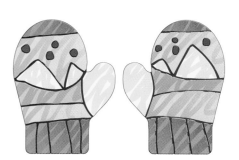

Matching Mittens

Mittens are a favorite article of winter clothing! Revisit the page in the book that shows a large illustration of the mittens. Guide students to notice the matching designs on the mittens. Then provide each child with a pair of mitten cutouts. Have the child paint a design on one mitten and then repeat the design on the other mitten. For younger students, press the second mitten cutout over the painted mitten to create a matching pair.

Clues About Clothes

Get your youngsters thinking with this small-group activity. To prepare, photocopy pages 14 and 15; then color the cards. Laminate them for durability and then cut them out. Set the cards at a center; then invite one or two children to join you. After briefly reviewing the story, identify the different articles of clothing on the cards. Next, give a child a clue about an article of clothing and then have him find the corresponding picture card. For example, you might say, "My neck is cold! What should I wear?" Repeat the activity in this manner until each of the cards has been identified.

Zipper Solutions

What happens to the zipper on the jacket in the story? It gets stuck! After reading the book, ask your preschoolers if they have ever had the zipper stick on their coats. Brainstorm different solutions for a stuck zipper; then invite youngsters to join you in singing the following song.

To sing additional verses, replace the underlined words, in turn, with other student suggestions.

(sung to the tune of "Skip to My Lou")

My little zipper's stuck! What do I do?
My little zipper's stuck! What do I do?
My little zipper's stuck! What do I do?
What do I do, my darlin'?

[Pull, pull, pull] 'til it moves!
[Pull, pull, pull] 'til it moves!
[Pull, pull, pull] 'til it moves!
[Pull] 'til it moves, my darlin'!

Snow-Clothes Mobile

What do your preschoolers wear in the snow? Find out by having each child make a snow-clothes mobile. To prepare, gather a class supply of inexpensive clothes hangers. Next, photocopy the clothing cards on pages 14 and 15 to make a supply; then cut them out. Invite each child to choose four cards that represent the different articles of clothing she likes to wear in the snow. Have her color the cards; then punch a hole in the top of each one. Thread a length of yarn through each hole and tie the cards onto a hanger. Program a strip of construction paper similar to the one shown and tape it onto the hanger. After each child has completed a mobile, invite her to show it to the class and talk about the different clothing items on it. "This is the hat I wear in the snow!"

These Are the Clothes
I Wear in the Snow

Patterns

Use with "Clues About Clothes" and "Snow-Clothes Mobile" on page 13.

Use with "Clues About Clothes" and "Snow-Clothes Mobile" on page 13.

CHICKA CHICKA BOOM BOOM

by Bill Martin Jr. and John Archambault
illustrated by Lois Ehlert

"Skit skat skoodle doot. Flip flop flee. Everybody running to the coconut tree." Why is everyone running to the coconut tree? Find out by reading this catchy alphabet book to your preschoolers. Then use the following story extensions. Your youngsters will be nuts about learning!

ideas contributed by Roxanne LaBell Dearman
Western NC Early Intervention Program for Children Who Are Deaf or Hard of Hearing
Charlotte, NC

CUCKOO FOR COCONUTS

sensory experience, visual discrimination, counting
Sure this story is about the letters of the alphabet. But you'll also find a crop of learning opportunities in the coconuts! Before reading the story, pass around a real coconut for youngsters to explore. Discuss the shape, sound, and texture of the coconut; then read the book aloud. After the reading, revisit each page and have students find and count the coconuts. To nurture thinking skills, ask your preschoolers why more coconuts appear at the beginning of the book before the tree falls over.

HERE COMES MY NAME UP THE COCONUT TREE!

name awareness, letter recognition
Here's a creative way to give your preschoolers practice spelling their names! Provide each child with a coconut-tree trunk and two or three leaves cut from construction paper. Direct him to glue the leaves onto the trunk to create a tree. When the glue is dry, provide a supply of alphabet stickers, rubber stamps, and ink pads. Invite the child to use the materials to spell out his name across the leaves. Glue a photo of the child onto a small coconut cutout; then have him glue the coconut onto his tree. Show off your youngsters and their work by displaying the trees on a bulletin board titled "Chicka Chicka Boom Boom! Look Who's in Our Classroom!"

EVERYBODY RUNNING TO THE COCONUT TREE
letter identification

Want to nurture literacy? Have youngsters climb a pretend coconut tree! Use colored masking tape to outline a large coconut tree shape on a carpeted area of your classroom. Then make two of each letter you wish to reinforce. Invite a small group of students to join you near the tree. Provide each child with one of the letters. Keep a set for yourself to use as calling cards.

To begin the activity, hold up a letter and instruct the child with the matching letter to walk to the top of the coconut tree and stand on a leaf. As the child moves to the top of the tree, have the remaining children say the chant shown. Continue the activity in this manner until each child is standing on the tree. Then say, "Oh, no! Chicka chicka…BOOM! BOOM!" and direct students to fall down gently. When the giggles have subsided, redistribute the cards and get ready to go again!

Here comes [*B*] up the coconut tree!
Chicka chicka boom boom!
Will there be enough room?

WHAT'S THAT SOUND?
letter-sound association

When the entire alphabet falls from the coconut tree, the letters make the sound "BOOM! BOOM!" But what would each letter sound like if it fell from the tree individually? Ask students this question as you begin the following literacy activity. Listen to their responses; then place a felt coconut tree on your flannelboard. Show students a felt letter and discuss its sound. Then move the letter up the coconut tree and invite youngsters to join you in saying the chant shown. After the letter falls off the tree, repeat the activity with a different letter moving up the coconut tree.

Here comes [*B*] up the coconut tree!
Oh, no! Chicka chicka…[B-uh! B-uh!]

CHICKA CHICKA YUM YUM
following directions, measurement

"Chicka chicka yum yum!" That's what youngsters will be saying when they make this simple treat. Help each child measure one cup of vanilla pudding and then place it in a small bowl. Have the child mix one tablespoon of coconuts (Cocoa Puffs cereal) into the pudding. Invite each child to munch on her snack as you read aloud *Chicka Chicka Boom Boom. A* told *B* and *B* told *C,* "This little snack is really tasty!"

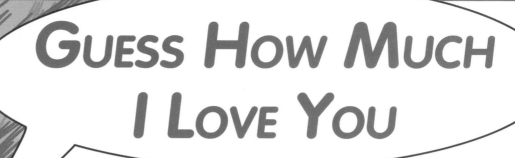

GUESS HOW MUCH I LOVE YOU

by Sam McBratney

Guess how much your preschoolers will love this sweet story of a father rabbit and his son. This much! After sharing the book, use these follow-up activities with your youngsters. They'll be all ears!

ideas contributed by Sue Fleischmann—PreK
Holy Cross School, Menomonee Falls, WI

Lights, Camera, Action!

"Read it again!" That's what your preschoolers will say after the initial reading of the book. After a few readings, your preschoolers will most likely know the book by heart. So offer your youngsters a chance to act it out! Invite one child to play the part of Big Nutbrown Hare and provide him with a rabbit-ear headband. Then invite a second child to use a small stuffed rabbit to play the part of Little Nutbrown Hare. As you read the story, have the two children dramatize it. Repeat the activity daily until each child has had a turn. Then set the props and an audio recording of the book at a center for students to use independently. ***dramatic play, story comprehension***

I Love You to the Moon and Back!

At the end of the story, Big Nutbrown Hare declares to Little Nutbrown Hare, "I love you right up to the moon—and back." What if the two rabbits took a trip to the moon and back? What would each one pack? Have your preschoolers help this father-son team sort the items in their suitcases with this size-discrimination activity. To prepare, gather pairs of big and little items such as the following: child-size and adult-size toothbrushes, child-size and adult-size T-shirts, child-size and adult-size sneakers, and child-size and adult-size jeans. Place the items in a laundry basket; then set the basket near a child-size suitcase and an adult-size suitcase. Invite each child to help the Nutbrown Hares pack by sorting the items by size into the suitcases. All systems are go. Blast off! ***size discrimination, sorting***

Some Bunny Loves You!

This cute card will help your preschoolers tell their parents just how much they are loved! To make a card, photocopy the pattern on page 20. Cut out the card along the bold lines and then fold it on the inside lines. Next, cut out the following shapes from tan construction paper: $3^{1}/_{4}$" x $3^{1}/_{4}$" heart, two $2^{1}/_{2}$-inch-long rabbit ears, $10^{1}/_{4}$" x $1^{1}/_{2}$" strip with rounded ends. Provide a child with the card and construction paper shapes. Direct her to glue the shapes in the middle of the open card as shown. Then have her add sticky dot eyes, crinkle strip whiskers, and a construction paper nose. When the glue is dry, have the child color and sign the card as shown. Refold the card; then fold and tuck the tip of the rabbit's paws inside. Encourage the child to let her love unfold by presenting the card to a special someone!
writing, literacy

Wide, High, and Far

Little Nutbrown Hare loves Big Nutbrown Hare as wide as his arms will stretch, as high as he can hop, and "all the way down the lane as far as the river." How wide, high, and far do your preschoolers love their parents? Find out with this booklet idea! To prepare, draw three identical hearts, each on a separate sheet of white copy paper. Program each of the hearts as shown. Then photocopy the hearts to make a set for each child. Cut out the hearts. Stack each set between two construction paper covers. Staple the pages together and then write "I love you…" on the front cover.

Work one-on-one with a child and ask him who will receive his booklet. Have him dictate a response for each booklet page and then illustrate it. When the booklet is complete, invite the child to sign his name. Write the date on the back of the booklet and parents will have a priceless keepsake! *literacy, thinking skills*

Nutbrown Hare Breadsticks

Your youngsters will agree. These Nutbrown Hare Breadsticks are nuttin' but good! Read through the recipe shown and gather the necessary ingredients and supplies. Have each child make a Nutbrown Hare Breadstick to munch, and she just might say, "I love this 'all the way up to my toes!'" *following directions*

Nutbrown Hare Breadsticks

Ingredients:
refrigerator breadstick for each child
cinnamon-sugar
raisins
tube icing
cinnamon heart candy for each child
shoestring licorice

Utensils and supplies:
cookie sheet
aluminum foil
access to an oven

Provide each child with an unbaked breadstick. Have her fold it as shown. Sprinkle it with cinnamon-sugar and then add two raisin eyes. Bake the breadsticks according to the package directions. Remove them from the oven. When the breadsticks are cool, have the child use dabs of icing to add a cinnamon-heart nose and shoestring-licorice whiskers.

Card Pattern
Use with "Some Bunny Loves You!" on page 19.

Today I heard the story
*Guess How Much
I Love You.*

Guess how much I love *you!*

©The Education Center, Inc.

Bulletin Boards and Displays

BULLETIN BOARDS

Ms. Smedley's Cute Cookies!

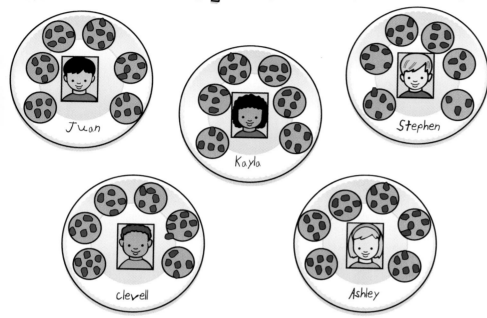

Are your preschoolers just so sweet you could eat them up? Here's a display idea that shows off the cute cookies in your class! Have each child glue brown paper scraps onto tan construction paper circles to create chocolate chip cookie cutouts. Glue a photograph of each child onto a personalized paper plate; then have the child glue her cookies around the photo. Display the plates on a bulletin board with a title similar to the one shown. Say! Those are some cute cookies!

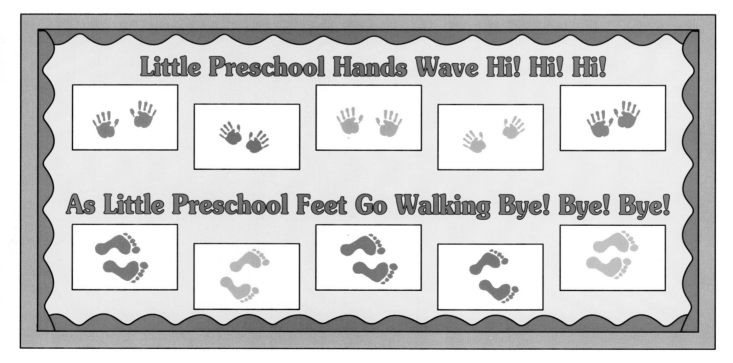

During your self-awareness study, set up this warm and welcoming display in a hallway. Staple students' handprints and footprints on a bulletin board as shown; then add the rhyme shown. As your preschoolers and other visitors pass the display, they won't be able to resist waving and smiling!

Jodi M. Kilburg, Bellevue Elementary School, Bellevue, IA

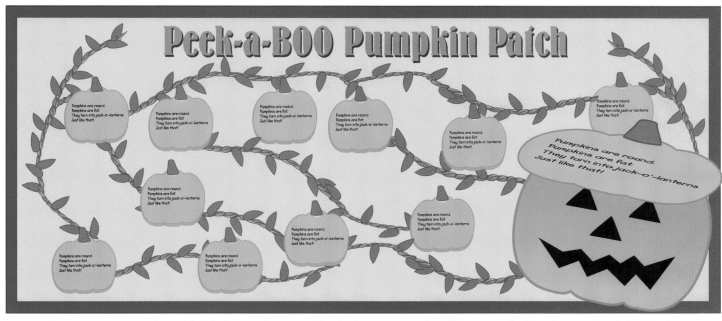

Peek-a-BOO Pumpkin Patch

Carve out some smiles with this interactive pumpkin display. Have each child create a jack-o'-lantern by gluing black construction paper shapes onto a pumpkin cutout. Program another pumpkin cutout as shown; then staple it over the child's jack-o'-lantern. Have the child glue a green construction paper stem onto the top pumpkin. Staple the pumpkins onto a bulletin board so they can be opened. Add twisted tissue paper vines and a title similar to the one shown. Come peek inside this pumpkin patch!

adapted from an idea by Sarah Booth—PreK, Messiah Nursery School, South Williamsport, PA

Here's a turkey that looks too good to eat! To make this display, provide each child with a large poster board feather. Set up a center with a variety of craft items, collage materials, and fingerpaints. Then direct each child to visit the area and decorate his feather as desired. Display the feathers around a large turkey cutout and add a holiday greeting.

Barb Olszewski—Special Education
Elmer Knopf Learning Center
Flint, MI

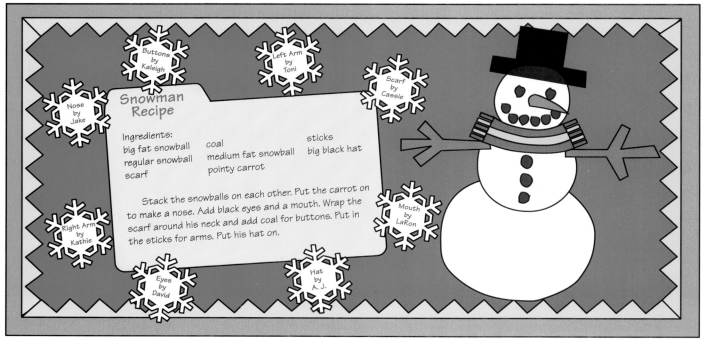

This silly snowman recipe is sure to stir up smiles from passersby! Have your class dictate a step-by-step recipe for a snowman, and write their dictation on a large recipe card shape. Display the recipe card on a wall or bulletin board beside a large snowman that students have created together. If desired, add snowflake cutouts, each programmed with a child's name and the part of the snowman he made. With this display, your class will be creating and cooperating at the same time. Cool!

Celeste Wiederholt, The Blake School, Hopkins, MN

Spread a little holiday cheer with a display that also lets parents in on their child's wish list! Have each child illustrate an item that he would like for Christmas or another upcoming holiday. Fold the paper in half. Tape a sheet of laminated gift wrap to the top half of the folded paper and then add a self-adhesive bow. Have the child dictate a few clues about the item; then write her dictation on a tag cutout similar to the one shown. Tape the tag onto the gift. Display each child's present on a wall or bulletin board in a prominent location for parents. When the holidays are over, untape the child's drawing and gift tag from the laminated gift wrap. Send the drawing home with the child and store the gift wrap to use again next year.

Sarah Booth—PreK
Messiah Nursery School
South Williamsport, PA

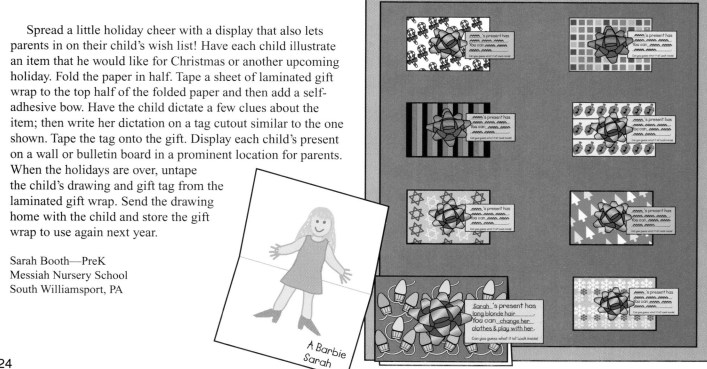

You just might have visions of sugarplums when you set up this display! Photograph each child pretending to be asleep. Cut out the child from the developed photo and glue the cutout onto a tagboard bed shape similar to the ones shown. Glue a piece of fabric over the bed to resemble a quilt. Display each child's bed cutout on a bulletin board titled "The Children Were Nestled All Snug in Their Beds." Right before your youngsters leave for the holidays, take down the display. Place a piece of self-adhesive magnetic tape on the back of each child's photo, and then send it home for parents to display on their fridge.

Nancy Dailey—Four-Year-Olds
Noah's Ark Preschool
Colonie, NY

The Children Were Nestled All Snug in Their Beds

Have a Sugar- and Spice-Filled Holiday!

A little holiday spice makes an oh-so-nice display! Have each child use sequins, glitter glue, and other craft items to decorate a gingerbread cookie cutout. Spread a little glue on the cutout and then sprinkle a little ground ginger onto the glue to add a touch of fragrance. Set the cutout aside to dry. Staple a large cookie jar shape onto a bulletin board. Add the completed cookie cutouts to the display; then title it as shown.

Leah Treen—Four-Year-Olds, Hillwood Baptist Preschool, Huntsville, AL

BULLETIN BOARDS

Do you like to dabble in papier-mâché? If so, this display idea is for you! Follow your favorite papier-mâché recipe to cover a round inflated balloon. When the papier-mâché is complete, paint it in valentine colors. Next, punch four equidistant holes near the bottom of the papier-mâché balloon. Then use a sharpened pencil to poke four equidistant holes under the rim of a Styrofoam cup. Thread lengths of pipe cleaners through the holes in the cup and then attach them to the balloon. Insert a partially straightened paper clip into the balloon to make a hanger. Enlist the help of parents and volunteers to make several of these hot-air balloons. Suspend the balloons from the ceiling of your classroom. Then, every few days, surprise youngsters by filling the baskets with valentine treats for the class to share.

Shannon Martin—Kindergarten
Provena Fortin Villa
Bourbonnais, IL

Give a Western flair to a valentine display with this idea. Make a class supply of the Wanted poster on page 30. Photograph each child wearing a cowboy hat; then glue the developed photo to the middle of the poster. Or use a digital camera and print each child's picture onto a poster as shown. Display the posters on a bulletin board and add the title shown.

Maria Niebruegge—Preschool Special Education, Blue Ridge Elementary, Columbia, MO

I'll Hand You My Heart on Valentine's Day

Samantha · Gregory · Chris · Jackson · Keesha · Suna · Lewis · Breanna · Thomas · Austin · A.J. · Nikita · Maggie · Juanita

There's nothing more precious than a display that has been handmade by preschoolers. Have each child dip her hands into a shallow pan of pink or red paint. Then have her press her hands onto a sheet of manila paper as shown. When the paint is dry, cut around the hands in a heart shape. Use a permanent marker to write the child's name across the heart. Display each child's heart on a wall or bulletin board with the title "I'll Hand You My Heart on Valentine's Day."

Kate Buschur—Preschool, Southern Elementary, Lexington, KY

Whether you're teaching about the circus or March weather, this lion display will be a "mane" attraction! Have each child finger-paint a lion cutout. Or place orange and red drops of paint in the middle of a lion-head cutout. Fold the head in half and rub it gently to create a symmetrical design. Unfold the head and have the child glue it onto a lion-body cutout. Repeat the process with the tip of the lion's tail; then have the child add facial features to the lion. Staple the lions to a bulletin board and add circus cutouts or weather cutouts, depending on your theme.

Sheree Jordan—K4
Rejoice Christian School
Owasso, OK

This jellyfish display will transform your classroom into an underwater wonder! Have each child turn a foam bowl upside down and paint the outside with a blue-tinted glue-and-water mixture. When the glue dries, have the child add construction paper eyes and iridescent cellophane tentacles. Make a hole in the top of the jellyfish. Thread a length of yarn through the hole and tape the lower end to the underside of the bowl. Suspend students' jellyfish from your ceiling; then add construction paper seaweed cutouts.

Stacey Teeple and Shelly Johns
Rainbow Castle Childcare
Carpentersville, IL

If your preschoolers are getting ready to fly off to kindergarten, bid them a fond farewell with this ladybug display. Cut a large potato as shown. Have each child use the potato half to make a red print on a large piece of white bulletin board paper. Then have her use the smaller potato pieces to make wing prints. When the paint is dry, direct the child to make black fingerprint spots and eyes on the ladybug. Label the ladybugs with students' names and then add the title shown.

We're Stepping Out Into Summer!

Anthony

Christy

Anne

Jackson

Celebrate the arrival of summer with this display. Have each child step barefoot into a shallow pan of washable glue. Then hold his hand as he walks across a length of bulletin board paper. At the end of the paper, have a supply of wet paper towels handy to wipe off any excess glue. Next, invite the child to sprinkle colored sand over his footprints; then have him write his name under them. If desired, provide summer-themed rubber stamps and stickers for each child to add to the display. Hang the sandy footprints in the hallway outside your classroom with the title "We're Stepping Out Into Summer!"

Kelly Drews—4K, St. John the Baptist, Plymouth, WI

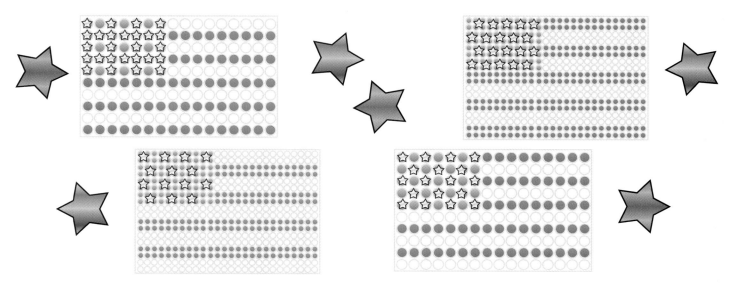

Why will this patriotic display be so "pop-ular"? The flags are made from bubble wrap! To prepare, cut a large rectangular piece of bubble wrap for each child. Next, mix a little liquid dish soap with red and blue fingerpaint (approximately 1 part soap with 3 parts fingerpaint). Have each child fingerpaint red stripes and a blue rectangle on the wrap to resemble an American flag. When the paint is dry, have the child add foil star stickers to the blue rectangle. Use loops of clear packing tape to display the flags in a window. Then add red and blue cellophane stars to complete this translucent display.

Diann Kroos—Preschool, Donald O. Clifton Child Development, Lincoln, NE

WANTED...

...FOR HUGS!

Note to the teacher: Use with the display idea on page 26.

BUSY HANDS

BUSY HANDS

Creative Learning Experiences for Little Hands

SENSORY ART

Stimulate youngsters' creativity and senses with this collection of open-ended art experiences.

ideas by Roxanne LaBell Dearman—Preschool
Western NC Early Intervention Program for Children Who Are Deaf or Hard of Hearing
Charlotte, NC

PA-RUM-PUM-PUM PAINTING

Now, hear this! When it comes to combining art and music, this activity is unbeatable! Prepare your work area by covering a table with newspaper. Next, half-fill a large empty margarine tub with sand to anchor it. Place the lid back on the tub. Have a child don a smock; then provide him with a wooden or metal spoon. Direct the child to dip the back of the spoon into a shallow pan of paint and then use the spoon to tap a drumbeat on the lid. Encourage your little one to repeat the drumming with other colors to create a vivid design on the lid. Carefully place a white construction paper circle on the lid. Rub the paper gently so the paint transfers onto the paper. Remove the circle, flip it over, and admire the design. Shall I paint for you? Pa-rum-pum-pum-pum.

JINGLE, JINGLE, JINGLE

Adding jingle bells to glitter containers will give this traditional art activity a new ring! To prepare, mix approximately 1/3 cup of water with 2/3 cup of white glue. Provide each child with a sheet of white construction paper and a paintbrush. Invite the child to dip the brush in the glue mixture and paint a design on her paper. Then place a tablespoon of glitter in a shaker and add a couple of jingle bells. Have the child shake and jingle the glitter over the glue. Hey! I like the sound of that!

FOILED AGAIN!

Aluminum foil is great for wrapping up leftovers, but did you know it also makes a wonderful sensory art medium? Stock your art center with foil and pieces of Con-Tact paper. Help each child remove the backing from the Con-Tact paper; then have him place it on a table adhesive side up. Invite each child to cut the foil into small pieces and stick them onto the adhesive. For added sensory stimulation and texture, encourage the child to crumple and then uncrumple the foil before adhering it to the paper. Cut out star shapes from the covered Con-Tact paper; then have the child glue the shimmering stars onto a sheet of black construction paper. Heigh-ho, silver!

SENSORY CIRCLES

There's no end to a circle. And there's no end to the creative possibilities with this activity! In advance, cut out a class supply of six-inch circles from clear Con-Tact paper. Also, cut out a supply of smaller circles from textured materials such as corrugated paper, fine sandpaper, and wallpaper samples. Place the circles in a center along with an assortment of textured items, such as cotton balls, plastic Easter grass, and crinkle craft strips. Help each child remove the backing from the Con-Tact paper. Then invite him to place the materials on the adhesive paper to create a textured, circular collage. Use loops of tape to mount the completed collage on a circular construction paper mat. Display the collages at children's level and invite them to gently touch the art.

TEXTURED PLAY DOUGH

Youngsters won't be able to resist squeezing and shaping this stimulating play dough. To begin, follow your favorite play dough recipe and add a little dry rice to the mixture. Knead the rice into the dough; then place the dough in an airtight container. Set the container at your play dough center and invite your preschoolers to make some sense-stimulating sculptures.

SANDY, BUBBLY FINGERPAINTING

What do you get when you combine sand, fingerpaint, and bubble wrap? A super sensory art experience that provides an abundance of stimulation! Mix a small amount of play sand with different colors of fingerpaint. Then invite each child to use the mixture to fingerpaint directly on a sheet of bubble wrap. Be sure to have plenty of bubble wrap and paint on hand. This gritty, bubbly activity is bound to be "pop-ular"!

BUSY HANDS

Creative Learning Experiences for Little Hands

FINE-MOTOR ART

With this collection of creative art experiences, youngsters will use their fine-motor skills to create fine works of art!

CUT AND CREATE

Here's an activity that has youngsters practicing scissor skills and exercising their creativity! To prepare, visit your local home improvement store and collect samples of paint chips in different colors. Set the chips at your art center and have students cut them into individual rectangles. Next, have each child glue his colorful rectangles onto a sheet of black construction paper to create a design. Display each child's creation on a sheet of construction paper that is slightly larger than the black paper, and the effect will be dazzling!

Lisa Page—Preschool
Learning Hutch Preschool
Hutchinson, MN

PLAY DOUGH IMPRESSIONS

A little paint. A little play dough. A little pressing…and presto! Youngsters can make a print! Provide each child with a ball of play dough. Have her roll out the dough and flatten it. Then encourage the child to make impressions with objects such as a plastic fork, small seashells, cookie presses, and bottle caps. Have the child remove the objects from the dough; then help her paint a *thin* layer of tempera paint over it. Place a sheet of paper on the dough and direct the child to gently rub the paper to transfer the paint onto it. Lift the paper, turn it over, and admire the print!

Heather Miller—PreK
Creative Play School
Auburn, IN

ABSTRACT ZEBRAS

What's black and white and ripped all over? An abstract zebra! Provide each child with a large sheet of white construction paper and a sheet of black construction paper. Direct the child to tear the black paper into long strips and then glue them onto the white paper. Have the child add construction paper eyes, ears, legs, and a tail, and the result will be one amazing-looking zebra!

Elena Weiss—PreK, School 21, Yonkers, NY

COLLAGE ON CONTACT

Don't toss out those scraps of colored Con-Tact paper! Save them for this collage idea, which helps develop fine-motor skills. Cut the scraps into pieces small enough to use in a collage. Set the scraps at your art area along with sheets of construction paper. Invite each child to peel the backings off the Con-Tact paper scraps and then stick them onto a sheet of construction paper to make a collage. Little fingers will enjoy peeling the paper, and little minds will enjoy creating the collage!

Cristin Cates—Preschool
Family Child Care, Ft. Gordon, GA

SQUEEZE ME

Dress up your classroom with colorful window clings that have been handmade by your pre-schoolers! Provide each child with a piece of overhead transparency (available at office supply stores). Secure the transparency to your work surface by taping the edges. Provide the child with bottles of colored glue in a variety of colors. (Adding a little dishwashing liquid to each bottle of glue will help the clings adhere to the glass.) Invite the child to squeeze the glue onto the transparency to create a design. (For best results, he should squeeze a thick amount of glue onto the surface.) Untape the transparency and set the child's work aside to dry for at least 24 hours. When the glue is dry, peel it from the transparency and display it in a window.

Taneka Henderson-Batiste—Four-Year-Olds
Lincoln Child Development Center
Redondo Beach, CA

35

BUSY HANDS

Creative Learning Experiences for Little Hands

COOPERATIVE ART

It takes two—or more—to try these art ideas. They're the perfect way to encourage cooperation *and* creativity!

CLASS COLLAGE

Everyone contributes to make this collage! To prepare, cut a large piece of clear Con-Tact paper and tape it sticky side up to your art table or sticky side out on a wall. Gather a large number of lightweight decorative items, such as craft feathers, construction paper scraps, paper doily pieces, bits of ribbon, or colored cellophane shapes. Invite children to stick the items onto the Con-Tact paper as an ongoing art project. Pieces can be peeled off and moved as the children desire.

Cristin Cates—Preschool
Family Child Care, Ft. Gordon, GA

Nancy M. Lotzer—PreK
The Hillcrest Academy, Dallas, TX

FRIENDSHIP PLATES

Colorful plates and plenty of sharing are the results of this group project! To begin, give each youngster a paper plate and a sheet of construction paper. Each child should have her own unique color of paper, so you may want to buy two brands of construction paper to get plenty of variation in shades. Guide each child to tear her paper into the same number of pieces as students in your class. Then have a few children at a time go around the room, each giving one of her paper pieces to each of the other children. When all the paper has been distributed, encourage youngsters to glue the paper pieces to their plates. Display these "friendship plates" to show off the sharing your preschoolers can do!

Mary E. Maurer, Kingston Elementary, Kingston, OK

SHADES OF BLUE (OR RED...OR PURPLE...)

Help youngsters understand variations in color as they cooperate to mix up many shades. First, give each child a square of cardboard and have her paint it with blue tempera paint (or another color of your choice). Next, give each child a small amount of the same paint and set out white and black paint on the table. Invite each child to mix either the white or black paint into her blue to make a new shade. Give out small pieces of cardboard for students to paint with their newly created colors. Next, have students switch colors with a friend and paint another small piece of cardboard with this shade. After all the cardboard has dried, have each student glue her smaller pieces of cardboard to her larger one, creating a unique piece of three-dimensional artwork.

Faustine Davis—Three-Year-Olds
First English Lutheran Preschool and Kindergarten
Baltimore, MD

"HALVE" A HEART

Take heart! This project is just right for Valentine's Day and it teaches cooperation, too! For each child, cut out a large paper heart. Cut each heart in half and ask a child to paint both halves. When the paint is dry, have him give one half to a partner. Tape together the two halves of each newly created heart. It's partner heart art!

PARTNERS ON A ROLL

Put a new twist on an old favorite with this variation of marble painting. Put a piece of paper in the bottom of a large box. Have two partner painters hold two sides of the box; then dip a golf ball into tempera paint and drop it into the box. Have the children tilt the box back and forth to roll the ball and create a design on the paper. Take the painting out and set it aside to dry. Then repeat the procedure with another sheet of paper so that each partner has a cooperative painting to keep.

SOCK SNAKES

This s-s-super art will be easy for your preschool painters! In advance, have each child bring in a plain white tube sock. Pair up children; then have one child in each pair slip a sock onto her arm. Have her partner use a brush to decorate the sock with tempera paints. Pull the painted sock off the child's arm and hang it to dry. Then have the partners switch roles to paint the other child's sock. Add two black marker eyes to each child's sock to transform it into a colorful snake!

Kate Buschur—Preschool
Southern Elementary, Lexington, KY

BUSY HANDS

Creative Learning Experiences for Little Hands

GROSS-MOTOR ART

Make the most of youngsters' gross-motor movements with these action-filled art activities.

by Lucia Kemp Henry

FINGERPAINTING WITH FEET!

This silly twist on fingerpainting has youngsters painting with their feet! To prepare, tape a large piece of bulletin board paper to the floor of your classroom. Place a few spoonfuls of fingerpaint on the paper. Invite a child to remove her shoes and socks and then step into the paint. Hold the child's hand to prevent her from slipping and then invite her to use her feet to paint a design on the paper. Encourage the child to create an intricate design by performing different actions, such as skating, marching, and tiptoeing.

TOSS 'N' PAINT

Does this sponge-toss art activity call for creativity or eye-hand coordination? It's a toss-up! To prepare, cover the floor of your work area with newspaper. Set a large cardboard box in the center of the paper. Place several shallow pans of paint and a supply of sponges a short distance away from the box.

To begin the activity, a child places a sheet of white construction paper inside the box. She dips a damp sponge into a pan of paint and then tosses the sponge into the box. The child retrieves the sponge and continues painting in this manner. When her design is complete, she removes the paper from the box and sets it aside to dry.

HIGH-FIVE DESIGNS

Youngsters will jump at the chance to participate in this moving art activity. Tape a large piece of black bulletin board paper slightly above students' eye level. (For easy cleanup, tape a layer of newspaper under the bulletin board paper.) Next, place a shallow pan of paint and a few child-size knit gloves near the paper. Invite a child to don a glove and then dip his palm and fingers into the paint. Then have him face the paper, jump, and swat the paper with the gloved hand, making a print. Encourage the child to repeat the process a few more times. Then invite a different child to don a glove and try his hand at this active art activity.

CHALK IT UP

Large arm movements will help youngsters chalk up a colorful mural. To prepare, use duct tape to attach pieces of sidewalk chalk to dowel rods. Tape a large piece of black bulletin board paper to the floor or a wall in your classroom. Place the chalk near the paper. Have a child hold the chalk by the rod and use exaggerated arm movements to draw on the paper. When he is finished, untape his artwork. Tape a new sheet of bulletin board paper to the area and invite another child to chalk it up!

ROLLING PIN PAINTINGS

This activity gets youngsters' creativity rolling and gives their little arms a workout! To prepare, use clear packing tape to adhere bubble wrap to a few rolling pins. Next, cover your work table with newspaper; then tape a large piece of painting paper to the table. Place the rolling pins at the table along with several shallow pans of paint. To use the center, a child dips a rolling pin in paint and then rolls it across the painting paper. He repeats this process with different rolling pins and colors of paint to create a design. As the child paints, encourage him to exercise his arm muscles by moving the rolling pin in a variety of directions, such as forward, backward, right, and left.

BUSY HANDS

Creative Learning Experiences
for Little Hands

PLAYGROUND PICASSOS

Who says the playground is only for recess? These process art activities are made for warm summer days, so grab some paint smocks and sunglasses and head outdoors for some fun-in-the-sun art! After each child completes these activities, provide her with a copy of the badge on page 42.

ideas by Danna R. DeMars, St. Charles, MO

CLOTHESLINE CANVAS

It takes a bit of skill to make your mark on this suspended canvas! String a clothesline across an area of your playground. Use clothespins to suspend a long piece of white bulletin board paper from the clothesline. Then give each young artist a paper cup of tempera paint and a brush. Encourage him to touch only his paintbrush to the paper—no hands! Watch as your students experiment with the best way to accomplish this artistic endeavor.

Gina Ashwell—PreK
St. Ann School, Gloucester, MA

MAKE TRACKS DOWN THE SLIDE

Painting with toy cars is always fun, but this variation will drive your preschoolers wild! First, cut a long piece of bulletin board paper to fit on your playground slide, and tape the paper in place. Set a shallow box at the bottom of the slide. Then climb with a child to the top. Have her squirt a bit of liquid tempera paint onto the top of the paper and then dip a small toy car into the paint. Have her send the car on a ride down the slide and watch the tracks it makes as it goes! Try a variety of paint colors and an assortment of cars to make this painting "wheel-y" neat!

Ada Goren
Winston-Salem, NC

BALL PAINTING

Ready…aim…paint! That's the whole idea behind this toss-and-create activity! To prepare, attach a large piece of bulletin board paper to a wall or fence. Pour some liquid tempera paint into trays and provide some light-weight Koosh balls and foam balls. Have a child dip a ball into paint and then toss it onto the paper. Talk about the impressions the different balls make on the paper. When the painting's done, clean up the paint splashes with a few squirts of the hose.

BODY PAINT

Planning a preschool water day when your little ones will be sporting their bathing suits? Consider body painting as one of your activities! Provide large paintbrushes and small cups of washable tempera paint with a bit of dishwashing liquid added to it. Invite your students to paint designs on their arms, legs, and tummies. What fun! And a quick shower under the hose will wash it all away at the end of the day.

CHALK 'N' PAINT

Do your youngsters love sidewalk chalk? Try this variation for added fun! After a child draws a design with the chalk, provide her with a small bucket of water and a large, clean, stiff-bristled paintbrush. Have her paint over her design and watch the colors blend. Or for a slightly different effect, have her wet her fingers and fingerpaint over her chalk design.

Jennifer Gleason—Preschool
Little Explorers, Youngsville, NC

SPRAY AND SQUIRT

Forget the brushes and find the bottles for this painting activity! Fill inexpensive spray bottles and dishwashing-liquid bottles with slightly diluted watercolor or tempera paint. Then clip a large piece of inexpensive white fabric (such as an old bedsheet) or a large piece of bulletin board paper to a fence on your playground. Invite your preschoolers to spray or squirt various shades of paint onto the canvas, observing as the colors blend. Hang the completed canvas in your classroom as a background for a bulletin board—it will be perfect for showcasing little ones' art.

Badge Pattern

Use with "Playground Picassos" on page 40.

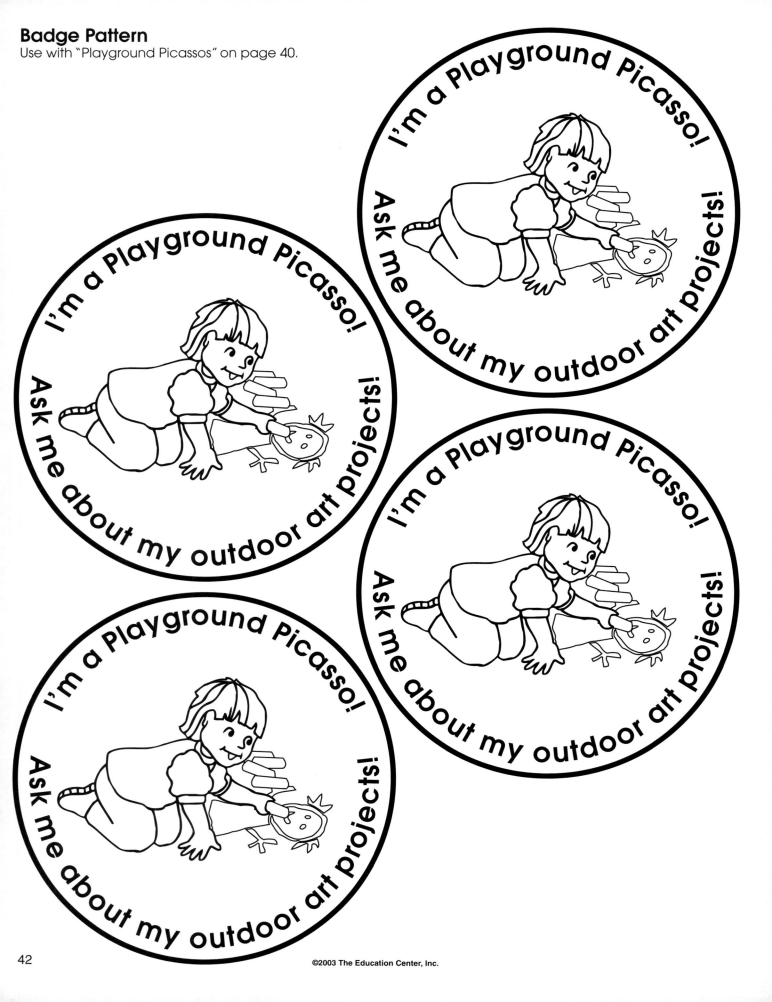

I'm a Playground Picasso!

Ask me about my outdoor art projects!

I'm a Playground Picasso!

Ask me about my outdoor art projects!

I'm a Playground Picasso!

Ask me about my outdoor art projects!

I'm a Playground Picasso!

Ask me about my outdoor art projects!

CENTER UNITS

A TEDDY BEAR BRIGADE!

Ah! There's something comforting about a soft, plush teddy bear. So imagine how comforting your classroom will be when you set up these teddy bear centers! Ready, Teddy? Let's go!

ideas contributed by Sue Fleischmann—Preschool
Holy Cross School, Menomonee Falls, WI

Games Area

Tic-Tac-Toe! Teddies in a Row!

Here's a game idea that tosses in a variety of learning opportunities! In advance, follow the directions in the box to make a supply of teddy bear beanbags. Then use strips of colored masking tape to make a tic-tac-toe grid on a clear shower curtain liner. Tape the liner to the floor and then set the teddy bear beanbags near it. Invite students to play a game of tic-tac-toe by tossing the teddies onto the grid. Or create a color-matching game by cutting out squares of construction paper that match the colors of the beanbags. Tape each square behind a different space in the grid. Invite students to toss the bears onto the matching grid spaces. For added learning fun, program each grid space with a symbol such as a letter or number. Direct each child to toss a teddy onto a space and identify the symbol in it. *taking turns, gross-motor skills, eye-hand coordination*

> **Teddy Bear Beanbags**
> **Materials needed to make one beanbag:**
> 2 felt teddy bear cutouts   dried beans
> hot glue gun   fabric paint
>
> Hot-glue the bear cutouts back-to-back, leaving a small opening in the top. Stuff the bear by pouring dried beans through the opening. Hot-glue the opening closed. Add features to the bear with fabric paint.

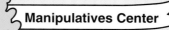
Manipulatives Center

Oh, Buttons!

This center idea can be used as a follow-up to Don Freeman's book *Corduroy* or as a simple stand-alone idea. To prepare, use the patterns on page 49 to create tagboard tracers. Then use the tracers to make a supply of craft foam bears and overalls. Hot-glue a pair of overalls onto each bear. Gather a pair of large craft buttons for each bear. Hot-glue one button from each pair onto a different bear. Place the remaining buttons in a container. Set the bears and buttons at a center. Then invite your preschoolers to match each button by placing it on the corresponding bear's overalls. *color matching, visual discrimination, fine-motor skills*

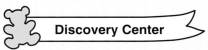
How Many Teddies Tall Am I?

Set up this center and exploring height will be a delight! To prepare, attach a long self-adhesive Velcro strip (loop side) to a wall. Next, use the pattern on page 49 to create a supply of colorful teddy bear cutouts. Laminate the bears and then place a hook-side Velcro strip on the back of each one. Set the bears near the strip of Velcro strip. Invite pairs of children to the area. Direct one child to stand with his back against the wall beside the Velcro strip. Then have the other child measure him by attaching the teddy bears to the strip. Invite the students to count the number of teddy bears to determine the child's height. Have youngsters remove the bears and then repeat the activity with the second child. If desired, record each child's height on a nearby chart or graph. *counting, measurement, graphing*

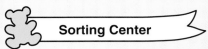
Sorting Center

Bears and Berries

Did you know that bears love to eat berries? Invite your preschoolers to play the part of a hungry bear with this sorting activity. To set up, place a container of large red and blue pom-poms in the area; then add a pair of brown "bear claws" (mittens). Invite each child to don the claws and then sort the pom-pom berries by color. *fine-motor skills, sorting*

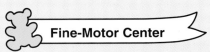
Fine-Motor Center

Feeling Punchy

Let your little cubs go to town with an activity that packs a punch! In advance, collect an assortment of bear-shaped hole punchers. Place the hole punchers near a supply of materials such as tissue paper, construction paper, craft foam, and wrapping paper scraps. Invite students to use the hole punchers to make a variety of teddy bear shapes. Collect the shapes in a box and then hide them in your sand table. (See "Bear Treasure" on page 46.) *fine-motor skills*

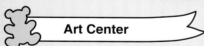
Bear Treasure

With this sand table idea, youngsters won't find buried treasures, they'll find *bear* treasures! In advance, collect a variety of teddy bear–shaped hole punchers; then punch out a supply of bears. (Or use the bears from "Feeling Punchy" on page 45.) Hide the bears in your sand table; then have youngsters sift through the sand to find them. *visual and sensory stimulation, fine-motor skills*

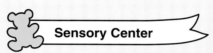

Sensory Center

In a Jam

Here's a simple sensory game that will quiet your little cubs. To prepare, place a few spoonfuls of jam in a resealable sandwich bag. Add two blue bear counters and two red ones to the middle of the bag. Then seal the bag with clear packing tape. To play the game, a child squeezes the bag and moves the bears through the jam until the red bears are on one side of the bag and the blue bears are on the other side. *fine-motor skills, sensory stimulation*

Art Center

What Is Brown?

Creating a bear at this center is not only fun, it's also a study of the color brown! To prepare, gather a supply of paper (or paint chips) in different shades of brown. Cut the paper into small pieces; then set them at the center. Provide each child with a piece of clear Con-Tact paper, adhesive side up. Have the child stick two construction paper eyes and a nose near the top of the paper. Then invite the child to cover the adhesive paper with pieces of brown paper. When the child is finished, cut another piece of clear Con-Tact paper; then place it on the collage, adhesive side down. Trace a large bear shape onto the Con-Tact paper and then cut on the resulting outline to create a teddy bear. What a work of art! *creativity, color exploration*

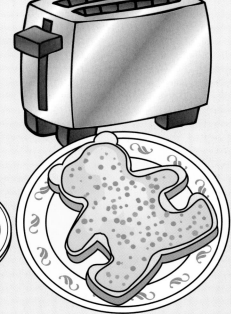
Tea for Me and Teddy

Here's a dramatic-play idea that will have your tots sipping and socializing with some plush pals. Place a child's tea set in the area; then add other items, such as dress-up clothes, costume jewelry, plates with play cookies, and an assortment of teddy bears. Invite your youngsters to dress the bears and themselves in the clothing and then throw a teddy bear tea party. There will be a lot of learning brewing at this party! *dramatic play, language development*

Snack Center

Teddy Bear Toast

Why does a teddy bear love this toast recipe so much? There's honey in the butter! In advance, make a batch of honey butter by mixing equal portions of whipped butter and honey. Place the honey butter at a supervised center with a toaster. Have each child use a bear-shaped cookie cutter to cut a slice of bread. Toast the bread. Help the child spread the butter onto the toast and then sprinkle it with cinnamon-sugar. Mmm! No wonder this is Teddy's favorite type of toast! *fine-motor skills, following directions*

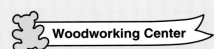

Woodworking Center

Tee Time

To set up this center, use a photocopier to enlarge the teddy bear pattern on page 49. Cut out the pattern and place it on a piece of Styrofoam. Then use a permanent marker to trace around the pattern. Place the piece of Styrofoam in the center; then place a rubber mallet and a supply of golf tees nearby. Invite each child to use the mallet to hammer the tees into the teddy bear outline. *eye-hand coordination, fine-motor skills*

Bears Afloat

Make a splash at your water table by adding colorful floating teddy bear shapes. In advance, use bear-shaped hole punchers to make a supply of craft foam teddy bear cutouts. Add the cutouts to your water table. Then invite your preschoolers to use strainers, soup ladles, and clean fishnets to catch the floating teddies. Provide plastic containers and encourage youngsters to sort the bears by color or by size. *color and size discrimination, sorting, fine-motor skills*

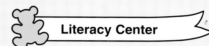 **Literacy Center**

B Is for Bear

Set up this literacy center and little ones will quickly learn that *bear* begins with B. In advance, die-cut a class supply of *B*s from construction paper or wallpaper samples. Set the *B*s at the center. Have each child choose a *B* and then use a teddy bear hole puncher to punch bear shapes in the letter. Collect the punched-out bears in a container. After each child has visited the center, place a class supply of construction paper *B*s in the area. Add a few glue sticks; then invite each child to decorate a *B* with the punched-out bears. *letter recognition, letter-sound association, fine-motor skills*

 **Play Dough Center**

Build a Bear

What will your youngsters do at this play dough center? Make customized play dough teddy bears! To prepare, stock your play dough area with bear-shaped cookie cutters and craft items, such as rickrack, pom-poms, large buttons, sequins, and beads. Have each child use the cookie cutters to make play dough teddy bears. Then invite the child to decorate the bears using different craft items. *creativity, fine-motor skills*

Teddy Bear Pattern

Use with "Oh, Buttons!" on page 44, "How Many Teddies Tall Am I?" on page 45, and "Tee Time" on page 47.

Overall Pattern

Use with "Oh, Buttons!" on page 44.

At the Firehouse

Your classroom will be ablaze with activity when you set
up these red-hot firehouse centers!

ideas contributed by Roxanne LaBell Dearman—PreK
Western NC Early Intervention Program for Children Who Are Deaf or Hard of Hearing, Charlotte, NC

Math Center

Lots and Lots of Dalmatian Dots

What animals can be found helping out at the
firehouse? Dalmatians! Use these dotty dogs to help
reinforce number recognition and counting skills. To
prepare, make two or three copies of the dog pattern
on page 54. Laminate them for durability and then cut
out each one. Set the patterns at the center along with
a supply of small black pom-poms and a numbered
die.

To use the center, a child rolls the die and identifies
the number rolled. She places that many pom-poms
on the dalmatian and then repeats the activity with the
other dalmatian patterns. If desired, reinforce early
addition skills by encouraging the child to count the
total number of pom-poms placed on the dalmatians.

Gross-Motor Area

Up and Down the Ladder

Here's a gross-motor idea that will have
your little firefighters on the move! To prepare,
use strips of masking tape to make a ladder
outline on the floor of your classroom. Place a
pile of stuffed animals at the top of the ladder.
Then encourage each child to walk up the ladder, placing one foot after the other on each
consecutive rung. When he reaches the top of
the ladder, have him choose an animal and
then walk backward down the ladder with it.
Encourage the child to continue the activity
until all the animals have been brought to
safety. Preschool firefighters to the rescue!

Hoses, Ladders, and Tires!

These fire truck cutouts need equipment! And your youngsters can make just the thing at your play dough center. First, photocopy the pattern on page 55 to make a supply of fire truck cutouts. Color the trucks. Laminate them and then cut out each one. Set the trucks in the center. Have youngsters make play dough hoses, ladders, and tires and then place them on the fire truck cutouts. Now these fire trucks are ready to respond!

Literacy Center

Tag—You're It!

Reinforce letter-sound association with this sensory idea, and youngsters will yip with delight. In advance, cut out magazine pictures of items beginning with letters you wish to reinforce. Enlarge the dog pattern on page 54; then use the enlarged pattern to make a dalmatian cutout for each magazine picture. Glue a firehat cutout onto each dog; then glue a magazine picture onto each hat. Draw spots and a collar on each dog. Then laminate the dalmatians for durability.

Next, make a dog tag for each dalmatian and program the tag with the appropriate letter. For added sensory stimulation, make the dog tags from a variety of textured materials, such as craft foam, felt, corrugated cardboard, and fine sandpaper. Then use squeezable fabric paint to program the tags with letters. Place the tags in a container and set the container near the dalmatians. Have each child match the tags with the pups according to letter-sound association. *D* is for dalmatian!

Fine-Motor Center
Ladder Up!

Offer your little firefighters the opportunity to build ladders as they build up their motor skills! To prepare, use a photocopier to make reduced and enlarged copies of the fire truck pattern on page 55. Color the trucks, laminate them, and then cut out each one. Next, cut heavy cardboard into strips to make ladder rails and rungs for each truck. Place the trucks and strips at the center. Then invite each child to use the strips to make an appropriately sized ladder for each truck. For added math reinforcement, encourage youngsters to estimate the number of rungs that will fit on each ladder and then count the results.

Flannelboard Center
The Wheels on the Fire Truck

If the wheels on the bus go round and round, what do the wheels on the fire truck do? They go fast, fast, fast! Teach youngsters the following fire truck song; then set up a flannelboard center that will encourage them to sing, sing, sing! To prepare, use the firefighter patterns on page 54 to make flannelboard cutouts. Then cut out the following shapes from felt: truck, siren, hose, ladder, and wheels. Set the pieces near your flannelboard. To use the center, a child places the fire truck on the board and then adds the remaining shapes to the truck as she sings the song.

(sung to the tune of "The Wheels on the Bus")

The wheels on the truck go fast, fast, fast!
Fast, fast, fast! Fast, fast, fast!
The wheels on the truck go fast, fast, fast
When there's a fire!

The siren on the truck goes woo, woo, woo!
Woo, woo, woo! Woo, woo, woo!
The siren on the truck goes woo, woo, woo
When there's a fire!

The hose on the truck goes squirt, squirt, squirt!
Squirt, squirt, squirt! Squirt, squirt, squirt!
The hose on the truck goes squirt, squirt, squirt
When there's a fire!

The ladder on the truck goes up and down!
Up and down! Up and down!
The ladder on the truck goes up and down
When there's a fire!

The firefighters help to put the fire out!
Put the fire out! Put the fire out!
The firefighters help to put the fire out!
Thank you, firefighters!

Water Table
Ready, Aim, Squirt!

Imagine aiming a 50-pound fire hose at a fire! That takes practice! Your youngsters might not have a 50-pound hose at this center, but they will have plenty of aiming practice! Cut out several craft foam flame shapes and place them in your water table. Then place several squirt bottles or liquid dish detergent bottles at the table. Direct your youngsters to fill the bottles with water and then use them to squirt the flames. Bull's-eye!

Putting Out Fires

Here's a prewriting idea that will have your preschoolers fired up about literacy! To begin, use a permanent marker to draw a simple house shape on a sheet of overhead transparency. Place the transparency at your writing center. Also place a cotton sock and yellow, orange, and red dry-erase markers in the area. Invite each child to use the markers to draw flames on the house. Then have her "put out" the fire by using the sock (fire hose) to erase the flames. Good work, little firefighters!

Art Center

Designing Dalmatians

Dalmatian dogs are famous for their spots. But did you know that dalmatian puppies are born all white? After sharing this information with your preschoolers, invite each child to design the dots on a dalmatian pup cutout. Photocopy the dog pattern on page 54 for each child. Then provide the child with an unsharpened pencil with an eraser. Have the child dip the eraser in an ink pad and then make spots on her pup. How dotty!

Snack Center

Bowwow Chow

After designing dalmatians, invite your preschoolers to make some pretend puppy food for their pooches. Set a large plastic dish at a center. Then fill each of three serving bowls with one of the following ingredients: Kellogg's Cracklin' Oat Bran cereal, miniature marshmallows, and chocolate chips. Invite each child to use a $\frac{1}{4}$-cup measuring cup to scoop each ingredient into the dish. Have the child use a large spoon to stir the mixture; then help him spoon it onto a paper plate or into a bowl. Encourage the child to serve the snack first to his fire dog friend and then eat any of the pup's leftovers. There's no need for a doggie bag at this snack center!

Dog Pattern

Use with "Lots and Lots of Dalmatian Dots" on page 50, "Tag—You're It!" on page 51, and "Designing Dalmatians" on page 53.

Firefighter Patterns

Use with "The Wheels on the Fire Truck" on page 52.

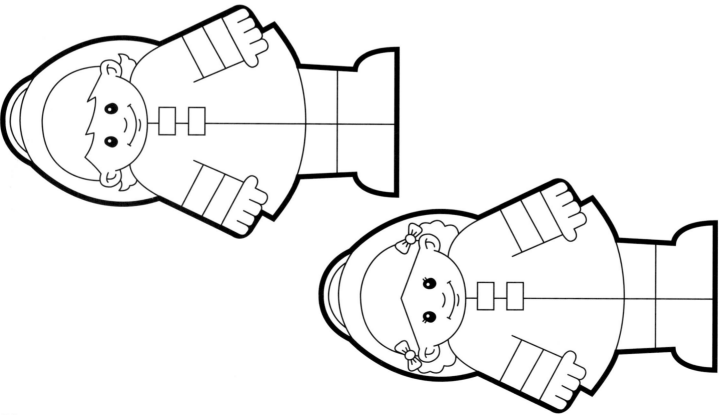

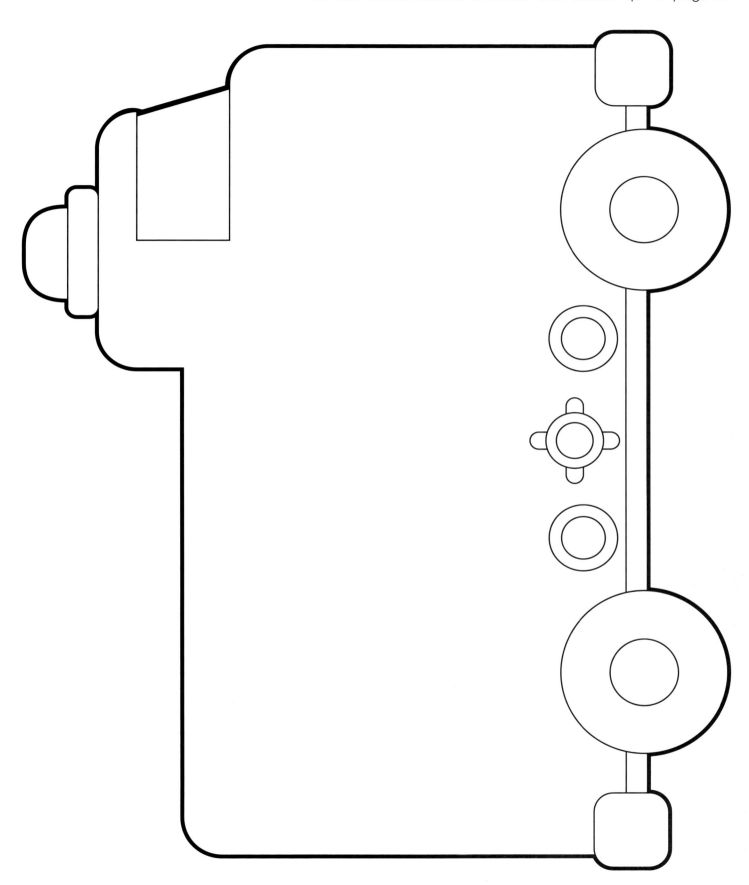

A Room Full of Penguins

Or, actually, a room full of penguin *centers!* Introduce your preschoolers to penguins; then try these ideas for your classroom centers to help youngsters learn more about these cool critters!

by Ada Goren

Reading Center

Welcome to the South Pole!

Simulate a South Pole environment in your reading area by covering the floor and furniture with old white sheets. Provide a basket of mittens for youngsters to wear while they read. Then put in a few stuffed penguins for company! Stock the book baskets or shelves with penguin stories such as these:

Little Penguin's Tale
By Audrey Wood

Tacky the Penguin
By Helen Lester
Illustrated by Lynn Munsinger

Splash! A Penguin Counting Book
By Jonathan Chester and Kirsty Melville

Puffins Climb, Penguins Rhyme
By Bruce McMillan

The Emperor's Egg
By Martin Jenkins
Illustrated by Jane Chapman

Plenty of Penguins
By Sonia W. Black
Illustrated by Turi MacCombie

Penguins and Preschoolers

What do an emperor penguin and a preschooler have in common? They're about the same size! Male emperors grow to about four feet tall, and the females are a little smaller. Make a life-size penguin cutout for your block area that will help youngsters compare themselves to penguins. Spread out a long length of black bulletin board paper on the floor. Ask a child to lie down on the paper. Using the size of the child as a guide, draw a penguin shape (as shown) on the paper. After the child stands up, cut out the shape. Then add paper features to make the cutout resemble a penguin. Display the penguin on a wall in your block area so its feet touch the floor. Invite a student to build a block tower to match the penguin's height. Then have him compare himself to the tower. Is he taller, shorter, or the same height?

Puzzle Area

A Kid-Sized Penguin Puzzle

This floor puzzle is as fun to make as it is to assemble! To make a life-size penguin cutout, follow the directions in "Penguins and Preschoolers" (above). Then cut the completed penguin into several puzzle pieces. Be sure to laminate the pieces for durability because your little ones will want to put this penguin puzzle together again and again!

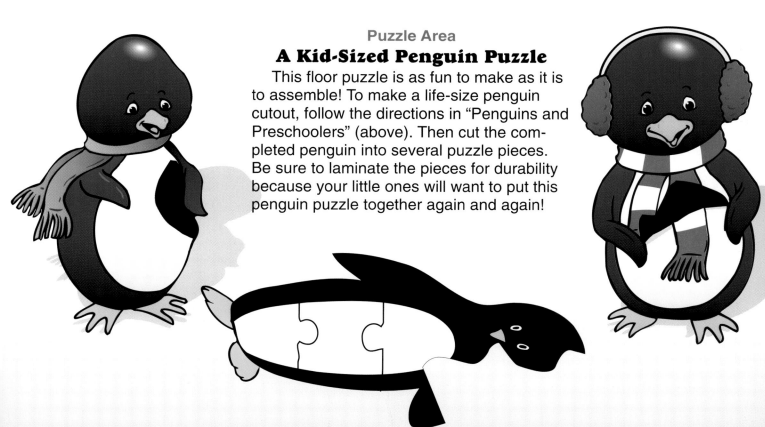

Ice Fishing

Penguins dive into icy waters in search of fish, squid, and krill (tiny shrimplike creatures) to eat. Invite your preschool penguins to visit your sensory table on a hunt for fish hidden below a layer of packing peanut "ice." To prepare, cut or die-cut a number of fish from light-colored craft foam. (For a challenge, cut the fish from *white* craft foam.) Lay the fish in the bottom of your sensory table; then pour on a layer of white packing peanuts. Give each child at the center a pair of small plastic tongs and invite him to use this "bill" to grab the fish hiding below the ice. If desired, tell youngsters how many fish are hidden and ask them to count their catch until they've found them all.

Snack Center
Penguin Food

After catching faux fish at your sensory table, little ones will be delighted to make this edible penguin treat! Put out bowls of pretzel Goldfish crackers, cheddar Goldfish crackers, and sunflower seed kernels (to represent tiny krill). Write out measurement cards (as shown), and have each youngster measure the appropriate amount of each snack food into a plastic sandwich bag. When she has all three ingredients in her bag, she can enjoy her snack of Penguin Food!

Science Center
A Simple "Eggs-periment"

Explain to your youngsters that after a mother emperor penguin lays an egg, the father penguin holds it on his feet, under a warm flap of skin. Then the mother penguin goes to the sea to eat and bring back food for the chick that will hatch from the egg. Father penguins hold the egg on their feet for about two months!

Invite your preschoolers to play the part of daddy penguins at your science center. Place a large plastic Easter egg or a Styrofoam egg, as well as a simple minute timer, at the center. Have a child place the egg on his feet and then set the timer for one minute. How does it feel to stand still for one minute and keep the egg from falling off his feet? Imagine holding the egg day and night for two months!

Art Center
A Penguin Portrait

Work one-on-one with your youngsters in your art center to create these personalized penguin pictures! To make one, use white tempera paint to paint an arch shape on the sole of a child's foot. Then paint the remainder of her foot (excluding the toes) with black paint. Ask her to step down onto a half sheet of yellow construction paper. Have her lift her foot straight up, and have an old towel ready to wipe off the paint. Next, paint the side of her hand—from the wrist to the tip of the little finger—with black paint, and have her press this onto the footprint, creating a flipper for the penguin body (as shown). Repeat this procedure to make another flipper. Next, paint her pinkie fingertip orange and have her press six penguin toes onto the base of the penguin body. Then repaint her pinkie fingertip with white paint and have her add two dot eyes to the penguin's face. Finish the face by adding pupils with a black marker and gluing on an orange construction paper or craft foam beak. Now your printed penguin is perfect!

Math Center
Penguins on Ice

Brrr! Things will look mighty chilly in your math center when you add some imaginary icebergs to the area! Cut five chunks of Styrofoam packing material; then label each piece with a number from 1 to 5. Next, duplicate the penguin manipulatives on page 61 onto tagboard. Cut them out; then laminate them for durability. To use this center, a child identifies the numeral on each iceberg and then counts out a corresponding number of penguins to place on it.

59

South Pole Scenery

Put some sparkling white play dough in your play dough center and invite little ones to create South Pole scenery for some penguin friends! Prepare a batch of Sparkling Snow Dough (see the recipe). Then duplicate the penguin manipulatives on page 61. Cut the manipulatives apart and laminate them for durability. Invite children at this center to shape the snow dough into hills, valleys, and icebergs for the penguins to stand on. If desired, extend the activity by sending each child home with a ball of play dough and a few laminated manipulatives. Now Mom and Dad can have some fun at the South Pole too!

Sparkling Snow Dough
2 c. water
2 c. flour
1 c. salt
4 tsp. cream of tartar
4 tsp. oil
iridescent glitter

Combine all ingredients in a heavy saucepan. Cook over medium heat, stirring constantly with a wooden spoon, until mixture thickens and pulls away from the sides of the pan. Form the dough into a ball, place on waxed paper, and allow to cool before kneading in a desired amount of iridescent glitter.

Pink and Purple Penguins

Reinforce the shape and sound of the letter *P* with this fun color-cut-and-paste activity. To prepare, outline a large letter *P* on a sheet of copy paper for each child. Then duplicate page 61 to make a class supply. Add the letter outlines and penguin papers to your literacy center, along with a supply of pink and purple crayons. Have each child at the center color a sheet of penguins with pink and purple crayons. Emphasize that he is using these two colors because their names begin with the /p/ sound, just like the word *penguin*. Have him cut out his penguins and then glue them onto a letter *P* outline. There you have it—*p*ink and *p*urple *p*aper *p*enguins on a *P*!

Penguin Manipulatives

Use with "Penguins on Ice" on page 59 and "South Pole Scenery" and "*Pink and Purple Penguins*" on page 60.

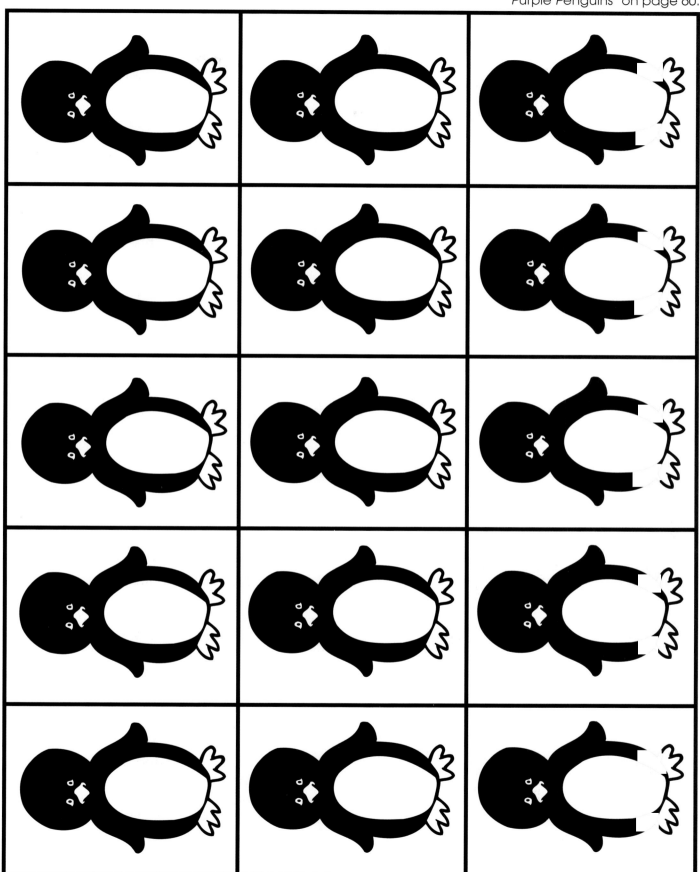

Totally Teeth!

February is National Children's Dental Health Month. What better time to talk about teeth with your youngsters? The following centers not only help reinforce basic preschool skills, but also introduce students to tooth topics, such as losing baby teeth, the importance of flossing, and recommended brushing techniques. So set up these centers and smile! It's time for a denture adventure!

ideas contributed by Roxanne LaBell Dearman
Western NC Early Intervention Program for Children Who Are Deaf or Hard of Hearing
Charlotte, NC

Math Center

Tooth on the Loose!

Do your preschoolers know that their baby teeth will eventually fall out? After explaining this phenomenon to your youngsters, set up this math center that introduces early subtraction concepts. To prepare, cut out a few mouth-shaped mats from red construction paper. Glue a pink tongue cutout onto each mat; then make Unifix cube outlines around the mat as shown. Set the mouths at a center along with a die and a supply of white Unifix cubes (teeth).

Send a small group of children to the center and have each one choose a mat. Then have each child place a cube on each outline on his mat. To play the game, the first player rolls the die, reads the number rolled, and then removes that many teeth from the mat. The game continues in this manner until each child has removed all of the teeth from his mat. The tooth fairy will be working overtime with this game!

Blocks Area

Smiles Under Construction

You'll see big smiles when you set up this visual-discrimination activity in your blocks area. In advance, cut out a large mouth shape from red bulletin board paper. Next, trace rectangular blocks and square blocks on the mouth to create teeth outlines. Glue on a pink tongue cutout; then laminate the mouth for durability. Tape the mouth-shaped mat to the floor of your blocks area; then invite each child to add teeth to the mat by placing matching blocks on the outlines.

Flossing Is Fun!

This flossing activity helps preschoolers brush up on their dental hygiene knowledge and develops fine-motor skills. Make a model of teeth with plaque by pushing bits of play dough (plaque) in between the pegs (teeth) on large interlocking building blocks. Set the blocks at a center; then add a supply of inexpensive dental floss. Explain to students the importance of flossing; then show them the model of teeth with plaque. Invite each child to visit the area and use the floss to remove the plaque. When the child is finished flossing, direct her to place play dough back on the blocks for the next little flosser to use.

Ann Rappelt—Preschool, St. Benedict Preschool Chicago, IL

Science Center

A Mouth Model

You'll need to make a set of tooth-shaped sponges for this center, but the results will have your students saying, "Ahh!" To make the sponges, photocopy the molar, canine, and incisor patterns on page 66. Cut them out and then trace each one onto a craft sponge. Cut out the shapes from the sponge; then hot-glue an empty film canister onto each sponge to create a handle. Place the sponges at the center. Then add a shallow pan of white paint, a supply of mouth and tongue cutouts, and a small mirror. Use the supplies to make a mouth model similar to the one shown. Display the completed model at the center.

Invite one or two children to the area. As you identify the different types of teeth, have the students examine their own teeth with a small mirror. Next, help each child, in turn, make the mouth model similar to the one on display. If desired, label each child's model with the names of the teeth. Encourage students to take their models home and share their tooth knowledge with their families. Incisors, canines, and molars—that's a mouthful!

adapted from an idea by Patricia Lewis—PreK, S.A.I.S. Jeddah, Saudi Arabia

Bristly Brushes

Stimulate little ones' sense of touch with this activity. In advance, ask parents for donations of new toothbrushes—some with soft bristles and some with hard. Set the toothbrushes in your sensory area. Then invite students to touch the brushes and feel the differences in textures. For added learning fun, place two plastic toothbrush holders in the area. Label one "soft" and the other one "hard." Direct youngsters to sort the brushes into the appropriate holders.

soft **hard**

Tooth Fairy Concentration

After stories and talks about the Tooth Fairy, your youngsters are sure to enjoy a game based on her nightly searches for lost teeth! To make the game, program pairs of tooth cutouts with matching letters, numbers, or shapes. Glue each tooth onto the back of a pillow cutout. Place the cutouts in the center and invite pairs of students to play a game of Concentration. Want to also sneak in some coin recognition? Photocopy pairs of the coin patterns on page 66. Glue each one onto a separate cutout and then add it to the deck. When a child flips over the cutout, she'll see that the Tooth Fairy has taken the tooth and left a coin!

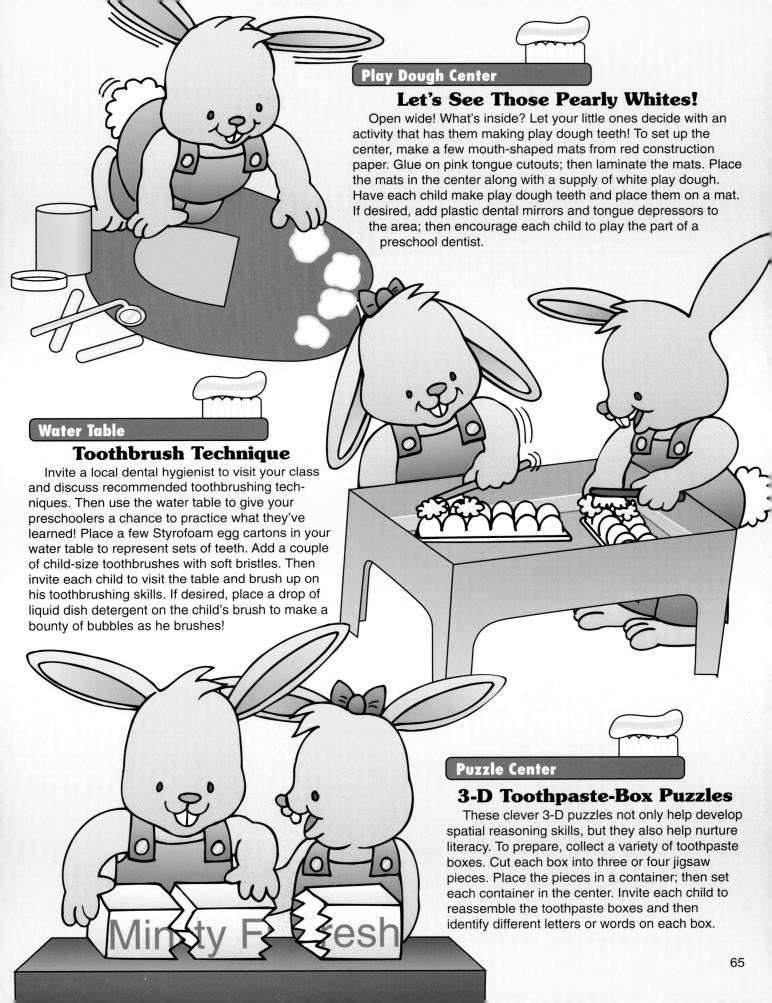

Let's See Those Pearly Whites!

Open wide! What's inside? Let your little ones decide with an activity that has them making play dough teeth! To set up the center, make a few mouth-shaped mats from red construction paper. Glue on pink tongue cutouts; then laminate the mats. Place the mats in the center along with a supply of white play dough. Have each child make play dough teeth and place them on a mat. If desired, add plastic dental mirrors and tongue depressors to the area; then encourage each child to play the part of a preschool dentist.

Water Table

Toothbrush Technique

Invite a local dental hygienist to visit your class and discuss recommended toothbrushing techniques. Then use the water table to give your preschoolers a chance to practice what they've learned! Place a few Styrofoam egg cartons in your water table to represent sets of teeth. Add a couple of child-size toothbrushes with soft bristles. Then invite each child to visit the table and brush up on his toothbrushing skills. If desired, place a drop of liquid dish detergent on the child's brush to make a bounty of bubbles as he brushes!

Puzzle Center

3-D Toothpaste-Box Puzzles

These clever 3-D puzzles not only help develop spatial reasoning skills, but they also help nurture literacy. To prepare, collect a variety of toothpaste boxes. Cut each box into three or four jigsaw pieces. Place the pieces in a container; then set each container in the center. Invite each child to reassemble the toothpaste boxes and then identify different letters or words on each box.

Teeth Patterns

Use with "A Mouth Model" on page 63.

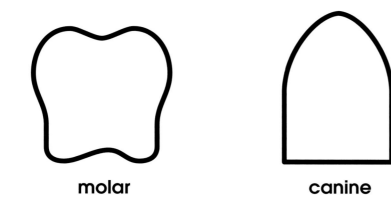

molar

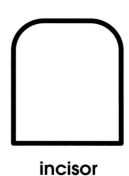

canine

incisor

Coin Patterns

Use with "Tooth Fairy Concentration" on page 64.

Creepy-Crawly Critter Centers

What's all the buzz about? These bug-themed centers! Use this collection of creepy-crawly critter ideas and your youngsters will be going buggy!

ideas contributed by Sue Fleischmann
Child and Family Specialist
Waukesha County Project Head Start, Waukesha, WI

How many ants balance the scale?

Math Center
weight measurement, counting, recording information

How Much Does a Picnic Weigh?

Believe it or not, ants are welcome at this pretend picnic! Set up a balance scale in your math area. Fill a picnic basket with toy food; then set the basket near the scale. Add a supply of plastic ant counters to the area. To use the center, a child places an item from the picnic basket onto the scale. Then she places ants on the opposite side of the scale until it is balanced. For more learning fun, make a supply of recording sheets similar to the one shown. Set the sheets near the scale and have students write the number of ants needed to balance each food item. The ants are weighing one by one! Hurrah, hurrah!

firefly
fly
ant

bee

Literacy Center
letter matching, comparing lengths, print awareness

B Is for Bee

Your little ones will swarm around this literacy center, which reinforces a variety of skills! In advance, photocopy the insect patterns on page 72. Color the patterns and then cut out each one. Glue each pattern to the left end of a sentence strip. Write the name of the insect on the strip; then write each letter from the name onto a different spring-type clothespin. Invite each child to the area and have him spell out the name of each insect by clipping the clothespins above the matching letters. Encourage the child to also compare the lengths of the different names and to find matching letters or similar letter groupings in the names.

67

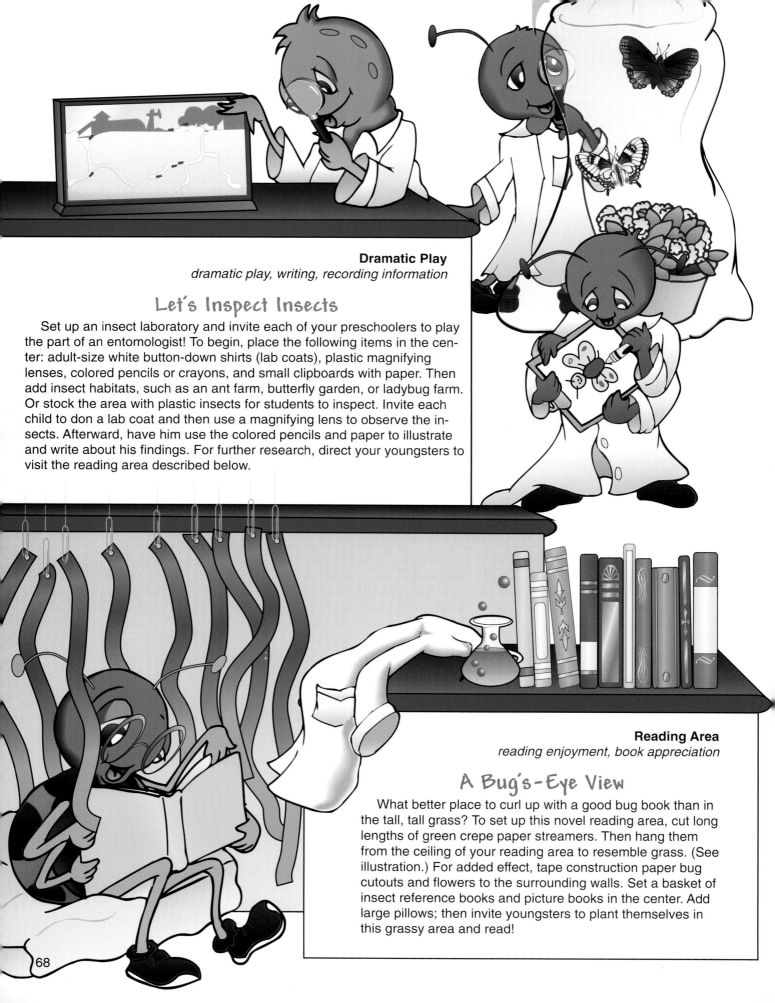

Dramatic Play
dramatic play, writing, recording information

Let's Inspect Insects

Set up an insect laboratory and invite each of your preschoolers to play the part of an entomologist! To begin, place the following items in the center: adult-size white button-down shirts (lab coats), plastic magnifying lenses, colored pencils or crayons, and small clipboards with paper. Then add insect habitats, such as an ant farm, butterfly garden, or ladybug farm. Or stock the area with plastic insects for students to inspect. Invite each child to don a lab coat and then use a magnifying lens to observe the insects. Afterward, have him use the colored pencils and paper to illustrate and write about his findings. For further research, direct your youngsters to visit the reading area described below.

Reading Area
reading enjoyment, book appreciation

A Bug's-Eye View

What better place to curl up with a good bug book than in the tall, tall grass? To set up this novel reading area, cut long lengths of green crepe paper streamers. Then hang them from the ceiling of your reading area to resemble grass. (See illustration.) For added effect, tape construction paper bug cutouts and flowers to the surrounding walls. Set a basket of insect reference books and picture books in the center. Add large pillows; then invite youngsters to plant themselves in this grassy area and read!

We're Goin' on a Bug Hunt

Don't worry! All the bugs in this discovery center are plastic and contained inside a bottle! To make a discovery bottle, half-fill a clean, empty plastic bottle with sand. Add a few plastic ants to the bottle and then hot-glue the lid on. Shake the bottle so that the ants are partially hidden in the sand; then invite each child to look for and count the ants inside the bottle.

To make a ladybug bottle, hot-glue small ladybug buttons (or attach ladybug stickers) to the leaves on a craft vine. Stuff the vine into a clear plastic bottle and then hot-glue the lid on. Provide plastic magnifying lenses and have students search for the ladybugs in the vines.

Peanut Butter Bug Bites

Little ones won't mind these bug bites one bit! Before setting up this supervised center, check with parents for student peanut allergies. (If there are allergies in your class, substitute soy-nut butter for peanut butter.) Next, follow the recipe shown to prepare a serving of edible play dough. Provide a child with the prepared dough and have her make a bug body with it. Next, provide her with six pretzel sticks to use as the bug's legs. Then offer the child an assortment of cereal pieces, cake sprinkles, shoestring licorice, and raisins to complete her bug's decorations.

For a literacy extension, photograph each child's play dough bug. Glue the developed photo to the right half of a sheet of construction paper. Then have the child dictate a story about the bug, and write her response on the left half of the paper. Display the completed stories on a wall or bulletin board for youngsters and visitors to enjoy!

Edible Dough
(makes one serving)

Ingredients:
2 tbsp. peanut butter (or soy-nut butter)
2 tbsp. honey
nonfat dry milk

Mix the peanut butter and honey. Add the dry milk until the mixture has a play dough consistency and does not stick to hands.

Science Center
observing, hypothesizing

Bobbing Water Bugs

Your youngsters will be amazed as you transform ordinary raisins into lively, diving water bugs! To begin, fill a clear drinking glass with seltzer water. Use food coloring to tint the water blue. Invite a small group of students to join you at the center. Show students the glass of water; then pass around a few raisins for them to examine. Drop the raisins into the glass. Direct students to observe closely as the raisins become water bugs and begin to dive up and down in the water. How does that happen? Invite your preschoolers to offer explanations; then explain that the wrinkles in the raisins trap the seltzer-water bubbles. The bubbles carry the raisins to the top of the water. When the bubbles pop, the raisins fall. New bubbles become trapped in the raisins and they start rising again.

Games Area
Earth awareness, eye-hand coordination, taking turns

Litterbug Toss

What's the worst bug of all? A litterbug! Recognize Earth Day (April 22) with a lesson on littering; then set up a game that encourages students not to be litterbugs! In advance, gather a supply of crumpled fast-food bags and balls of scrap paper. Cut out a large poster board litterbug and tape it to a clean, empty wastepaper basket. Place the litterbug basket in your games area; then set the litter a short distance away from the basket. Invite students to visit the area and take turns tossing the litter into the trash.

Art Table
creative development, color identification

Lovebugs

Youngsters are sure to get hugs when they give these lovebug frames! To make one, cut out a photo-frame opening in a 9" x 5½" sheet of white construction paper. Then have a child make blue, yellow, pink, and red fingerprints around the opening. When the paint is dry, help the child use permanent markers to add features to each bug. Tape a photo of the child to the back of the frame so that the picture shows through the opening. Then program the bottom half of the paper with a poem similar to one of those shown. Have the child sign the frame. Laminate it for durability and then attach a self-adhesive magnetic strip to the back.

The blue bug says, "Have a wonderful day!"
The yellow bug says, "You're special in every way!"
The pink bug says, "I love you."
The red bug says, "You love me, too!"

The blue bug says, "Have a wonderful day!"
The yellow bug says, "You're special in every way!"
The pink bug says, "Jesus loves you."
The red bug says, "I love you, too!"

Sand Table
counting, social development, color recognition

Insect Seek

Set up this center for pairs of students to seek insects. Place a supply of plastic bug counters near your sand table. To use the center, one child covers her eyes while another child hides several bugs of the same color in the sand. The second child recites a chant similar to the one shown; then the first child uncovers her eyes and tries to find the bugs. After finding the bugs, the students switch roles and play again.

Little bugs, come out and play.
[Six red] bugs are hiding today!

71

Insect Patterns
Use with "*B* Is for Bee" on page 67.

Beep, Beep! Bubble, Bubble!

Car Wash Centers for Your Classroom

Got some spare sponges and a bevy of buckets? Then you're ready to give your classroom centers a car wash theme! From math to painting, these centers are bubbling over with squeaky-clean fun!

by Ada Goren

Dramatic-Play Center
Our Own Car Wash

Mix things up a bit by moving your dramatic-play area *outdoors* for this unit. Turn an area adjacent to your classroom into a class car wash, servicing ride-ons and play cars usually used at playground time. Just add a few buckets and big sponges, an old garden hose, some chamois cloths, and a few squeegees. Nearby, set up a table with a toy cash register where customers can pay for their car washes. Encourage little ones to use pretend water to keep things neat and tidy!

Flannelboard Center
Dirty, Clean, and in Between

Have youngsters practice sequencing with the car cards on page 77. Simply photocopy the page, color the pictures, and then cut the cards apart. Prepare the cards for use on your flannelboard by attaching a piece of self-adhesive felt to the back of each one. Ask a child at this center to put the cards in the correct sequence from left to right, showing the progression of a car being washed.

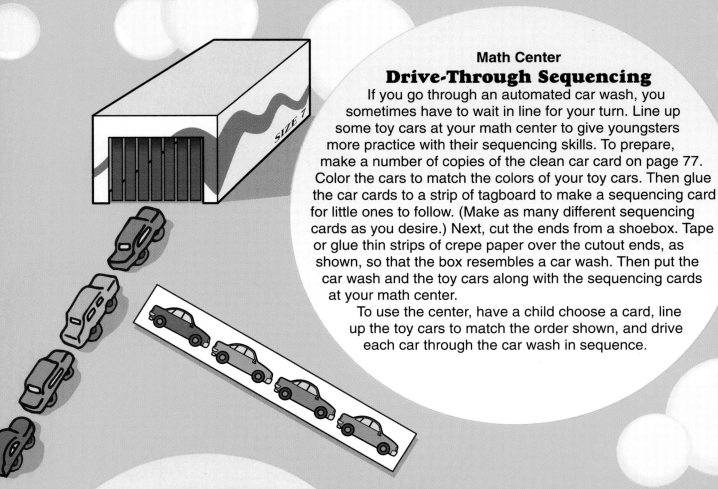

Math Center
Drive-Through Sequencing

If you go through an automated car wash, you sometimes have to wait in line for your turn. Line up some toy cars at your math center to give youngsters more practice with their sequencing skills. To prepare, make a number of copies of the clean car card on page 77. Color the cars to match the colors of your toy cars. Then glue the car cards to a strip of tagboard to make a sequencing card for little ones to follow. (Make as many different sequencing cards as you desire.) Next, cut the ends from a shoebox. Tape or glue thin strips of crepe paper over the cutout ends, as shown, so that the box resembles a car wash. Then put the car wash and the toy cars along with the sequencing cards at your math center.

To use the center, have a child choose a card, line up the toy cars to match the order shown, and drive each car through the car wash in sequence.

Painting Center
Squeegee, Please

Which is more fun, painting or "un-painting"? It's hard to tell in this activity, which involves an important car wash tool—the squeegee! To prepare, purchase one or two clear Plexiglas acrylic sheets at your local home-improvement store. Invite youngsters to fingerpaint on the surface of the acrylic sheet using fingerpaint that's had a bit of dish soap added to it. Give each child her own squeegee and encourage her to use it to "erase" her painting whenever she wishes. When the surface is clean, she can start all over again!

Literacy Center
Wash 'n' Write

This activity is letter-formation and tactile fun, all in one! To wash cars in your literacy center, first enlarge the dirty car card on page 77 to full-page size. Make a few copies; then laminate them to make mats. At your literacy center, invite a child to squirt a bit of nonmenthol shaving cream onto a mat. Have him spread the cream over the car and give it a good scrubbing! Then encourage him to use his finger to write letters (or numbers or words) in the shaving cream. Provide a damp sponge for wiping off the shiny, clean car. Oh…Still dirty? Better wash it again!

Art Center
Sporty Sponge Cars

Use some of those big car wash sponges to create these cool cars! Set out large shallow pans of tempera paint in a few colors. Have a child dip a car wash sponge into the color of her choice and then press it onto a sheet of construction paper. Allow the paint to dry. Then invite the child to transform the sponge print into a car with a few paper shapes and a bit of glue! Give each child a small white square for the driver's window and two black circles for wheels. Have her glue the shapes in place. Then encourage her to complete her car by drawing herself as the driver! Vroom, vroom!

Water Table
Sponge Sorting

There are three sizes of sponges for this activity, which is BIG on fun! Partially fill your water table with water and squirt in some mild dish soap. Toss in a few small, medium, and large sponges for youngsters to investigate. Below the table, set three buckets labeled "small," "medium," and "large." (Draw a corresponding sponge on each sign to help nonreaders.) After little ones squeeze and squish to their hearts' delight, ask them to sort the sponges into the buckets. Have some towels handy for drying off when the sudsy sorting is complete!

Which Towel Is Tops?

Once a car is washed, it has to be dried. But which kind of towel does the best job? Encourage little ones to experiment at your science center to find out! Provide a tub of water, some small toy cars, and two types of towels—paper towels and chamois cloths. Have a child dip a toy car into the water and then dry it with a paper towel. Repeat the process until the paper towel is too wet to use. How many cars did he dry with the paper towel? Try the experiment again with a chamois cloth. Can your youngsters see why a chamois is the towel of choice for car washes?

Writing Center
Signs of All Kinds

No doubt youngsters will be building car washes from wood or plastic LEGO blocks during this unit. Encourage them to create signs for their car washes at your writing center. Duplicate the open reproducible on page 78 to make at least a class supply. Then choose from the following sign-making options that best fit your preschoolers' needs and abilities. (Note: This reproducible would also be great for a note to parents telling them all about the car wash commotion in your classroom!)

- Have a child write his name and draw a picture of a car or cars.
- Leave a space or blank for the child's name; then draw dotted letters that say "CAR WASH." Have the child add his name and trace the letters.
- Have the child write his name and copy from a sign you've made the letters to spell "CAR WASH."
- Have the child use alphabet stamps to stamp his name and the words *CAR WASH.*

Car Cards

Use with "Dirty, Clean, and in Between" on page 73. Use the clean car card with "Drive-Through Sequencing" on page 74. Use the dirty car card with "Wash 'n' Write" on page 75.

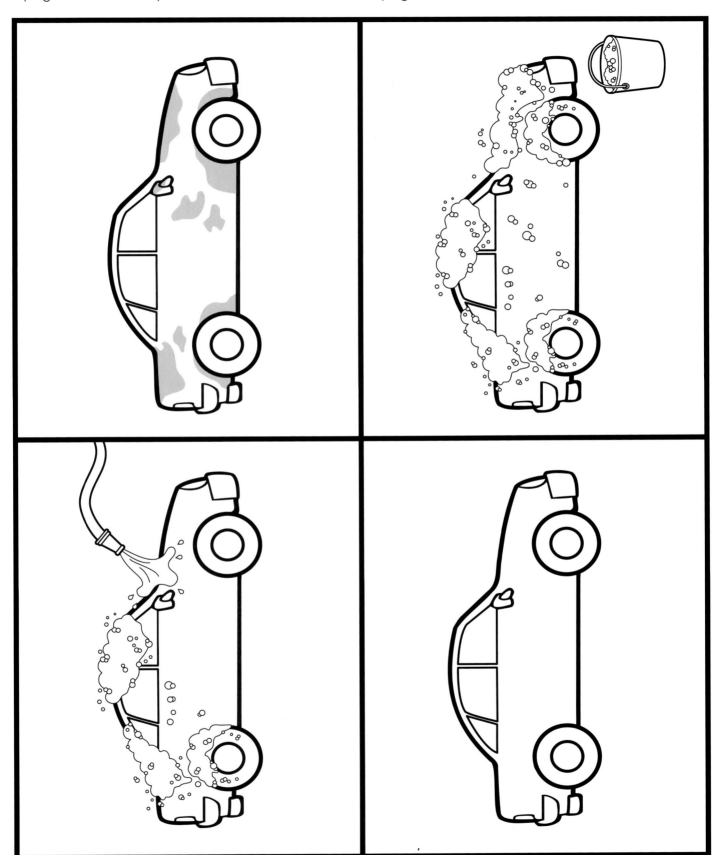

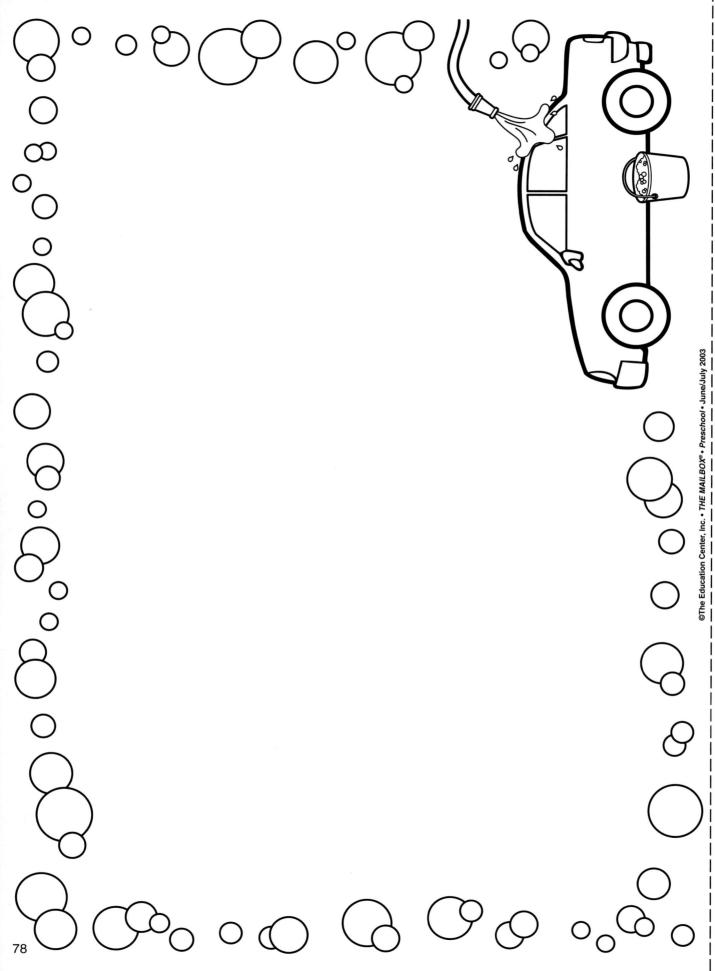

Note to the teacher: Use with "Signs of All Kinds" on page 76.

CRAFTS FOR LITTLE HANDS

Crafts for Little Hands

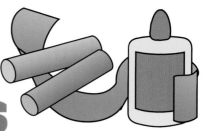

Pansy Picture Frame

What will parents say about this pressed-pansy picture frame? "Wow! Impressive!" In advance, press a supply of pansy flowers in a heavy book for approximately one week. Cut out a tagboard picture frame for each child and have her paint a watercolor design on it. When the paint is dry, provide the child with a few pressed flowers and direct her to glue them onto the frame. Tape a photo of the child behind the frame. Laminate the frame and then add a strip of magnetic tape to the back of it. Pressed and complete! This picture frame can't be beat!

I'm a Preschool Artist!

Making a personalized paint smock will have each of your preschoolers feeling like Picasso! In advance, obtain an adult-sized white T-shirt for each child. Slip a piece of cardboard inside the shirt to prevent paint from bleeding through it. Use Slick black fabric paint to outline an artist's palette on the front of each shirt; then write "Preschool Artist" on the shirt. Set the shirt aside to dry; then cut a few small potatoes in half. When the paint is dry, work with one child at a time to make colorful fabric-paint potato prints on the palette. Keep the completed smocks in your classroom for each artist to wear when creating a masterpiece.

Ada Goren, Winston-Salem, NC

Egg Carton Critters

It's a bug! It's a bird! It's a bee! There's no limit to what your preschoolers can make with this open-ended craft. To prepare, cut cardboard egg cartons into individual cups or pairs of cups. Punch holes in opposite sides of each cup; then set the cups at your art center. Demonstrate how to thread lengths of pipe cleaner through the holes to create legs. Then invite each child to use craft items to create an egg carton critter.

"Hand-some" Thanksgiving Card

Fingers become feathers for this holiday greeting card. For each child, cut out a simple turkey head and body shape (about ten inches high) from brown construction paper. Add a red paper wattle to each child's turkey cutout and write the message shown. Next, have each child decorate a 5" x 8" piece of tagboard with your choice of spin art, bingo markers, paint, or markers. When it's dry, turn the tagboard over and trace the child's hands. Cut out the hand shapes and arrange them behind the precut body to look like feathers. Have the child draw eyes for the turkey and add her name below the message. Gobble, gobble!

Cheryl Helaire—Preschool
Monarch Nursery School
Wolcott, CT

Ahhh...Autumn!

These autumn leaves are lovely—and easy to make! To prepare, cut simple leaf shapes from tagboard (at least one per child). Next, use kitchen graters or pencil sharpeners to grate crayons in autumn colors into paper cups. Lay a leaf shape on a covered work surface. Have a child take a pinch or two of crayon shavings and sprinkle them onto her leaf shape. Then lay a sheet of waxed paper over the shavings and press the leaf with a hot iron (the child should be at a safe distance from the iron). Oooh—how pretty!

Carol Hammill—Two-Year-Olds
Community Christian Preschool
Fountain Valley, CA

Mr. Scarecrow

All it takes are a few simple craft materials to create this scarecrow cutie! To prepare each project, precut a circle face from tan construction paper, a hat from any color construction paper, and a sunflower shape from yellow construction paper. From fabric scraps, cut two small hearts for cheeks, a triangle for a nose, and a hatband. To assemble the scarecrow, glue raffia strips to each side of the face to make the scarecrow's hair; then glue the hat to the top of the head. Glue the hatband and flower in place. Glue a black pompom to the center of the sunflower. Glue on two button eyes and the fabric nose and cheeks; then use a black crayon to draw a mouth. Hello, Scarecrow!

Bonnie Martin—Three- and Four-Year-Olds
Hopewell Country Day, Pennington, NJ

Crafts for Little Hands

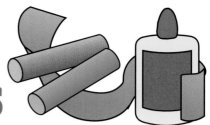

Peppermint Pretty

This cute candy cane smells as good as it looks! To prepare, add a few drops of peppermint extract to some red tempera paint. Cut a candy cane shape from white construction paper for each child. Working with one child at a time, place a candy cane cutout in a box lid. Put a bit of the peppermint-scented paint in each corner of the lid. Then drop in a marble. Have the child tilt the box lid back and forth to make the marble roll through the paint and over the candy cane cutout. Look—stripes!

Christa J. Koch—PreK, Circle of Friends School, Bethlehem, PA

Sonya Bussan—Preschool, Third Presbyterian Head Start, Dubuque, IA

What Dear Reindeer!

Moms and dads are sure to treasure these Rudolph wall hangings! To make one, paint a cardboard cake or pizza circle with red tempera paint. Using two different shades of brown construction paper, trace a child's shoe on one color and both his hands on the other. Cut out the shoe and hand shapes; then glue them to the painted circle as shown. Add sticky dot eyes, a red pom-pom nose, and a merry red bow. Hot-glue a picture hanger to the top of the back and your gift is complete. How neat!

Cheryl Songer—Preschool
Wee Know Nursery School
Hartland, WI

Angelic Art

Here's a handy little project that may seem heaven-sent! To prepare, cut a class supply of seven-inch-tall triangles from inexpensive lace fabric and three-inch circles from white or skin-toned construction paper. Have each child glue a triangle body and a circle face onto a sheet of construction paper as shown. Then have her press her hands into white tempera paint and onto the paper to make the angel's wings. Have her use crayons to add facial features and glitter glue to add a halo. If desired, copy the poem shown for each child and have her glue it to the bottom of the angel.

Sarah Booth—Four- and Five-Year-Olds
Messiah Nursery School
South Williamsport, PA

I'm just a little angel,
So sweet and heavenly,
Made from lace and handprints
For all the world to see!

Holiday Candle

These pretend candles will make super centerpieces for holiday tables! To make one, first paint a toilet tissue tube with red tempera paint. While the paint is wet, sprinkle on iridescent glitter; then set the tube aside to dry. Meanwhile, glue several 5" x 5" squares of green tissue paper to a small paper plate as shown. Glue a few clusters of small red pom-poms (holly berries) onto the green tissue paper. When the paint on the tube is dry, tuck small pieces of yellow, orange, and red tissue paper into one end to resemble a flame. Then glue the opposite end of the tube to the center of the paper plate.

Carrie A. Gross—Three-Year-Olds
Davis Child Care Center
Oshkosh, WI

Star Light, Star Bright

Invite youngsters to top their holiday trees with these sparkly stars! To make one, lay a flattened coffee filter atop a thin white paper plate. Color the coffee filter with washable markers (blues and greens work well). Then use an eyedropper to drip water over the filter, making the ink spread into unique designs. Remove the coffee filter to see the design left behind on the plate. Allow the plate to dry. Cut it into a star shape; then add squiggles and lines of glitter glue in a color that complements the ink. Hot-glue a tagboard ring to the back of the star (as shown) and it's ready to top the tree!

Carol Hargett—PreK
Kinderhaus III
Fairborn, OH

A Peaceful Picture

This super simple craft is ideal for little ones to complete as you study Martin Luther King Jr. Use a die-cutter to punch out a class supply of Martin Luther King Jr. silhouettes from black construction paper. Have each child glue her cutout silhouette on one side of a half sheet of blue construction paper. Next, brush white tempera paint onto a large dove rubber stamp (also use green paint if your stamp shows an olive branch). Have the child press the stamp next to the silhouette of King. Easy!

Daisy Green—Three-Year-Olds
Surrey Child Care Center
Hagerstown, MD

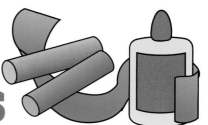

Crafts for Little Hands

Valentine Boxes

These boxes are red, white, and just right for taking home valentines! To make one, first spray-paint a class supply of empty tissue boxes red. Then set out heart-shaped sponges and white tempera paint in shallow containers. Have a child sponge-paint hearts all over a red tissue box. When the paint is dry, use a permanent marker to label the box with the child's name. On the day of your party, slip valentines into the box openings and youngsters will have sturdy totes to carry home their cards!

Sarah Booth—Four- and Five-Year-Olds
Messiah Nursery School
South Williamsport, PA

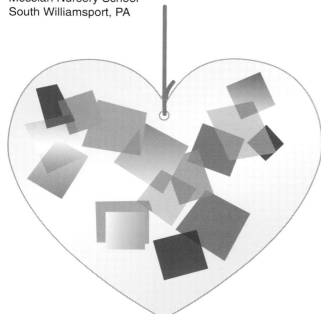

Seasonal Suncatchers

Hang these hearts in a window for a splash of valentine color! To make one, dilute some white glue and tint it pink with a few drops of red food coloring. Have a child paint the pink glue onto a piece of waxed paper. Have him add small, precut squares of tissue paper and cellophane in valentine colors. Then help him lay a second piece of waxed paper on top of the glued design. When the glue is dry, trace a large heart shape onto the paper. Help the child cut out the heart and punch a hole at the top. Thread a piece of yarn through the hole, tie a knot, and hang the suncatcher in a window. Don't you just love it?

Julie Whiting—PreK
Julie's Day Care
Alexandria, MN

Celery Roses

Sure, celery is good for a healthy snack, but is it good for *painting?* Of course! A bunch of celery makes these realistic roses—perfect for a Valentine's Day greeting! To prepare, cut off the bottom two inches from a bunch of celery (leave the rubber band in place to hold together any stalks that come loose). Next, dry the bunch with a paper towel, or allow it to air-dry. Have a child dip the bottom of the bunch into red paint and then print a few roses near the top of a sheet of white construction paper. Have her add green fingerpainted stems and glue on a flowerpot cutout. Then write a Valentine's Day message at the top and the child's name on the pot.

Molly Mosely—PreK
Wee Little Ones Preschool
Pana, IL

84

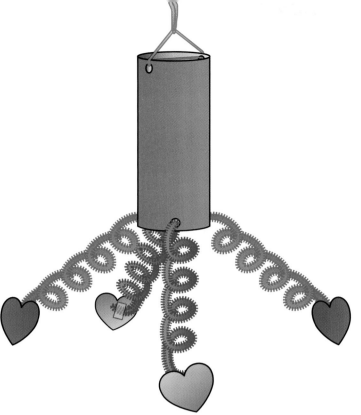

Special Spirals

This Valentine's Day mobile will have little ones doing the twist—twisting pipe cleaners, that is! To make one, paint a toilet paper tube red (or another valentine color). When the paint is dry, punch four equidistant holes at one end of the tube and two holes at the other. Thread a piece of yarn through the two holes on one end; then tie the ends of the yarn together to make a hanger. Next, twist together two pipe cleaners in valentine colors to make an X. Thread each end of the X into one of the four holes in the tube and bend it downward. Wrap each section of pipe cleaner around a pencil to make a spiral. Tape a small heart cutout to the free end of each spiral. Then hang the mobiles for everyone to admire!

Cathie Sarvis—Three-Year-Olds
Park Avenue School
Wilmington, NC

Tooth Fairy Wands

Make Dental Health Month a delight with these whimsical wands! To make one, have a child paint a paper towel tube with pastel paint; then allow it to dry. Cut a tooth shape from a sponge; then help the child sponge-paint several white teeth over the painted tube. When the paint is dry, use a black permanent marker to outline each tooth. Next, gather a few lengths of curling ribbon in the center. Staple or tape the gathered ribbon to one end of the tube. Complete the tooth fairy wand by stapling a large white construction paper tooth over the gathered ribbon.

adapted from an idea by Lucia Kemp Henry, Fallon, NV

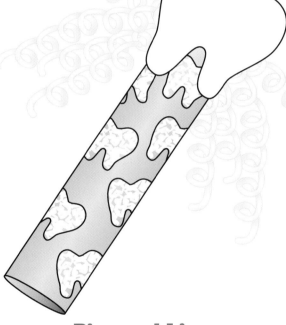

Diamond Lions

Is March coming in like a lion where you live? Make these shapely creatures to welcome this marvelous month! For each child, precut a large diamond and two small squares from brown construction paper, as well as a large supply of long, thin diamonds from yellow and orange tones of paper. Trace the large diamond onto the middle of a white sheet of construction paper. Then have a child glue the thin diamonds all around the outline to make the lion's mane. Next, help the child glue the large diamond and two small squares over the mane as shown. Have her use markers to add facial feature to her lion. Then ROAR!

Shelley Williams—Three- and Four-Year-Olds
Children's College, Layton, UT

85

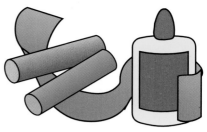

Crafts for Little Hands

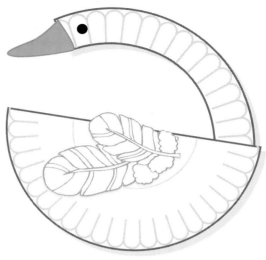

Lovely Swans

Swim into spring with these simple swans! To make one, cut a thin white paper plate in half; then cut away the rim of the plate from one half. Glue the rim to the intact plate half, as shown, to form the swan's neck. Then glue on an orange construction paper beak and add a sticky dot eye. Add a few pretty white craft feathers to complete this beautiful bird!

Leita Oberhofer, Newport News, VA

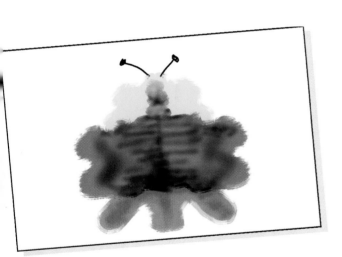

Push-Paint Butterflies

Have your preschoolers flutter on over to the art table to make these easy butterfly paintings! To make one, fold a 12" x 18" sheet of white construction paper in half. Open the paper; then have the child choose two to four different colors of tempera paint. Spoon a bit of each color onto the fold of the paper. Refold the paper; then have the child press from the fold outward to spread the paint. Open the paper and allow the paint to dry. Then use a marker to add features. There you have it, a one-of-a-kind butterfly!

Jackie Grasso—Three-Year-Olds
Good Shepherd Episcopal School
Friendswood, TX

Stripes in the Jungle

Make jungle animals in a jiffy with this easy painting idea! Use the pattern on page 90 to make a tracer. Trace the pattern onto orange construction paper to make a tiger. Have a child use painter's tape to mark off stripes on his tiger. Then have him fingerpaint with black paint over the entire tiger. When the paint is dry, cut out the tiger and peel off the tape to reveal the stripes. Invite the child to draw facial features on the tiger to complete it. What fun!

Susan Rust—PreK
Thompson Elementary School
Jacksonville, NC

Koosh Ball Bouquet

Koosh balls help make pretty flowers for a springtime display! Have a child dip a small Koosh ball into one or two colors of tempera paint and then press the ball onto a sheet of construction paper. After making several flowers, allow the paint to dry. Then have the youngster use a green marker to add stems and leaves.

Donna Leonard
Dyersville Head Start
Dyersville, IA

Mother's Day Corsage

Make moms feel special with these crafty corsages. To make the flowers, cut four equal-size circles from two flattened coffee filters. Pinch each circle in the center; then dip the edges into diluted food coloring. Allow the flowers to dry; then add a stem to each one by twisting a five-inch-long piece of green pipe cleaner around the pinched center. Add leaves to each flower stem by poking the free end of the pipe cleaner through scraps of green crepe paper streamer. Then twist all four flower stems together and poke them through the center of a four-inch doily. Add a ribbon bow to complete this cute corsage!

Cheryl Cicioni—Preschool
Kindernook Preschool
Lancaster, PA

Ladybug Card

Wish moms a happy Mother's Day with the help of these lovely little ladybugs! To make a card, trace a simple ladybug shape on a half sheet of red construction paper as shown. Program the card with the text shown. Then cut a circle from red paper to match the size of the ladybug's body. Have a child make black tempera paint fingerprints over one side of the circle to resemble the ladybug's spots. Help him cut the circle in half. Then use a brad to attach the two halves over the ladybug body as shown. Have the child sign his name and take this creepy-crawly card home for Mom to read!

Peggy Miller—Four- and Five-Year-Olds
Rabbit Hill Nursery School
Springfield, PA

Crafts for Little Hands

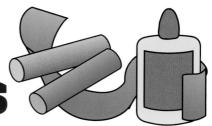

Sparkly Fish

Wait 'til you "sea" these fanciful fish! To make one, cut a simple fish shape from brightly colored construction paper; then cut out the center portion as shown. Next, squirt some glitter glue onto the center of a piece of waxed paper slightly larger than the fish shape. Use a paintbrush to spread the glue with short strokes, making the design resemble fish scales. When the glue is dry, trim the waxed paper and then glue or tape it behind the opening in the fish cutout. Add a dot eye and a friendly fishy smile, and this project is ready to display!

Barb Stefaniuk—Three- and Four-Year-Olds
Kerrobert Tiny Tots Playschool
Kerrobert, Saskatchewan, Canada

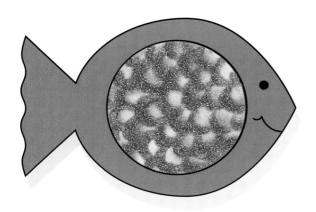

Dandy Dragonflies

These bugs are big, blue, and beautiful! For each child, gather four thin white paper plates—three small and one large. Have each child paint the back of each plate with blue tempera paint. When the paint is dry, staple the four plates together, as shown, to form a dragonfly. Glue on two large eyes cut from white and black construction paper scraps. To make wings, tie a knot in the center of an 8" x 15" piece of white tulle netting; then hot-glue the knot to the dragonfly's body. Hang the finished dragonflies from your classroom ceiling and say, "Welcome, summer!"

Shelley Williams—Three- and Four-Year-Olds
Children's College
Layton, UT

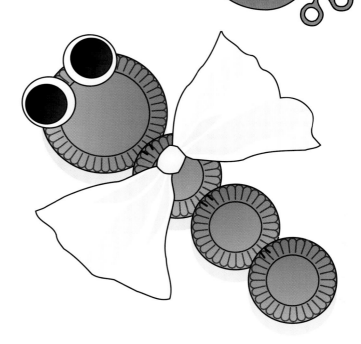

Paper Bag Octopus

What has eight arms and is a cute craft? A paper-bag octopus, of course! To make one, paint a small paper lunch bag with purple tempera paint. When the paint is dry, stuff some tissue paper into the bottom and then use ribbon or string to tie the bag closed above the stuffed section. Cut the remainder of the bag into eight strips; then twist each one to form an arm. Flip the bag over and add two sticky dot eyes and a sweet smile to what is now the octopus's head. What a friendly ocean critter!

Crystal Hampton
Kare Nursery, Arcadia, CA

Shaving Cream Scoops

Youngsters will flip for ice cream that drips! To make this melting ice-cream cone craft, first mix together one part glue, one part shaving cream, and a few drops of food coloring. Glue a tan cone shape onto a sheet of construction paper. Dab a bit of the mixture over the top of the cone and gently form it into the shape of an ice-cream scoop. Then hang the project to dry for 24 hours. The ice-cream mixture will puff up and some of it will run, giving the effect that the ice cream is melting!

Brandy Fletcher—Preschool
Hand in Hand
Springfield, IL

Magic Flags

There'll be stars, stripes, and surprises when you help youngsters create these American flags! To prepare, cut a 6" x 10" rectangle of white construction paper for each child; then fold back about two inches on one short side of each paper. Using a white crayon, draw a rectangle in the upper left corner of each flag-to-be; then add stars. Next, use waxed paper to mask the area inside the white rectangle you drew. Then invite a child to use a mini paint roller to paint seven red stripes over the rest of the rectangle. When the red paint is dry, have the child remove the waxed paper and color the upper left corner with a blue bingo marker. The stars will magically appear! When the blue paint is also dry, wrap the folded edge of the paper around a drinking straw and glue it in place. Then watch those flags wave!

Donna Pollhammer—Three- and Four-Year-Olds
YMCA Chipmunk Preschool
Westminster, MD

Watercolor Sunset

There's nothing like a spectacular sunset at the beach! Invite each of your preschoolers to make her own version of this summer scene with watercolor paints. First, have her use a spray bottle to dampen a sheet of white construction paper with water. Then have her use watercolors to paint bands of colors across the paper. Hold the paper by the top corners over a tray, allowing the paint to drip and the colors to blend together. When the paint is dry, have the child glue a half circle cut from fluorescent orange paper near the bottom of the scene. Finally, help her glue on a torn strip of blue paper to simulate the ocean's waves. Beautiful!

Nancy O'Toole—Preschool
Ready Set Grow
Grand Rapids, MN

Explorations

Explorations

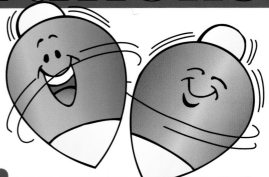

Top This!

Get youngsters' minds spinning by giving this color-mixing exploration a whirl!

Use a red marker to color one half of a white cardboard circle. Use a yellow marker to color the other half of the cardboard circle.

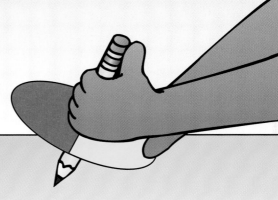

Poke a short, sharpened pencil through the center of the circle to create a top (a teacher's job).

Instruct students to observe the top carefully as you spin it on a table. The top will appear orange!

Have students continue to observe the top as its spinning slows down. When it stops, the red and yellow will reappear. How did *that* happen?

Science You Can Do

To explore colors, you will need the following:

white cardboard circle
red marker
yellow marker
short, sharpened pencil
tape

STEP 3

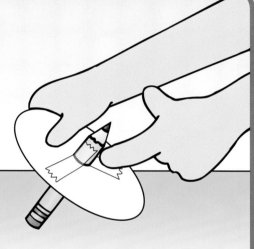

Place small strips of tape under the circle to secure it in place.

STEP 4

Have students examine the top and identify the two colors.

This Is Why

Red and yellow combined make orange. The top was spinning so fast the red and yellow colors appeared to be mixed together, making the top look orange.

What Now?

Make other tops with different color combinations such as red and blue (purple) or yellow and blue (green). Or make a six-sectioned top and color the sections in the following order: red, orange, yellow, green, blue, and purple. Spin the top, and it will appear white!

Explorations

It's All About Balance!

All eyes will be on this balance exploration, which involves gravity-defying potatoes.

STEP 1

Gather a potato and an empty plastic bottle for each child in a small group. Half-fill each bottle with water or sand to help weigh it down; then replace the cap. Set the potatoes and bottles at a center.

STEP 2

Invite a small group of students to join you at the center. Provide each child with a potato and a plastic bottle. Have the child find a way to balance the potato on top of the bottle.

STEP 5

Have the child make another attempt at balancing the potato on the bottle. (Adjust the position of the forks if needed.)

STEP 6

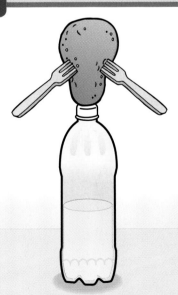

Ta-da! It's a "spud-tacular" balancing act!

Science You Can Do

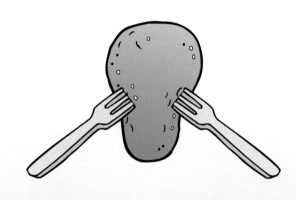

To explore balance, you will need the following:
small oval-shaped potato for each child in a small group
empty plastic bottle for each child in a small group
water or sand to half-fill each bottle
pair of metal forks for each child in a small group

STEP 3

Direct each child to find the smaller end of her potato. Then challenge the child to stand the potato on its smaller end and balance it on the bottle.

STEP 4

Provide each child with a pair of metal forks. Help the child insert the forks into the potato as shown.

This Is Why

Items that are heavier at the bottom balance more easily than those that are top-heavy. Placing the forks in the potato added weight near the bottom, making it easier to balance.

What Now?

If you and your youngsters are planning a trip to the circus, have students carefully observe the high-wire act. Why does the high-wire artist walk with a pole? The pole adds weight near the lower half of her body, making it easier for her to balance.

Explorations

Rain Check!

How much pollution is in rainwater and puddles? Try this water-filter investigation to find out!

Collect a sample of rainwater or puddle water in a clear container.

Invite students to use plastic magnifying lenses to closely examine the water in the container. Encourage youngsters to discuss their observations and then record their observations on a sheet of chart paper.

Invite students to compare the filtered water with the unfiltered water. Discuss any differences and invite students to explain why the filtered water is more clear. Record students' responses on the chart.

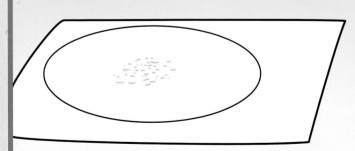

Remove the filters from the funnel. Lay the top filter flat on a sheet of white copy paper. When the filter is dry, invite students to examine the particles trapped by it.

Science You Can Do

To explore pollutants in water you will need the following:
2 white coffee filters
funnel
2 clear containers
rainwater or puddle water
plastic magnifying lenses
chart paper

STEP 3

Place two white coffee filters in a funnel. Then set the funnel in a clear, empty container.

STEP 4

Slowly pour half the water from the container through the funnel into the empty container.

This Is Why

The water is clearer because the filter traps larger particles in the water and keeps them from passing into the container.

What Now?

Repeat the experiment with other water samples such as tap water, distilled water, or pond or lake water. Label each of the filters and compare the particles on each one.

Explorations

Wrinkles and Raisins

You'll be raisin' great learning fun with a science exploration that answers the question "Why are raisins wrinkled?"

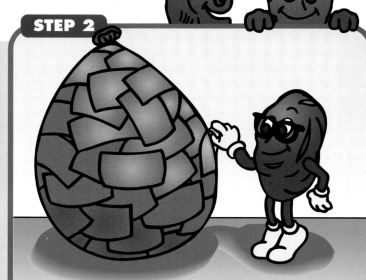

STEP 1

Prior to the exploration, make a model of a grape by filling a round purple balloon with water.

STEP 2

Be sure the balloon is completely dry; then cover it with small pieces of clear packing tape. Set the balloon aside and out of students' reach.

STEP 5

Direct students to carefully observe the outside of the balloon as the water drains into the tub. Gently squeeze the balloon to empty all of the water into the tub.

STEP 6

Have students examine the deflated balloon and compare it to the raisins. Both are wrinkled!

Science You Can Do
by Nancy Lotzer

To explore wrinkles in raisins, you will need the following:

round purple balloon
access to a water faucet
chart paper
clear packing tape
fresh grapes

raisins
resealable plastic bags
straight pin
plastic tub

STEP 3

Place a few grapes and raisins in resealable plastic bags. Have students examine the two bags and describe the differences between the grapes and the raisins. Guide students to notice the wrinkles in the raisins and then ask them why raisins have wrinkles. Write their responses on a sheet of chart paper.

STEP 4

Explain that raisins are grapes without the juice. Show students the model of a grape (water-filled balloon). Hold the balloon over the plastic tub and use the pin to poke several holes in the balloon.

This Is Why

The tape on the balloon stays the same size, even after the water is released from the balloon. Without the water inside the balloon to keep it stretched out, the tape wrinkles up. The same thing happens to grapes. When the juice inside the grape dries up, the skin on the grape becomes wrinkled, and the grape becomes a raisin! So why are raisins wrinkled? Their skin is too big for them!

Looking for a home-school connection? Provide each child with a copy of the badge on page 100, and prompt parents to ask, "Why are raisins wrinkled?"

What Now?

You can take the water out of a grape, but can you put the water back in a raisin? Try it and see! Soak a few raisins in a bowl of water. After a few days, check on the raisins. Do they look like grapes?

I know
why raisins
are wrinkled.
Ask me!

I know
why raisins
are wrinkled.
Ask me!

I know
why raisins
are wrinkled.
Ask me!

I know
why raisins
are wrinkled.
Ask me!

Fingerplays, Poems, & Rhymes

Five Fast Race Cars

To prepare for this action poem, label five paper plates (steering wheels), each with a different number from 1 to 5. Provide five students each with a different steering wheel. Invite the students to stand in front of the class; then watch those five fast race cars go!

Five fast race cars speeding round the track.
The first car said, "I can't look back!"
The second car said, "Oh, no! I'm out of gas!"
The third car said, "Beep! Beep! I'm fast!"
The fourth car said, "Watch my tires spin."
The fifth car said, "Vroom, vroom. I win!"

Then beep went a horn and flash went the lights,
And five fast race cars sped out of sight!

Angela Neimann—Preschool/Special Education
J. F. Burns Elementary
Kings Mills, OH

Poems, & Rhymes

Rudolph to the Rescue!

All the reindeer are here.
They are ready to go!
But how can they see
Out in the snow?

They need a little light
To show them the way.
Here comes Rudolph!
Hip, hip, hooray!

Put hands to head for antlers.
Prance in place.

Shrug shoulders.

Hand to brow, eyes straining to see.

Point finger.
Throw up hands and cheer.

Barb Stefaniuk—Three- and Four-Year-Olds
Kerrobert Tiny Tots Playschool
Kerrobert, Saskatchewan, Canada

Five Little Astronauts

In 1992, Dr. Mae Jemison became the first Black American woman to explore outer space. During Black History Month (February), teach youngsters about Dr. Jemison's accomplishments; then perform the following finger-play in her honor!

Five little astronauts floating in outer space,
The first one said, "Let's get out of this place!"
The second one said, "Let's race to the moon."
The third one said, "We'll be there soon."
The fourth one said, "The space shuttle's ready!"
The fifth one said, "Now, hold it steady."
Then, ZOOM, they took off and started their flight,
And five little astronauts flew out of sight!

adapted from a fingerplay by Renee Farrand—Three-Year-Olds
Union Methodist Church Preschool
Irmo, SC

Poems, & Rhymes

Hearts in Hands

After youngsters learn this fingerplay, they'll want to make heaps of hearts! So follow up the fingerplay by providing a variety of materials such as pipe cleaners, thin strips of paper, and glue sticks. Then lead youngsters to discover that this heart poem works for making all kinds of hearts!

Now's the time to make a heart.

Form a V—it's the place to start.

A big hump on one side,

And now another.

This heart shows the love we have for each other!

LeeAnn Collins—Director
Sunshine House Preschool
Lansing, MI

Fingerplays,

From April Showers to May Flowers

Little ones will enjoy performing this fingerplay from the month of April through the month of May!

Here come the April raindrops.	*Wiggle fingers like falling raindrops.*
They sprinkle and splash on my face.	*Tilt head up and wiggle fingers over face.*
Now here comes May.	*Circle arms above head to form a sun.*
The raindrops go away,	*Wiggle fingers while raising arms up.*
And flowers sprout up every place!	*Pantomime picking and smelling flowers.*

Poems, & Rhymes

Busy Bees

Here's a honey of a fingerplay for your preschoolers! To make this fingerplay even sweeter, hot-glue a craft bee to each finger on a right-hand glove. Then use the glove to perform the fingerplay. Buzz! Buzz! Buzz!

Five little bees   *Wiggle fingers on right hand.*
Up in the trees.   *Wiggle fingers above head.*
Busy,   *Wiggle fingers to the left.*
Buzzing   *Wiggle fingers to the right.*
Bumblebees.   *Wiggle fingers to the left and the right.*
First, they go to a flower.   *Hold left hand open; wiggle right hand toward it.*
Next, they go to the hive.   *Make fist with left hand; wiggle right hand toward it.*
Then they make some honey.   *Pat stomach.*
What a busy family of five!   *Wiggle fingers around.*

Donna Getzinger, Toluca Lake, CA

107

Five Spotted Cows

Celebrate National Dairy Month (June) by teaching youngsters the following poem about cows. Then invite five students to stand in front of the class and act out some bovine behavior.

Five spotted cows, standing in a line.
The first one said, "I'm feeling fine!" — *Point to self.*
The second one said, "How do you do?" — *Turn to third cow and hold out right hand.*

The third one said, "Moo! Moo! Moo!" — *Take second cow's hand and shake it.*

The fourth one said, "I'm grazing in the grass." — *Make chewing motion.*
The fifth one said, "I'm full at last!" — *Pat tummy.*
So the cows stood together and said,
"We're through! Let's take a bow and all say, 'MOO!'"

Lisa Thayer—PreK
Bunche ECDC
Tulsa, OK

GET MOVING!

Get Moving!

Movement Ideas for Preschoolers

Yee-haw!

Visiting the Wild West in your classroom? Hand each of your little cow-pokes a streamer and have her pretend it's a rope. Demonstrate how to swing the streamer as a cowboy would a lasso. Then teach youngsters the song that follows. Ready? Let's ride 'em and rope 'em!

(sung to the tune of "Did You Ever See a Lassie?")

Did you ever see a lasso, a lasso, a lasso?
Did you ever see a lasso swing this way and that?
Ride tall in your saddle,
And herd up the cattle!
Did you ever see a lasso swing this way and that?

Emily Lloyd
Dolley Madison Community Library
McLean, VA

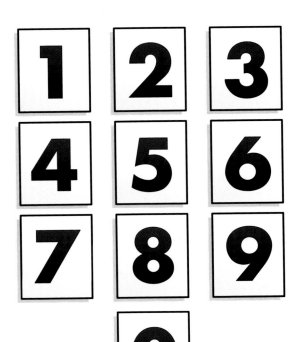

Jump 'n' Dial

Little ones will jump at the chance to practice their phone numbers with this activity! At your local craft store, purchase ten 9" x 12" pieces of white felt, as well as several pieces of black felt. From the black felt, cut the numbers 0 through 9; then glue each black number to a rectangle of white felt. Arrange the felt numbers on your floor to resemble the layout of a telephone keypad. Then invite each child to take a turn jumping from one square to another in the sequence of his phone number. Have him call out the numbers as he jumps. Memorizing a phone number has never been so much fun!

Katrina Stratford—Preschool
Libbie Edward Co-op Preschool
Salt Lake City, UT

Leaves Everywhere!

Pile on the fun when you invite youngsters to play in some realistic-looking leaves! To make leaves, crinkle and then flatten sheets of tissue paper. Laminate the sheets before cutting out leaf shapes. Make a big pile of paper leaves; then give directions for a movement—such as shuffle, hop, jump, or toss—for each child to perform on her turn to move through the pile. Then focus on body parts with the following song. Have youngsters place one or two paper leaves on each body part as it's sung. At the end, have little ones grab leaves from the ground and toss them into the air!

(sung to the tune of "Twinkle, Twinkle, Little Star")

Leaves, leaves, everywhere—
On my hands, my feet, my hair!
On my shoulders, on my toes,
One right here upon my nose!
Leaves, leaves, everywhere—
On the ground and in the air!

Christy Thomas—Preschool
Southern Baptist Theological Seminary CDC
Louisville, KY

Ribbons on Rings

Make some sturdy streamers for your preschoolers after a quick visit to the office supply store! Purchase a class supply of metal binder rings there. Then tie long lengths of curling ribbon to each binder ring and use your scissors to curl the ribbon. Have youngsters use the streamers as they move to recorded music. If desired, instruct little ones to freeze when you stop the music. Or add some skills by placing colored circles on the floor. When you stop the music, have each child run to the circle that matches her streamer color. Or distribute two of each color streamer. When you stop the music, have youngsters find a child whose streamer color matches her own. Then invite the partners to dance together when the music begins again!

Wendi Fleer—PreK
Emanuel Lutheran Preschool
LaHabra, CA

Get Moving!

Movement Ideas for Preschoolers

These Feet Were Made for Moving!

When the music stops in Hot Potato, the potato stops. So what stops moving in a game called Hot Feet? Youngsters' feet, of course. To begin this activity, name a movement such as hopping on one foot, running in place, or skipping. Start the music and have students perform the named action. Periodically stop the music and direct students to sit down wherever they are. After everyone is seated, name another action. Resume playing the music and have students perform the action until the music is stopped again.

Stacey Burton—Preschool
Memorial Education Center

Rockin' and Rollin'

Even your shyest preschooler will want to move to the music with this idea! Collect a colorful flyswatter for each child in your class. (See the parent note on page 116.) Demonstrate how to use the swatter as a pretend guitar. Play an upbeat musical selection such as Greg and Steve's "ABC Rock" or "The Number Rock." Then invite your youngsters to strum their "guitars" and move to the beat of the music. Have students play their flyswatter guitars often. By the end of the school year, you might want to include a lively number for them to perform during a program. Come on, everyone! Let's rock!

Kris Kelly—Preschool
Country Kids Preschool
Spanish Fork, UT

Tiptoe, Reach, Wiggle

From following directions to moving to counting, this simple poem is packed with preschool learning fun! Recite the poem shown and then have students perform the actions as directed. Repeat the activity, replacing the underlined word with other action words, such as *hop, clap,* and *jump.* For added learning fun, recite the poem at a different speed each time, and have students perform the actions to match the tempo of the poem.

Stand on your tiptoes.
Reach for the sky.
Wiggle your nose
And blink one eye.
Snap your fingers.
Okay, then…
[Count] with me from one to ten.
1, 2, 3, 4, 5, 6, 7, 8, 9, 10!

Kathleen Hershey
Valencia, CA

Humpty Dumpty Sat on a Wall

Your preschoolers will have a ball and a great fall with this movement activity. Invite a few students to play the part of Humpty Dumpty, and direct them to sit as shown. Have the remaining children serve as "all the king's horses and all the king's men." As you recite the rhyme, have the Humpty Dumptys "fall down" at the appropriate time. Direct the king's horses and men to gallop to the Humptys and then attempt to put them together by gently wiggling their feet. Repeat the activity and have students switch roles.

Amy Wilson—PreK
Wee Care Daycare
Kearney, MO

Get Moving!

Movement Ideas for Preschoolers

SQUAWK! SQUAWK!

Birds in the Nest

This group game is perfect to play outdoors on a spring day! Choose six children to form a circle (the nest), holding hands and keeping their arms raised. Have the remaining children form a line and weave in and out of the circle, passing under the raised arms. As the line of children runs in and out, say, "Little birds, little birds, run don't walk! Run 'til you hear a squawk, squawk, SQUAWK!" On the third "squawk," the children forming the nest lower their arms. Any children trapped inside the nest joins the circle for the next round, making the nest larger. Keep playing until all the players have been caught.

Barb Stefaniuk
Kerrobert Tiny Tots Playschool
Kerrobert, Saskatchewan, Canada

Animal Moves

Invite youngsters to act out each line of this movement poem. Then say the poem a second time at a faster tempo, having youngsters move quickly. Then try it a third time, saying the poem slowly and moving slowly. And just watch those wonderful wiggles when you recite the last line!

Walk like an elephant.
Hop like a frog.
Swim like a fish.
Wag like a dog.

Fly like a butterfly.
Flit like a bee.
Gallop like a horse.
Wiggle like me!

Suzanne Moore
Irving, TX

Jump on Your Name

This fun idea will get preschoolers moving *and* spelling their names! Use sidewalk chalk to write each child's name on a sidewalk or blacktop area. Write the letters of each name in a vertical column. Have each child stand at the base of her name. Then call out a movement, such as "Jump!" Ask each child to jump on each of her letters, saying them as she goes. After having each child return to the first letter in her name. Call out a different movement, such as "Tiptoe" or "Hop on one foot."

Dawn Schu—Preschool
Resurrection Preschool
Chicago, IL

Puddle Jumping, Hopping, and Crawling

If a spring rain keeps you inside, help your students get out their wiggles and work their muscles with some indoor puddles! Give each child a scarf to lay on the floor and serve as a puddle. Call out various actions, such as "Hop into your puddle," "Skip around your puddle," or "Leap over your puddle." Not only will youngsters be working on motor skills, but they'll be practicing positional words too!

Amber Peck—Preschool
Little Learners Preschool
Lehi, UT

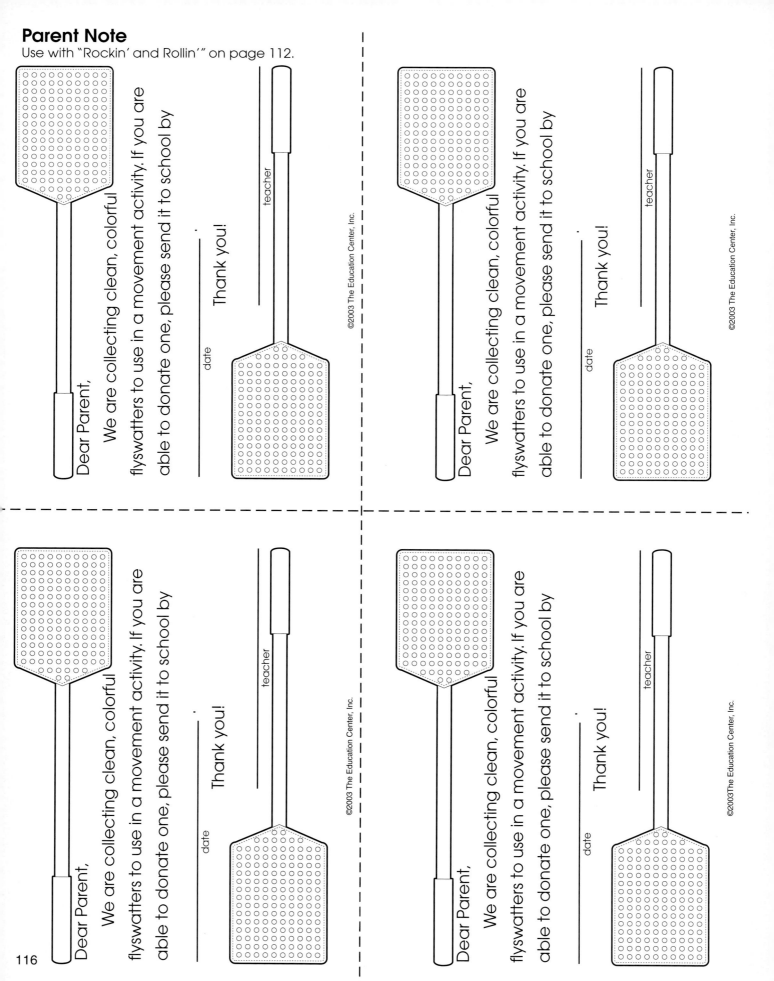

Dear Parent,

We are collecting clean, colorful flyswatters to use in a movement activity. If you are able to donate one, please send it to school by _____.

date

Thank you!

_____ teacher

©2003 The Education Center, Inc.

Dear Parent,

We are collecting clean, colorful flyswatters to use in a movement activity. If you are able to donate one, please send it to school by _____.

date

Thank you!

_____ teacher

©2003 The Education Center, Inc.

Dear Parent,

We are collecting clean, colorful flyswatters to use in a movement activity. If you are able to donate one, please send it to school by _____.

date

Thank you!

_____ teacher

©2003 The Education Center, Inc.

Dear Parent,

We are collecting clean, colorful flyswatters to use in a movement activity. If you are able to donate one, please send it to school by _____.

date

Thank you!

_____ teacher

©2003 The Education Center, Inc.

Getting Your Ducklings in a Row

Getting Your Ducklings

Step Up to the Line

Help little ones line up with these fun footsteps! To make a set, cut a pair of construction paper footprints for each child in your class. (See the pattern on page 126.) Label each pair with the color of the paper, a number, and the words *left* and *right*. Then attach the footprints (labeled side up) to the back side of a clear carpet runner. Place the runner near your classroom door. The cutouts will help your youngsters know just where to stand, and you can reinforce colors and numbers every time you line up. What neat feet!

Joyce Takak—Preschool
Kawerak Head Start/Aniguiin
Elim, AK

Ping-Pong Ball Calendar

Your class will have a ball at calendar time when you try this tip! To begin, attach a blank calendar grid and the appropriate monthly heading to a bulletin board. Attach the loop side of a small piece of self-adhesive Velcro fastening tape to each square on the grid. Then number 31 Ping-Pong balls with the numerals 1–31. Add the hook side of the Velcro tape to each ball. Each day, have a child stick the ball with the date onto the appropriate square on the calendar.

If desired, use colored markers to draw simple pictures on the balls for special days or holidays.

Shirley Zeamer—PreK
    and Kindergarten
St. Luke's Lutheran
Kenosha, WI

Boo-Boo Box

Keep first-aid supplies close at hand when you're outside on the playground by creating a boo-boo box! Fill an inexpensive toolbox with bandages, wipes, first-aid cream, and other first-aid supplies. And, if you don't want to carry the box back and forth each time you take little ones outdoors, set up a rural mailbox on your playground and keep the toolbox inside it. Your supplies will stay dry and ready for any boo-boos that happen during outdoor play.

Jo Wallace—Preschool
Ms. Jo's Preschool
Crockett, TX

in a Row — Tips for Getting Organized

Transition Timer

Do your preschoolers have a bit of trouble making the transition from one activity to another? Try a kid-friendly timer! Shop discount stores for a timer in a cute design that will appeal to your little ones. Then set the timer when youngsters begin an activity. Explain to your preschoolers that when the timer rings, it will be time to move on to the next activity. When it rings, say something such as, "Oh, listen! Mr. Bear is reminding us that it's time to clean up for lunch. Let's go!" Before you know it, transitions will be a treat!

Laurie Podd—Three-Year-Olds
Pinnacle Learning Center
Mahwah, NJ

Getting Into Centers

Looking for an easy way to get your preschoolers from group time into centers? Choose a number of items from each center that corresponds to the number of children allowed in the center. For example, if two children can paint at the easel, take two paintbrushes. If four children can go to dramatic play, choose four dress-up items. Place all the representative items on a tray. Call youngsters up one at a time to choose an item from the tray and take it to the chosen center. When the items are gone, the centers are full!

Kellie Kochensparger—Director
Mini University, Inc.—MVH Child Care Center
Dayton, OH

A Color-Coded Carpet

Guide your preschoolers to your preferred seating arrangements for storytime or group time with the help of colored Velcro fastening tape. Choose one color of Velcro tape and attach strips to your carpet in rows for storytime. Choose another color and attach strips in a circle for group time or show-and-tell. Then just name a color and little ones will know where to sit for the planned activity.

Crystal Young—PreK
Rodriguez School
Austin, TX

Getting Your Ducklings

Overalls Organization

Monitoring the number of children at each center is a snap with this idea! Staple an old pair of adult-sized overalls to a bulletin board. Or make a pair of overall cutouts from poster board. Label each pocket with the name of a different center. Next, use a photocopier to enlarge the tool patterns on page 260. Write the name of a different center on each enlarged pattern. Photocopy the programmed patterns to make tools equal to the number of children allowed at each center. (For example, make two tools for the blocks center to indicate that two children are allowed in the area.) Color and laminate the patterns. Cut them out and then punch a hole in the top of each one. Place the tools in the corresponding pockets on the overalls.

To use the overalls organizer, a child chooses a center, removes that tool from the pocket, and then hangs it on a self-adhesive hook at the center. An empty pocket indicates a center has the maximum number of children allowed, and the child must choose a different center.

Sue Fleischmann—Preschool, Holy Cross School, Menomonee Falls, WI

No More Lost Notes!

Here's a quick and easy way to send home reminders about important school events. Use a computer to print your reminder on address labels. At the end of the day, peel off the labels and stick each one onto a different child's clothing. Students will love showing off these nifty notes, and parents will be grateful for a reminder that sticks!

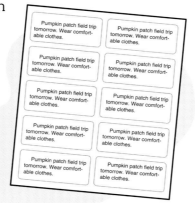

Karen Griffin
Cair Paravel–Latin School
Topeka, KS

Stickers by Season

If you're stuck on stickers, this organization tip is for you! Sort your stickers by season or theme; then place each set in a separate resealable sandwich bag. Use a permanent marker to label each bag; then file them alphabetically or by month in a small shoe box. Now finding that perfect seasonal sticker is a snap!

Deborah Wright—Preschool
SonShine Day Care
Okemos, MI

120

in a Row Tips for Getting Organized

Border in a Bottle

Use this idea to get your bulletin board border in order! In advance, collect clean two-liter plastic soda bottles. Remove the labels; then cut off the top half of each bottle. Coil the borders and then place them inside the bottles. For compact storage, stack the bottles inside one another. The clear plastic sides make it easy to find just the right border at a glance!

Linda Dammann—Preschool, Immanuel Lutheran School, Columbus, NE

A Place for Puppets

If the shoe rack fits, store puppets on it! Purchase an inexpensive shoe rack that is made to hang over doors. Set up the rack in your classroom and place hand puppets on it. If you have puppets for teacher use only, hang them on the higher racks; then place puppets for student use on the lower racks. How neat!

Cathy Consford—Director, Buda Primary Early Learning Center, Buda, TX

May I Have Your Attention, Please?

Need a catchy way to catch youngsters' attention? Try this call-and-response song and invite youngsters to repeat each line after you. By the end of the tune, you'll have a captive audience!

(sung to the tune of "Are You Sleeping?")

Teacher: Pay attention.
Students: Pay attention.
Teacher: Eyes on me. *Point to eyes.*
Students: Eyes on me.
Teacher: Children, are you listening? *Cup hands around ears.*
Students: Children, are you listening?
Teacher: One, two, three. *Point to eyes and ears and then put finger over lips.*
Students: One, two, three.

Betsy Gaynor—PreK, Creative Nursery School, Naperville, IL

Getting Your Ducklings

Glitter Bag

Love glitter but hate the mess? The answer to neater glitter application is in the bag! Pour about a half cup of glitter into a gallon-size zippered plastic freezer bag. Then have a child paint glue onto the project to which you want to add glitter. Place the project in the bag with the glitter, seal the bag, and have the child give it a shake! Then remove the item and give it one last shake over a trash can. *Much* neater!

Irene Miller—Preschool
WSOS Child Development Program
Elmore, OH

Straw Solution

If your children bring their own snacks or lunches to school, you've probably encountered drink boxes or pouches with missing straws. Keep a supply of coffee-stirring sticks on hand to solve this problem! They're the perfect size to fit drink boxes or pouches, and just as easy to insert as the original straws.

Linda Bille—Three- and Four-Year-Olds
Riviera United Methodist Preschool
Redondo Beach, CA

Spy Toy

Encourage your preschoolers to clean up with this version of I Spy. As youngsters begin to clean, tell them that you spy a special toy, but don't tell them which toy it is. When the room is clean, reveal which toy was the special "spy toy" for the day and reward the youngster who put it away with a small treat or special token.

Laura Seidensticker—Preschool Special Education
Decorah Elementary
West Bend, WI

in a Row Tips for Getting Organized

Sweet Savings

If your little ones sometimes need to save a toy, a seat, or a project as they step away, have them use this sweet idea—a Save Pop! To make one, cut two same-sized circles from the same color of tagboard. On one circle, glue the child's picture. On the other, write her name. Glue the circles back-to-back around a craft stick, and you have a Save Pop! Store the pops in an upside-down egg carton with a hole punched in each cup. Encourage a child to retrieve her Save Pop and use it to sweetly tell others that an item is in use!

Kellie Murphy—Preschool
Clubhouse for Kids
Cross Plains, WI

A Banner Idea

Tired of cutting or die-cutting letters to make titles for your bulletin boards? Try this tip! Print out banners from your computer instead! You can adjust the lettering size and add clip art to make a professional-looking title in no time!

Sarah Booth—Four- and Five-Year-Olds
Messiah Nursery School
South Williamsport, PA

Tissue Paper Totes

Check this out! Check boxes make handy storage containers for tissue paper pieces! Ask a few parents to donate the boxes they get when they order new checks. Keep each color of tissue paper scraps or precut squares in a separate box labeled with the color. They stack easily on a shelf or in a basket of supplies. When it's time to use the tissue paper for an art project, open a box, separate the lid from the bottom, and you have two boxes for little hands to reach into!

Hallie Michealson
Hallie's Child Care
Ramsey, MN

123

Getting Your Ducklings

Sorting Songs

Here's a simple summer project that will help keep you organized throughout the next school year. Make photocopies of all your favorite children's songs and glue each one onto a large index card. Sort the songs by theme and file them in an index-card box. Or punch a hole in one corner of each card and use a loose-leaf ring to bind the cards together by theme. Then store each set of songs with your other items for that theme. Now finding that perfect seasonal song is a snap!

Rachel Sutherland—Preschool
KIDS FIRST Learning Place
Middleville, MI

Dena Warner—PreK
Kendall-Whittier Elementary
Tulsa, OK

Use Your Noodle!

During the summer, swim noodles are everywhere! Stock up on a few to help keep your sand table area spick-and-span! Use a sharp knife to carefully cut the noodles to match the length and width of your sand table. Then slice through the noodles and attach them to your table as shown. The noodles will help prevent sand from spilling onto the floor. They will also provide a soft surface for little ones to wipe their hands on when finished. Want a money-saving tip? Wait for end-of-summer sales and then stock up on discounted noodles. Now *that's* using your noodle!

Elisa Goldman—PreK
St. Martin's Head Start
Philadelphia, PA

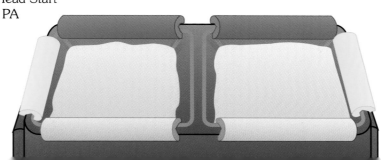

Dust Busters

Keep the dust bunnies at bay with this tip for summer storage! Place all of your books, toys, and manipulatives on shelves in your classroom. Then tape plastic painting tarps over the front of the shelves. When returning to your classroom after summer vacation, simply remove the plastic from the shelves. Wipe down the outside of the shelves with a damp cloth, and your dusting is done!

Peggy Morin Bruno, Squadron Line School, Simsbury, CT

in a Row
Tips for Getting Organized

Scrub-a-dub-dub

Do you have a Water Day planned for your preschoolers? If so, take the opportunity to have your swimsuit-clad students help you clean the class chairs! Set your classroom chairs outside near a supply of sponges and cans of shaving cream. Invite each child to squirt a little shaving cream onto a sponge and then scrub the chairs. Next, have each child take a turn with the hose and spray the chairs clean. Can't you just hear the squeals over such squeaky-clean chairs?

Kathy Rollins—PreK, The Children's Creative Corner, Springfield, MA

Sew Cute!

Summer is the perfect time to start sewing for the next school year, so start now to make a class supply of cute chair covers for your next class! First, measure the back of a classroom chair to find out how much fabric you will need to cover each chair back. Next, visit your local fabric store and purchase a variety of inexpensive fabric remnants to use for the covers. Sew three sides of the fabric together, leaving one side open to slip over the chair. Next, sew a clear plastic pocket on the back of each cover. Write each child's name on a separate index card and then slip each card into a different pocket. The variety of fabrics will not only brighten your classroom, but it will also help each child recognize her chair and name more quickly. When students are familiar with their chairs, keep your classroom interesting by mixing up the names in the pockets and having students find their new seats.

Amy Flori—PreK
Grace Lutheran CDC
Paris, IL

Summer Reading

Want to get a jump start on planning for next year? Spend a summer afternoon thoroughly reviewing those teacher resources that you put aside during the school year. When you come across an idea that you would like to use in the upcoming year, write the title of the idea, the name of the resource in which it appears, and the page number on an index card. Take note of each idea on a separate card; then place each card in your corresponding file. Throughout your next school year, you won't have to search to find that perfect idea—it will already be documented in your files!

Sherry McClure—Three-Year-Olds
Western School
N. Lauderdale, FL

Footprint Pattern
Use with "Step Up to the Line'" on page 118.

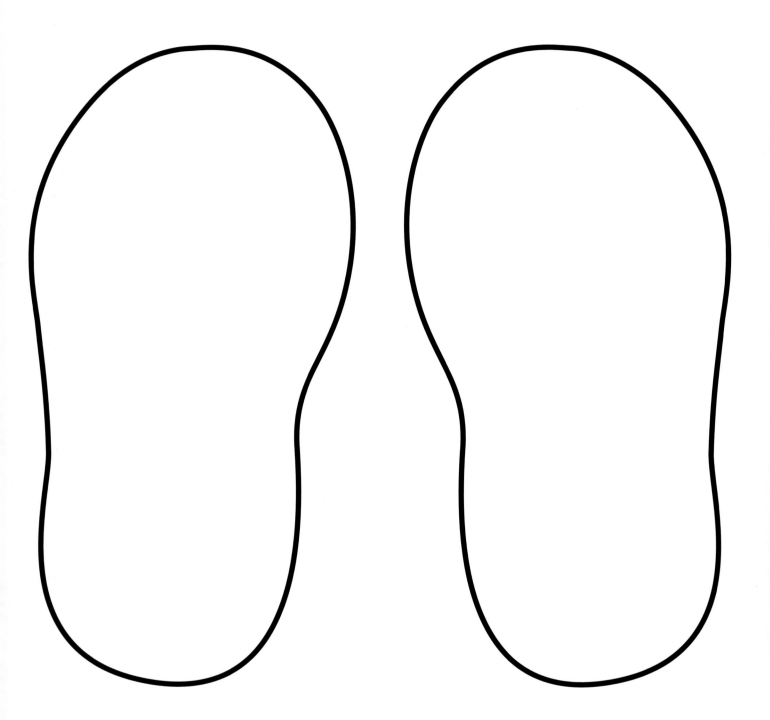

IT'S CIRCLE TIME

Bring a Friend to Show-and-Tell!

Introduce show-and-tell at the beginning of the year by asking each child to bring in a stuffed animal friend to share with the group. As little ones tell about their stuffed friends, talk about real friends too. Then, each month, specify a different theme for show-and-tell that will help this activity continue to tie into your curriculum. For example, ask youngsters to bring in pictures of loved ones near Valentine's Day or items in their favorite colors during a unit on colors.

Bess McGrath—PreK
St. Rita School
Hamden, CT

Musical Names

This twist on Musical Chairs will help your youngsters recognize their names! First, print each child's name on a separate index card. Then place a class supply of chairs in a circle and put a name card on each chair. Play recorded music and have youngsters walk around the circle of chairs. When the music stops, have each child find the chair with her name, pick up the card, and sit down. Then switch the cards to different chairs, restart the music, and play again! No losers—just winners in *this* name game!

Dorothy Hso—Four- and Five-Year-Olds
Grace Brethren Preschool
Westerville, OH

Kid-in-the-Box

Focus on students' names with this active circle-time activity! Ask your preschoolers to gather in a circle and pretend to be jack-in-the-box toys. Have them crouch down, put their heads down, and cover their heads with their hands. Say the chant below; then encourage your little ones to pop up to a standing position and shout, "Yes, I will!" Continue by having each child, in turn, crouch in the center of the circle. Then have the other students recite the chant with you, substituting the child's name for "Jack."

Jack-in-the-box sits so still....
Won't you come out, Jack?

Beth Lemke—PreK, Highland Headstart, Coon Rapids, MN

My Little Turkey

"Wattle" you get when you put feathers on your flannelboard? A colorful turkey, of course! To prepare, cut a simple turkey head and body from brown felt. Use a marker to draw the turkey's face. Cut a class supply of simple feather shapes from red, blue, green, yellow, and orange felt. Place the turkey head and body on your flannelboard; then gather youngsters and give each one a feather. Teach them the following song. When a child hears her feather color sung, she adds her feather to the turkey. After singing the verse for each color, your turkey will be one beautiful bird!

(sung to the tune of "Short'nin' Bread")

My little turkey
Has feathers, feathers.
My little turkey
Has feathers of [red].

LeeAnn Collins—Director
Sunshine House Preschool
Lansing, MI

What Do You See?

Get your preschoolers thinking and talking with the help of some magazine pictures. Cut interesting pictures from old magazines and mount each one on a sheet of paper. At circle time, hold up a picture and ask student volunteers to tell you about it. Guide students as necessary by asking questions such as the following: Who is in this picture? Where do you think this picture was taken? How can you tell? How do you think this person feels? If desired, have youngsters make up a story about the picture for you to record. A daily dose of picture talk will make students' oral language skills soar!

Melissa Weimer—Hearing Impaired Preschool
Stepanski ECC
Waterford, MI

129

Story Starter in a Stocking

A stocking stuffed with story starters is sure to give youngsters' language skills a lift! Before students arrive in the morning, place a few small items inside a Christmas stocking. During your group time, begin the story by saying, "Once upon a time…" Then pull an object out of the stocking and incorporate it into the story. Continue pulling items from the stocking and using them in the story. Repeat the activity daily, using different objects each time. When students are familiar with this storytelling process, invite each child, in turn, to pull an object from the stocking and add to the tale.

Carole Watkins—Librarian
Holy Family Child Care Center
Crown Point, IN

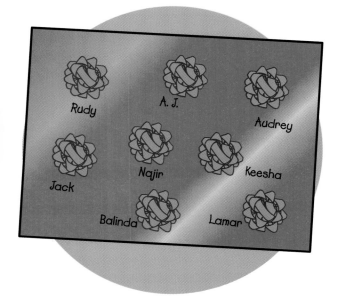

Pin the Bow on the Present

With the holiday season here, presents are everywhere! Invite students to practice their gift-wrapping skills with this fun adaptation of Pin the Tail on the Donkey. To prepare, wrap a sheet of poster board in holiday gift wrap and then laminate it. Hang the "present" at children's level. Line up your class a short distance away from the present. Hand the first child in line a self-adhesive bow. Blindfold the child and then have her walk to the present and stick the bow on it. Remove the blindfold; then write her name beside the bow. Continue the activity until each child has had a chance to add a bow to the present.

Sonya Bussan—Preschool
Third Presbyterian Head Start
Dubuque, IA

Silent I Spy

This circle-time game will settle your youngsters and help develop their visual discrimination skills. In advance, purchase an I Spy fabric panel. Or laminate a large piece of seasonal wrapping paper with large pictures. Display the I Spy fabric or wrapping paper in your circle-time area. Name an item for students to find by saying something like "I spy a red scarf." Then invite each child to find the named item and silently raise her hand to indicate she has found it. Allow students to search for a minute or two. Then choose one child with a raised hand to reveal the I Spy item.

Sharon Sipos—Three-Year-Olds
Prince George Christian Preschool
Prince George, VA

Let It Snow! Let It Snow! Let It Snow!

Put on some lively holiday music and get ready to rev up youngsters' motor skills! Have students hold the edges of a parachute. Open two bags of cotton balls and toss them into the center of the parachute to represent snow. Then throw in a few large jingle bells. Play upbeat musical selections such as "Let It Snow!" or "Jingle Bells." Have students vigorously shake the parachute to send the "snow" flying and get the jingle bells jingling. It's beginning to look and sound a lot like Christmas!

Lisa Waechter—Preschool
YMCA Cedear Lake Child Care Center
West Bend, WI

Who Me? Yes, You!

Adapt that favorite chant "Who Took the Cookies From the Cookie Jar?" into a lively hunt for a missing letter. Before students arrive in the morning, cover a letter from an alphabet strip displayed at children's level. During your group time, guide students to notice the missing letter from the chart; then invite students to join you in reciting the chant shown. Invite the last child named in the chant to uncover the letter from the chart.

Teacher: Who has the [F] from the alphabet? [Child's name]
      has the [F] from the alphabet.
Named child: Who me?
Class: Yes, you!
Named child: Couldn't be!
Class: Then who?
Named child: [Child's name] has the [F] from the alphabet.

Repeat the chant from the second line on, until each child has been named.

Marilyn Miller—Preschool
Preschool Potpourri
Richboro, PA

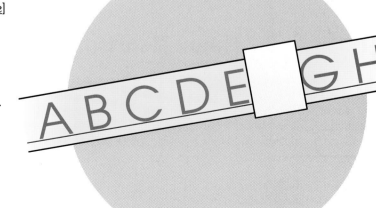

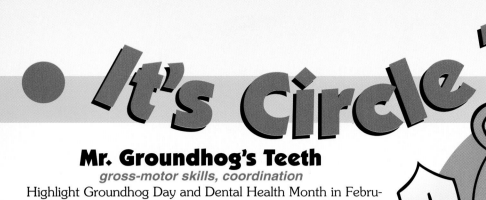

It's Circle Time

Mr. Groundhog's Teeth
gross-motor skills, coordination

Highlight Groundhog Day and Dental Health Month in February with this twist on Pin the Tail on the Donkey. Sketch a simple groundhog face and a few sets of "groundhog teeth" onto white poster board (see illustration). Laminate everything; then cut apart the sets of teeth. Post Mr. Groundhog on a wall at a child's eye level; then put Sticky-Tac adhesive on the back of each set of teeth. To play, blindfold a child and hand him a set of teeth. Spin him around; then set him on a course toward Mr. Groundhog. Have him try to stick the teeth in the correct place.

Amy Cowin
Washington County Educare
Potosi, MO

Who Is Hiding?
thinking skills, language

Put thinking skills to the test with this Valentine's Day activity. Seat your group in a semicircle; then spread a large blanket in front of them. Have everyone turn around and close his eyes as you secretly choose one child to hide under the blanket. Have students sing the song below; then have the child under the blanket say, "Happy Valentine's Day! Guess who?" Once the children have correctly guessed the identity of the hider, play again until everyone has had a turn to hide.

(sung to the tune of "Oh Where, Oh Where Has My Little Dog Gone?")

Oh who, oh who is our valentine friend?
Oh who, oh who can it be?
Give us a clue and we'll figure it out!
Oh who, oh who can it be?

Val Wilson—Preschool
Cove School
Beverly, MA

Name Hearts
literacy, name recognition

Send youngsters on a hunt for hearts in an activity that reinforces student names. To prepare, cut out a class supply of paper hearts; then label each one with a child's name. Scatter the hearts throughout your classroom. When you are ready to begin, have each child find a heart, read the name on it, and deliver it to that child.

Nancy Vogt—Preschool
Boothbay Head Start
Boothbay, ME

132

Emotions the Clown
social development

Help your preschoolers develop empathy and better understand emotions with the help of a clown face. Draw a simple head shape wearing a colorful clown hat, but leave off the facial features. Laminate the picture and post it on a wall near your group area. Each day at group time, lead youngsters to talk about feelings by recounting an event that took place in your classroom. For example, if there was a disagreement in the block area, talk about how the children involved felt. Use dry-erase markers to draw a face on the clown to represent the feeling they describe. Talk about how Emotions the Clown feels and why. Then invite youngsters to brainstorm ways to make Emotions feel better.

Diane Marks—Three- and Four-Year-Olds
Cedarburg Preschool
Cedarburg, WI

Leprechaun's Gold
number identification

Send your wee ones on a hunt for gold that will also sharpen their number-identification skills! In advance, make a supply of gold coins by cutting circles from yellow tagboard; then label each coin with a number from 1 to 10. Scatter the coins throughout your classroom. Sit at the front of the room with a pot and teach youngsters the following chant. Then send them hunting for gold! When a child brings you a coin, ask her to identify the number on it before adding it to the class collection.

Leprechaun, Leprechaun, I've been told
Hiding in our room are coins of gold!
Find them, find them, quick as can be.
Put them in the pot for you and me!

Lori Sazinski—Three-Year-Olds
The Villages Early Learning Center
The Villages, FL

It's Circle Time

What Do You Think About...?

thinking skills, language development

Get your preschoolers thinking and speaking with this idea for an ongoing display. Each day or each week, post a question, such as "What do you think about the dark?" or "What do you think about eating vegetables?" Working with one child at a time, ask the question and jot down the child's response to post on the display. At circle time, share what each child said and talk about the subject. Compile each child's answers into a booklet to send home at the end of the year.

Sharon Swenson—Toddler and PreK
Hazel Lake Montessori
Staples, MN

What do you think about taking a nap?

I like to snuggle with my toy rabbit.   Kavi

I don't like to take a nap.   JT

A Basket Full of Choices

management idea

Fill some plastic eggs with fresh ideas for making circle time fun! On slips of paper, write the titles of seasonal songs to sing, as well as simple directions for students to follow, such as "Hop on one foot" or "Count to ten." Put each slip of paper inside a plastic Easter egg; then put all the eggs in a basket with some Easter grass. Keep the basket in your group area. Each day, invite a child to pick out an egg and open it. Have the class sing the song or follow the directions together.

Cathy Consford—Director
Buda Primary Early Learning Center, Buda, TX

Christine Jenkins—PreK
Johnson Early Childhood Center, Weymouth, MA

Hop on 1 foot.

Where Was It?

positional words, language development

Reinforce positional words with this twist on a traditional egg hunt. Hide plastic Easter eggs throughout your classroom; then ask each youngster to find one. Ask each child to try hard to remember exactly where she finds her egg and to bring the egg back to your circle. Then ask each child, in turn, to describe where she found her egg. Emphasize any positional words she uses, such as "*on* a chair" or "*under* the art table."

Shelly Post—Preschool
ECSE Helping Hands Preschool
Great Bend, KS

My egg was behind a desk.

Carrot Hunt

letter-, number-, and shape-identification

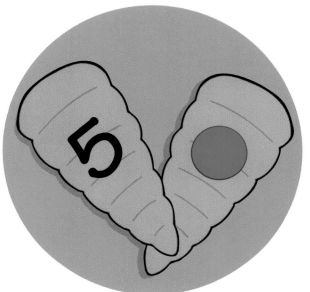

Put some crunch into your Eastertime scavenger hunt by hiding carrots instead of eggs! In advance, cut out a supply of paper carrots. Label each one with a letter, a number, or a shape for youngsters to identify. Then hide the paper carrots in your classroom. As little ones hunt for the carrots, have them sing the song below. When all the carrots have been found, have children take turns identifying the symbols or shapes on the carrots. Then celebrate with a fun treat of baby carrots and dip!

(sung to the tune of "Pawpaw Patch")

Pickin' up carrots and puttin' 'em in my basket,
Pickin' up carrots and puttin' 'em in my basket,
Pickin' up carrots and puttin' 'em in my basket,
Way down yonder in the bunny patch!

adapted from an idea by Jennifer Barton
Elizabeth Green School
Newington, CT

Five Little Bunnies

ordinal numbers

Make a set of five felt bunnies to use on your flannelboard with this countdown rhyme that reinforces ordinal numbers. Invite one child at a time to make a bunny "hop home."

[Five] little bunnies hopping down a trail.
The [fifth] one stepped on the [fourth] one's tail.
"Ouch!" said the bunny.
"I'm sorry," said his friend.
Then the [fifth] hopped home, and the [fourth] was on the end.

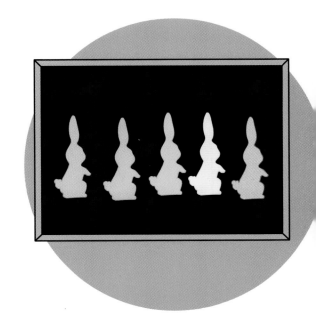

Repeat the verse two more times, substituting four *and* three *in the first line and the appropriate ordinal numbers in lines two and five. Then finish the poem with the following final verse:*

Two little bunnies hopping down a trail.
The second one stepped on the first one's tail.
"Ouch!" said the bunny.
"I'm sorry," said his friend.
Then the second hopped home, and the first said, "The end!"

Belinda Adkins—Preschool
Sissie Cares Preschool
Weston, WV

Watermelon, Watermelon

counting, fine-motor skills, early addition

It's summertime! Watermelons are ripe with learning opportunities! Provide each child with a slice of watermelon with seeds. Invite students to join you in singing the song shown. Then direct each child to remove the seeds from her slice of watermelon and count them. As students are counting seeds, draw a large watermelon on a dry-erase board. Then have each child tell the class how many seeds she counted; draw the corresponding number of seeds on the watermelon. After each child has had a turn, tally the total number of seeds from all the slices. Now that the seeds have been removed and counted, what should youngsters do next? Eat up, of course!

(sung to the tune of "Are You Sleeping?")

Watermelon, watermelon,
Red and green! Red and green!
Let's take all the seeds out.
Let's take all the seeds out
And count them! And count them!

Kathryn Davenport—PreK Special Education, Partin Elementary, Oiedo, FL

From Tadpole to Frog

science, sequencing

Sing this simple song at circle time to help youngsters learn the life cycle of a frog. If desired, sing the song and show sequencing cards that depict the transformation. (For a set of cards, see page 138.) Now hop to it!

(sung to the tune of "Twinkle, Twinkle, Little Star")

The tadpole hatches from an egg.
Then it sprouts two strong back legs.
Soon it gets its front legs too.
Can you guess? What do they do?
Now the tadpole is a frog
Jumping on a great big log!

adapted from a song by
Julie Hughes—Three-Year-Olds
Baxter YMCA Preschool
Indianapolis, IN

A Beautiful Day at the Beach
dramatic play, gross-motor development

Have each child bring in a favorite beach towel to make this movement activity seem more like a *real* day at the beach! Ask everyone to spread his towel in a large open area. Then say, "It's a beautiful day at the beach. Let's go swimming!" Have children pantomime running into the waves and swimming through the water. Then invite them to head back to their towels to take a rest. Next, say, "It's a beautiful day at the beach. Let's go fishing!" Have students stand up, bait their hooks, and cast their imaginary fishing lines out into the water. Of course, everyone will catch a *giant* fish and struggle to reel it in! After they take another rest on their beach towels, make more suggestions for beach activities, such as jogging, surfing, or playing ball!

Ada Goren, Winston-Salem, NC

Go Fish for a Wish
management tip

Promote children's choices by inviting your students to choose activities for your circle time. Ask each child to dictate a circle-time wish; then write her response on a paper fish cutout. For example, a child might say, "I wish we could sing 'Twinkle, Twinkle, Little Star,'" or "I wish we could play Duck, Duck, Goose." Collect these fishy wishes and keep them in a fishbowl in your group area. Each day at group time, invite a child to fish for a wish. Have her draw out one fish; then read and grant the wish! When the bowl is empty, restock it with more requests!

Ada Goren, Winston-Salem, NC

Sing
"Twinkle, Twinkle,
Little Star."

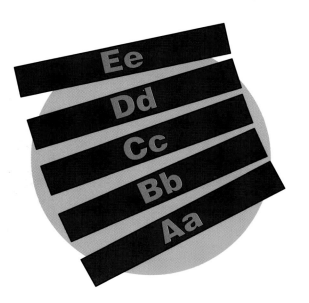

All Aboard!
letter or number identification and sequencing

Have youngsters make a play railroad, and preschool skills will be right on track! To prepare, cut out a class supply of black poster board strips to resemble railroad tracks. Program each track with a sequence of letters or numbers. Laminate the tracks and then place a self-adhesive strip of the hook side of a Velcro fastener on the back of each one. During your group time, provide each child with a track. Have the group work together to lay the tracks in sequence on a carpeted area. When the tracks have been laid, line up youngsters to create a train and then chug across the tracks. We've been working on the railroad!

Cathy Fontana

137

Frog Sequencing Cards
Use with "From Tadpole to Frog" on page 136.

KIDS IN THE KITCHEN

KIDS IN THE KITCHEN

Put on your apron and step into the kitchen—with your kids, of course! What's on the menu? A generous portion of learning opportunities served up with a batch of fun. Savor the following hands-on cooking activities, perfectly measured for preschool fun and teacher ease.

Here's what to do:

- Collect the necessary ingredients and utensils using the lists on one of the recipe cards below.
- Follow the teacher preparation guidelines for that cooking activity.
- Cut out the step-by-step recipe cards on pages 141 and 142.
- Display the cards on a bulletin board or chart in your cooking area so that the students can see the directions for the recipe you've selected. (The hand-washing card can be placed at the beginning of either recipe.)
- Discuss the directions with a small group of kids; then encourage them to get cooking!

Learning has never been so delicious!

Tasty Turkey Roll-Up

Ingredients for one:

flour tortilla
whipped cream cheese
2 slices of turkey sandwich meat
cranberry sauce

Utensils and supplies:

jumbo craft stick
paper plate for each child
spoon

Teacher preparation:

Keep turkey slices refrigerated until ready to use. Arrange the ingredients and utensils near the step-by-step recipe cards (see page 142).

First-Day Float

Ingredients for one:

cup of orange soda
scoop of orange sherbet
orange sprinkles

Utensils and supplies:

1 c. measuring cup
clear plastic cup for each child
ice-cream scoop
straw for each child

Teacher preparation:

Arrange the ingredients and utensils near the step-by-step recipe cards (see page 141). Help each child pour orange soda into a one-cup measuring cup

Recipe Cards
Use with "Tasty Turkey Roll-Up" on page 140.

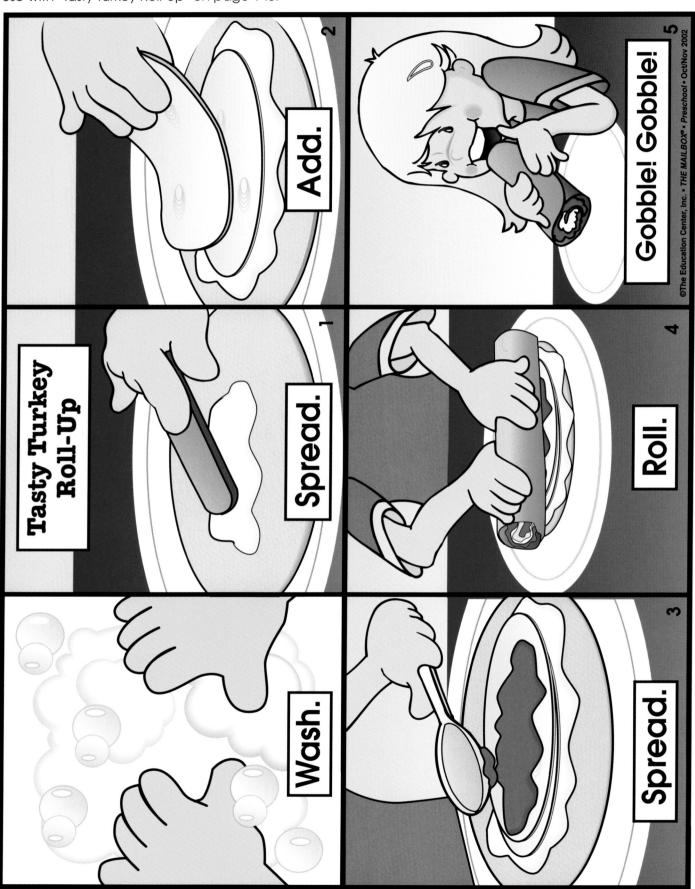

KIDS IN THE KITCHEN

Put on your apron and step into the kitchen—with your kids, of course! What's on the menu? A generous portion of learning opportunities served up with a batch of fun. Savor the following hands-on cooking activities, perfectly measured for preschool fun and teacher ease.

Here's what to do:

- Collect the necessary ingredients and utensils using the lists on one of the recipe cards below.
- Follow the teacher preparation guidelines for that cooking activity.
- Photocopy the step-by-step recipe cards on page 144 or 145.
- Color the cards; then cut them out.
- Display the cards on a bulletin board or chart in your cooking area so that the students can see the directions for the recipe you've selected.
- Discuss the directions with a small group of kids; then encourage them to get cooking!

Learning has never been so delicious!

Easter Egg Salad Sandwich

Ingredients for one:

2 slices of bread
egg salad
shredded carrot sticks
red and green pepper strips
sprouts

Utensils and supplies:

paper plate for each child
egg-shaped cookie cutter
serving bowl
serving spoon

Teacher preparation:

Prepare the egg salad. Peel and shred carrots. Slice red and green peppers. Arrange the ingredients and utensils near the step-by-step recipe cards (see page 144).

Mary Anne Quick
Middletown, RI

Peanut Butter and Banana Burrito

Ingredients for one:

flour tortilla
peanut butter
jelly
2 spoonfuls of sliced bananas

Utensils and supplies:

plastic knife
2 plastic spoons
paper plate for each child

Teacher preparation:

Peel and slice the bananas. Arrange the ingredients and utensils near the step-by-step recipe cards (see page 145).

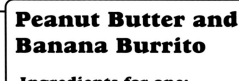

Recipe Cards

Use with "Easter Egg Salad Sandwich" on page 143.

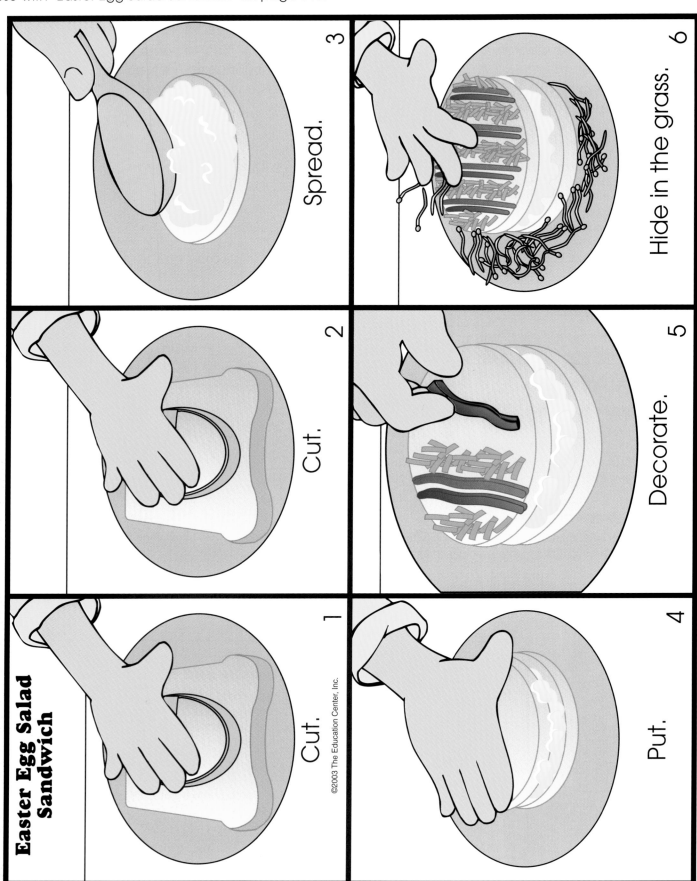

Easter Egg Salad Sandwich

1 Cut.

2 Cut.

3 Spread.

4 Put.

5 Decorate.

6 Hide in the grass.

©2003 The Education Center, Inc.

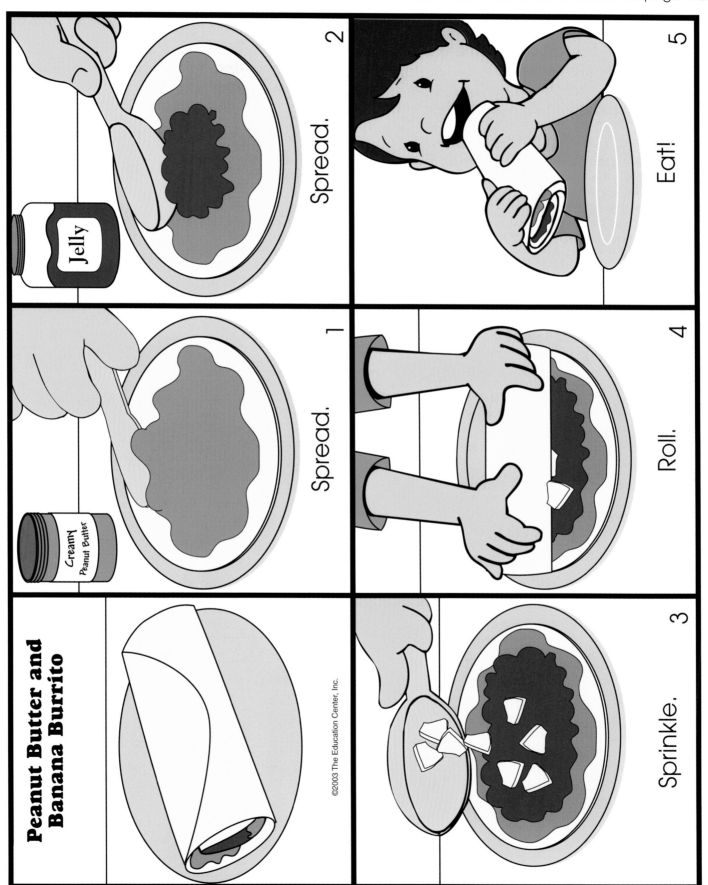

2 Spread.

5 Eat!

1 Spread.

4 Roll.

Peanut Butter and Banana Burrito

3 Sprinkle.

KIDS IN THE KITCHEN

Put on your apron and step into the kitchen—with your kids, of course! What's on the menu? A generous portion of learning opportunities served up with a batch of fun. Savor the following hands-on cooking activities, perfectly measured for preschool fun and teacher ease.

Here's what to do:

- Collect the necessary ingredients and utensils using the lists on one of the recipe cards below.
- Follow the teacher preparation guidelines for that cooking activity.
- Photocopy the step-by-step recipe cards on page 147 or 148.
- Color the cards; then cut them out.
- Display the cards on a bulletin board or chart in your cooking area so that the students can see the directions for the recipe you've selected.
- Discuss the directions with a small group of kids; then encourage them to get cooking!

Learning has never been so delicious!

Delicious Lily Pad

Ingredients for one:
slice-and-bake sugar cookie dough
green-tinted icing
flower-shaped cake decoration

Utensils and supplies:
paper plate for each child
jumbo craft stick for each child
knife *(for teacher use only)*
oven *(for teacher use only)*

Teacher preparation:
Slice sugar cookie dough; then cut out a small triangle shape from each slice to create a lily pad. Bake the cookies as directed on the package. Arrange the ingredients and utensils near the step-by-step recipe cards (see page 147).

Lari Junkin—Three-Year-Olds, Cathedral School
Natchez, MS

Tuna Toast

Ingredients for one:
slice of bread, toasted
1 tbsp. tuna salad
black olive slice

Utensils and supplies:
fish-shaped cookie cutter
tablespoon
paper plate for each child
toaster *(for teacher use only)*

Teacher preparation:
Prepare a batch of tuna salad. Toast a slice of bread for each child. Arrange the ingredients and utensils near the step-by-step recipe cards (see page 148).

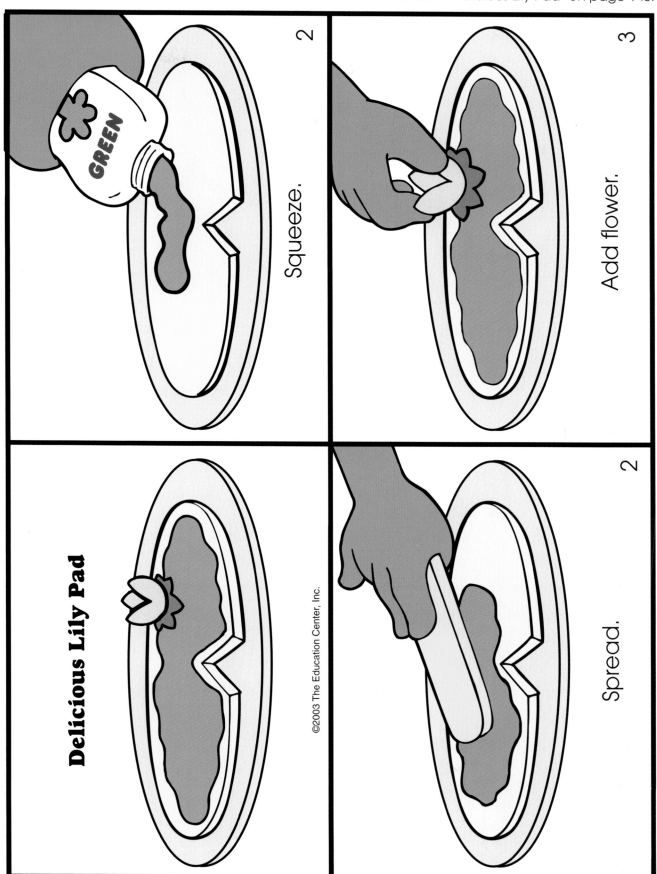

2

Squeeze.

3

Add flower.

Delicious Lily Pad

©2003 The Education Center, Inc.

2

Spread.

Recipe Cards

Use with "Tuna Toast" on page 146.

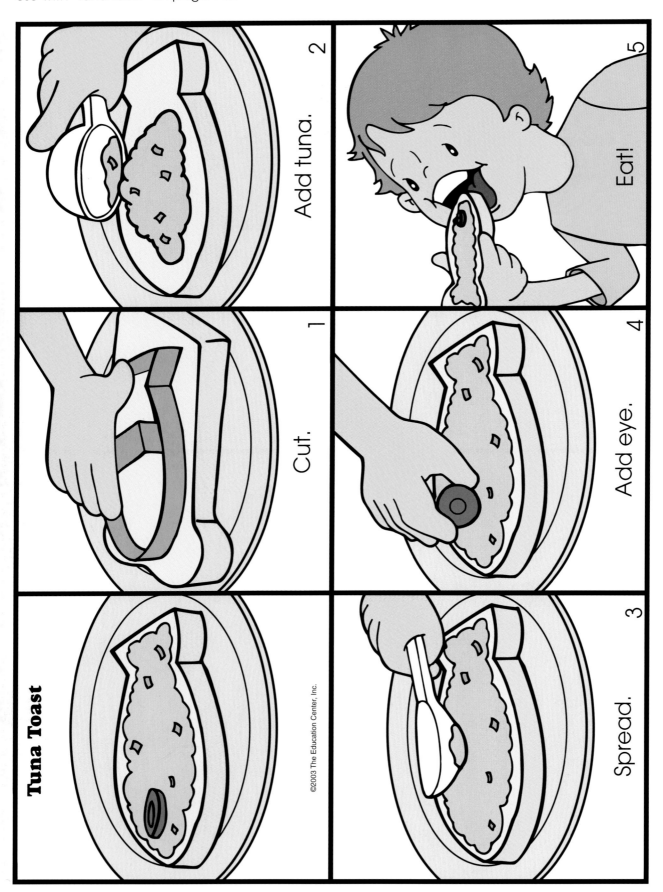

Tuna Toast

Cut. 1

Add tuna. 2

Spread. 3

Add eye. 4

Eat! 5

LEARNING CENTERS

Learning Centers

Games Center

A Place for Everything

Sharpen categorizing skills with this game involving household items. To prepare, cover six large coffee cans with felt, three with one color and three with another. (Overlap the felt to the inside on each can to cover any sharp edges.) Then add room labels and magazine photos to each set of cans as shown. Next, cut out magazine pictures of a variety of household items that might be found in any of the rooms. Mount each picture on a labeled index card.

To play, two students each take a set of cans. The pair places the pile of picture cards facedown between them. Each child takes a turn turning over a card and deciding in which room the item belongs. (Some items might be found in more than one room.) She then drops the picture card into the corresponding can. The pair continues until all the picture cards are sorted.

Holly Creep—Four- and Five-Year-Olds
Otterbein Day Care
Mt. Wolf, PA

Literacy Center

Stamps and Sounds

Do your preschoolers love rubber stamps? Then they'll love this stamping activity that reinforces letter sounds! As you study each letter of the alphabet, place large outlines of the letter in your literacy area, along with one or more rubber stamps of items beginning with that letter. Invite a child at this center to stamp the images within the outline of the letter. *B* is for butterflies, bears, and balloons!

Shelley Williams—Three- and Four-Year-Olds
Children's College
Layton, UT

Manipulatives Center

Top Matching

Give little fingers a workout at this matching center. Save plastic bottles or jars in a variety of sizes, along with their tops. Clean all the containers and tops thoroughly. Then place them in a tub, but leave the tops separate from the containers. Encourage youngsters to find and screw on the matching top for each bottle or jar.

Elytta Durkee—Four-Year-Olds
Lambs of Peace Preschool
Sun Prairie, WI

Dramatic-Play Area

The Three Pigs' House

This giant prop will be a BIG hit for imaginary play! Decorate three sides of a refrigerator box to resemble the three pigs' houses. On one side of the box, paint yellow straw (or glue on real straw). On the second side, paint or glue on sticks. Paint the third side red; then add strips of black electrical tape to resemble bricks. Cut a window in each decorated side; then cut a large door in the last side of the box. Add some simple pig and wolf masks and your preschoolers can start pretending!

Staci Dodson—Preschool
HCCD Head Start
Huntingdon County, PA

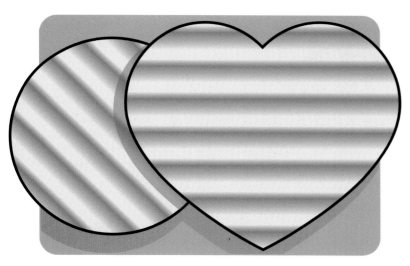

Math Center

Feelin' Good About Shapes

Add a textural element to a shape-matching activity by cutting the shapes from lightbulb holders instead of construction paper. Cut pairs of basic shapes from the ribbed inserts used to hold lightbulbs in their boxes. Then mix the shapes together and invite your little ones to match the pairs.

Lisbeth Taylor—Three- and Four-Year-Olds
Vernon Child Development Center
Big Bend, WI

Puzzle Area

A Puzzle of...Me!

Your youngsters will love putting together these life-sized puzzles of themselves! To make one, unroll a length of white bulletin board paper a little longer than the child's height. Have the child lie down on the paper as you trace around her body with a marker. Then encourage her to use crayons to color in her outline and add her facial features and hair. Cut along the outline; then cut the puzzle into several pieces (depending on your students' abilities). Be sure to label each piece with the child's name. Laminate the pieces; then place them in a large zippered plastic bag labeled with the child's name. At center time, invite preschoolers to piece together these personal puzzles!

Suzanne Godfrey—Preschool
FCCDC
Madison, FL

Learning Centers

Math Center

Monster Footprints

Make a supply of wacky footprints for some monstrous fun in your math area! From black construction paper, cut monster footprints in odd shapes and with varying numbers of toes. Laminate the footprints for durability. Invite little ones to count the toes on each footprint, sort or match the footprints by shape, or create a trail with a specific number of footprints. Hey—monster feet are neat!

Annette Hulen—Preschool
Glendale, AZ

Painting Center

Fall Leaf Paintings

Use those beautiful leaves your preschoolers pick up on nature walks for this painting activity. Have each child tape a few leaves onto a sheet of paper. Attach the paper to your easel; then invite the child to paint the entire paper with orange and yellow paint. When the paint dries, remove the leaves and look at the design that's left behind!

Angie Jenkins—Two-Year-Olds
Love to Learn
Knoxville, TN

Discovery Center

See the Seeds

Help little ones understand the concept of seeds growing into specific plants with this addition to your discovery area. Gather several packets of vegetable, fruit, and flower seeds. Cut one end off each packet, leaving as much of the front panel picture intact as possible. Pour the seeds from each packet into a separate zippered plastic bag; then slip the open packet into the bag too. Seal the bags and add clear tape to discourage youngsters from dumping the seeds. Place the bags in your discovery area and invite children to examine them. Encourage them to note how the seeds look alike and different. Take seeds from a few of the packages and plant them. Ask youngsters to predict what will happen. Will the plants look like the pictures on the packets?

Meghan Painton—Preschool, Brunswick Head Start, Brunswick, ME

Sweet Harvest Farms
GREEN BEANS 49¢

Sweet Harvest Farms
TOMATO 59¢

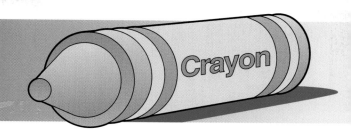

Games Area

Boo Bowling

Roll into Halloween with a game of Boo Bowling! To make ghostly bowling pins, drape circles cut from an old white sheet over several tall plastic containers, such as those used for powdered coffee creamer. Tie a length of black yarn around the neck of each container to hold the fabric in place; then use a black marker to add eyes. Set the ghost pins in bowling formation; then invite a child to roll a heavy ball toward the pins to try to knock them down.

Jeanie Young—Special Education
Lake Orion Community Schools L.O.O.K. First Program
Lake Orion, MI

Reading Center

Hayride Reading

Park a wagon in your reading center and add some props to give it the feel of an old-fashioned hayride! Add some straw, an old quilt, and one or two small pumpkins. If none of your students are allergic to hay, set some hay bales around the wagon and stack a few more pumpkins on top. Then fill a wooden crate with pumpkin books and encourage your preschoolers to "fall" into reading!

Christy McClellan—Preschool
Songwoods
Waynesboro, PA

Puzzle Area

A Real Pumpkin Puzzle

Youngsters will be piecing together this pumpkin puzzle again and again when you try this imaginative carving idea! Cut off the top of a large pumpkin and clean the inside as you would for carving a jack-o'-lantern. Next, draw a wavy line all around the pumpkin, about two inches below the cut-off top. Cut on the line; then set aside the resulting ring of pumpkin. Draw a different type of line, such as a zigzag, about two inches from the current top. Cut along that line to create a second pumpkin ring. Keep going, using a unique cut for each layer. Then challenge your students to visit the puzzle area to reassemble the pumpkin by stacking the rings atop one another. Cool!

Marie Drake—Five-Year-Olds
Younger Years, Inc.
Meadville, PA

Learning Centers

Ice Fishing

Put a wintry twist on your dramatic-play area when you send little ones ice fishing! Bring in a small plastic wading pool and cover the top of it with an old white sheet or some white plastic. Cut a hole in the center large enough to hold a plastic bucket or gallon ice-cream tub. Toss in some magnetic fish (or fish cutouts to which you've attached paper clips). Then provide a fishing pole (a dowel or yardstick) with a magnet tied to one end and another bucket to hold the "catch." Invite youngsters at this center to catch some fish and take them to the play kitchen to fry!

Peggy Coggins—Preschool Special Education
Stewart Elementary
Cincinnati, OH

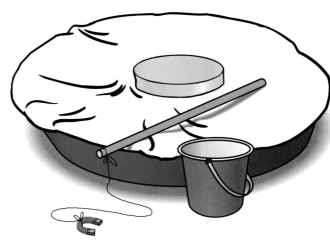

Games Center

Flip the Latke

Your little ones will flip for this game that helps them practice hand-eye coordination! To make a frying pan perfect for flipping latke look-alikes, first cover a sturdy paper plate with aluminum foil. Use heavy-duty tape to attach the flat blade of a spatula to the bottom of the foil-covered plate so that the handle of the spatula serves as the handle of the frying pan. Next, cut a potato latke from tagboard and paint it brown. Punch a hole in the latke cutout and another hole in the pan, opposite the handle. Thread an 18-inch length of yarn through both holes and tie one end to the latke and one to the pan. Then let the flipping begin! Can *you* get the latke into the pan?

Robbin Sigman—PreK Special Education
Just Kids
Lindenhurst, NY

Math Center

Tops and Bottoms

Focus on size matching with a center that makes good use of holiday gift boxes and wrapping paper. Collect gift boxes in assorted sizes. For a challenge, include a few that are the same size. Wrap the tops and bottoms of the boxes in holiday wrapping paper, but don't make the tops and bottoms match. Ask students at this center to find the right top for each box bottom by paying attention to size, not the patterns on the papers.

Sharon Jefferies and Susan Tornebene—Preschool ESE
Palma Sola Elementary
Bradenton, FL

January

Sunday	Monday	Tuesday	Wednesday	Thursday	Friday	Saturday
						1
2	3	4	5	6	7	8
9	10	11	12	13	14	15

Writing Center

Calendar Crazy

'Tis the season to toss out last year's calendars! So why not use them in your writing area to help preschoolers practice writing numbers? Collect a supply of old calendars and place them at your writing center. Invite children to trace over the numbers on larger calendars or to reproduce each number in the box for that date. After lots of practice with writing numbers, print off some blank calendar grids from your computer and invite youngsters to fill in all the numbers for the current month. Pretty soon they'll be making whole calendars!

Kaylene Killebrew—Birth to Age 5
Tuscola, IL

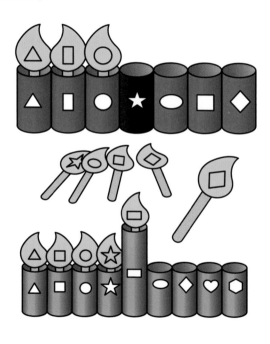

Math Center

That's a Match!

Light the way to shape matching with this center idea! Construct a simple menorah from eight toilet tissue tubes and one paper towel tube. Or create a Kwanzaa kinara from seven toilet tissue tubes. Cover each tube with paper; then glue or staple the tubes together side by side (as shown). Next, cut out a yellow construction paper flame for each tube. Be sure the base of each flame is wider than the tube openings. Laminate the flames for durability; then attach a craft stick to the back of each one. Lastly, program each flame and each tube so that you have pairs of shapes.

To use the center, a child "lights" each candle by slipping in the flame that corresponds to the shape on the candle.

Meg Townsend—Three-Year-Olds
Elbow Lane Nursery School
Warrington, PA

Painting Center

A Cookie Sheet Palette

Looking for easy-to-use painting materials? Look in the kitchen! First, fold a few paper towels so that they fit on the bottom of a cookie sheet. Squirt liquid tempera paint in two different (complementary) colors onto the paper towels. Place a sheet of art paper on another cookie sheet. Invite a child at this center to press cookie cutters onto the paint-soaked paper towels and then press them onto the paper to make prints. Encourage her to keep going until she has a whole tray of yummy-looking cookies!

Cynthia Sayman—Toddlers
All My Children Daycare Center
Binghamton, NY

Learning Centers

Handpicked Hearts

Making these simple Valentine's Day gifts will improve youngsters' fine-motor skills. Set a cookie sheet of candy conversation hearts in your fine-motor center, along with a pair of small tongs. Give each child at this center a small zippered plastic bag. Have him use the tongs to pick up ten or more of the small candies and deposit them in the bag. Then slip in a copy of the poem on page 162 and have little ones take the treats home as a gift for Mom or Dad!

Sarah Booth—PreK, Messiah Nursery School
South Williamsport, PA

This bag is full of love
And lots of kisses too!
I picked out every heart
Especially for you!
Happy Valentine's Day!
Love, Max

Painting Center

Salad-Spinner Art

Take an old salad spinner out of the kitchen and into the classroom for some painting fun! Place paper in the bottom of a salad spinner. (Use one without drainage holes in the outer tub, to avoid any mess.) Then put in the colander insert. Drop in a bit of paint and add a touch of glitter, if you like. Then put the top in place and invite a child to make the paint spin! The mess will stay inside the tub, and the painting will be "spin-tacular"!

Nancy Morgan, Care-a-Lot In-Home Daycare and Preschool
Bremerton, WA

Math Center

Valentine Chain

This heart-to-heart paper chain will help your preschoolers with patterning! To prepare, cut a large supply of 1" x 12" strips from valentine colors of construction paper. Fold each strip in half. At your math center, demonstrate how to fold the two ends of each strip together to make a heart shape (see illustration); then glue the ends together with a glue stick. Have each child make a heart from a strip of her choice. Then have her choose a different color. Have her thread the strip into the heart she's made before folding and gluing it into another heart shape. Have her then make a third heart using her original color. Have her continue following the two-color pattern to make a chain of the desired length. When every child has made a pattern chain, connect them all together and display the chain of hearts on your classroom ceiling or wall.

Shelly Post—Preschool and PreK, Helping Hands Preschool, Great Bend, KS

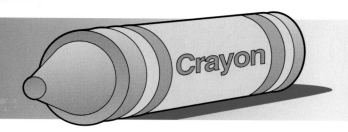

Crayon

Giant Conversation Hearts

What Valentine's Day messages do your little ones like? Find out when they make their own giant-sized candy conversation hearts! Invite a youngster at your writing center to trace a heart-shaped candy box onto a sheet of pastel construction paper. Post a list of appropriate messages, such as "I love you" and "Be mine," at the center. Have a child copy the message of her choice onto her heart shape before cutting it out. Display all the candy conversation hearts in your classroom or invite each youngster to take hers home to a special valentine!

adapted from an idea by
Susan Bailey—TMD Special Education
Douglas Elementary
Trenton, SC

Spool Shamrocks

Lucky for you, this painting idea is just in time for St. Patrick's Day! To prepare, gather some thread spools that have a three-space design at each end (see illustration) and pour white tempera paint into a shallow container. Have a child dip one end of a spool into the paint and then press it onto a sheet of green paper to make prints. When the paint dries, have the child use a green marker to add stems to the prints. There you have it—shamrocks from spools!

Angelia Dagnan—Preschool
Royale Childcare and Learning Center
Knoxville, TN

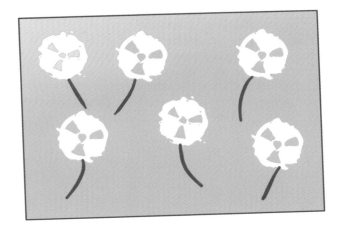

Clip Those Coupons!

If your preschoolers enjoy having a grocery store in your dramatic-play area, add this twist to develop math and motor skills! Ask parents to donate the coupon sections from your local paper. Put the coupon sections in a shallow box, with several pairs of safety scissors nearby. Invite youngsters to clip coupons before they begin their shopping trips at your imaginary store! Try to stock up on empty containers for items shown on the coupons so your young shoppers can put their matching skills to the test too!

Andrea Henderson—PreK
Jefferson Brethren Preschool
Goshen, IN

SOUP 50¢ OFF

SOUP

TATER CHIPS

BUY ONE GET ONE FREE!

Learning Centers

Literacy Center

Juice-Can-Lid Letters

Here's a letter-making activity preschoolers are sure to stick with! Use masking tape to outline letters on the floor or carpet in your literacy center. Add a shoebox filled with metal juice can lids and a magnetic wand. Have a child at this center lay the lids on top of the lines of a letter to trace its shape. When she's done, have her use the magnetic wand to "erase" her work!

Melody Yardley—Two- to Five-Year-Olds
Ms. Peg's Country Care
Odin, IL

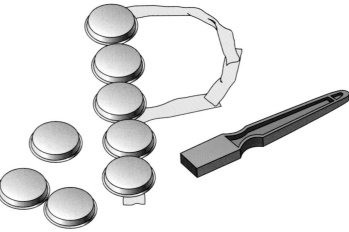

Block Center

Rock Garden

Add a bit of springtime fun to your block center by providing little ones with the materials to create a rock garden. Gather a few sand pails filled with interesting rocks (fist-size or smaller). Also provide a variety of silk flowers. (Be sure to check both the rocks and the flowers for sharp points or edges.) Then invite youngsters to arrange the rocks and flowers as they choose.

Nancy O'Toole—Preschool
Ready Set Grow
Grand Rapids, MN

Listening Center

Five Little Ducks

A few fun props will get your preschoolers waddling on over to your listening area! Provide a tape of the traditional song "Five Little Ducks." Purchase some rubber duckies—five small ones and one larger one to be the mama. Add a large blue plastic bowl to the area too. Then invite a child to listen to and act out the song using the toy ducks and the blue bowl pond.

Cathy Consford—Director
Buda Primary Early Learning Center
Buda, TX

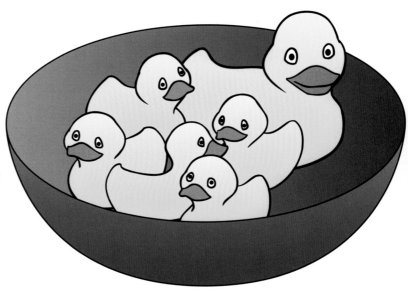

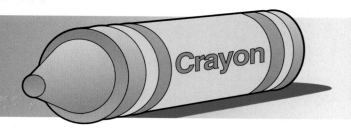

Sensory Tub

Shaving Cream Rainbow

This shaded shaving cream is fun to see *and* to touch! To prepare, half-fill a clear sensory tub with water. Squirt shaving cream on top of the water, nearly to the top of the tub. Then put a different shade of liquid watercolor—red, orange, yellow, green, blue, and purple—into each of six cups. Dilute each color half-and-half with water. Have children use eyedroppers to squeeze the diluted paints onto the shaving cream. After they observe the water turning colors and admire the rainbow in the tub, scoop out the shaving cream onto a tabletop and invite youngsters to fingerpaint with it!

Taneka Henderson-Batiste—Four-Year-Olds
Lincoln Child Development Center
Redondo Beach, CA

Manipulatives Center

Bow Tie Bonanza

Teaching about butterflies? Then this pasta project is perfect! To color a large supply of dried bow tie pasta, simply put some of the dried pasta into a zippered plastic bag along with a few drops of food coloring and a bit of rubbing alcohol. Shake the bag to coat the pasta with color. Then spread the pasta on paper towels or newspaper to dry. Make several different colors; then invite your preschoolers to count, sort, or pattern with these pretty pasta butterflies.

Cindy Lazaroe—Three-Year-Olds
United Methodist Children's Learning Center
Houma, LA

Painting Center

Carrot Painting

This spring, break away from brushes and try painting with produce! Set out your painting cups with a raw carrot tucked into each one. Encourage youngsters to paint and draw with the pointed ends of the carrots instead of fingers or brushes. Then display their "24-carrot" creations for everyone to admire!

Shelley Hoster—PreK
Jack and Jill Early Learning Center
Norcross, GA

Learning Centers

Picnic Art

Make painting a real picnic with this idea! Cover a table with a vinyl red-and-white-checked tablecloth. Set out plastic ketchup and mustard bottles filled with red and yellow tempera paint. Then fill an old set of salt and pepper shakers with white and black sand. (Make your own colored sand by mixing powdered tempera paint with clean play sand.) Then set a white paper plate at each place, and watch the squirting and shaking begin as your youngsters create picnic art!

Cathy Consford—Director
Buda Primary Early Learning Center
Buda, TX

Classroom Ocean

Can't take your preschoolers to the ocean? Then bring the ocean to your preschoolers! Set up a small plastic wading pool in your discovery area. Cover the bottom of the pool with sand; then add water. Put in a variety of shells, as well as plastic or vinyl sea creatures and some toy boats. Have students wear plastic smocks as they play and explore in this miniature ocean!

Maegen Johnson—PreK
Keene Adventist Elementary
Keene, TX

How Many Scoops?

Dish up some counting fun with the help of some pretend ice cream! To prepare, write a different numeral from 1 to 10 in the bottom of each of ten foam bowls. Put the bowls in your math center, along with an ice-cream scoop and some play-dough balls in a variety of cool and creamy ice-cream colors! Invite a pair of children to visit the center. Have one child choose a bowl and put in the corresponding number of play-dough ice-cream scoops. Have him serve it to his partner, who pretends to eat the ice cream while counting to check the server's work. Then have the children switch roles and dish up more fun!

Shelley Banzhaf
Maywood, NE

Science Center

See the Stars

Create a petite planetarium for your young stargazers! Affix a variety of glow-in-the-dark stickers shaped like stars, moons, and planets to sheets of dark construction paper. Tape the paper to the underside of a table; then cover the table with a dark sheet. Add a few books about space and a couple of flashlights. Then invite your preschoolers to take turns under the table, lying back to look up at the stars and using the flashlights to read all about them!

Rhonda Hixson—Four-Year-Olds
St. Christopher's Center for Children
Vandalia, OH

Dramatic-Play Area

Going to Kindergarten

Will your preschoolers be moving on to kindergarten next year? Help them get ready with this fun transformation of your dramatic-play area! After discussing what they think kindergarten will be like, add props to your play kitchen area to make it resemble a scaled-down classroom. Hang up a calendar, an alphabet strip, and posters showing shapes and numbers. Add a small rug for a group area and set up a work table with pencils, paper, crayons, and copies of reproducible sheets. Put up a small dry-erase board or chalkboard, and make nametags for everyone to wear. Then get ready for some kindergarten commotion!

Cathy Lubold—Preschool
All Saints Lutheran Preschool
Albuquerque, NM

Literacy Center

Letter Learning

Help your students practice letter formation and sounds with this simple activity. In advance, use a pencil to make a large outline of a letter on each of several sheets of white copy paper. Provide small incentive stickers or rubber stamps that show pictures of items beginning with that letter. Encourage a child to place the stickers along the outline of the letter or to stamp the image repeatedly along the outline.

As a variation, provide two different stickers or stamps, and challenge a child to use both images to create an ABAB pattern along the letter's outline.

J. Gaye Drummond—Three- and Four-Year-Olds
Redeemer Lutheran Preschool and School
Tucson, AZ

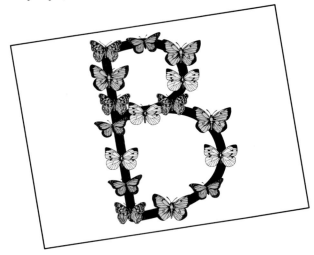

Poem

Use with "Handpicked Hearts" on page 156.

This bag is full of love
And lots of kisses too!
I picked out every heart
Especially for you!
Happy Valentine's Day!

This bag is full of love
And lots of kisses too!
I picked out every heart
Especially for you!
Happy Valentine's Day!

This bag is full of love
And lots of kisses too!
I picked out every heart
Especially for you!
Happy Valentine's Day!

This bag is full of love
And lots of kisses too!
I picked out every heart
Especially for you!
Happy Valentine's Day!

This bag is full of love
And lots of kisses too!
I picked out every heart
Especially for you!
Happy Valentine's Day!

This bag is full of love
And lots of kisses too!
I picked out every heart
Especially for you!
Happy Valentine's Day!

Once Upon a Story...

Once Upon a Story...

Stellaluna

Extend youngsters' enjoyment of *Stellaluna* by Janell Cannon by making this bat craft. For each child, cut one end of a toilet tissue tube to resemble two pointy ears as shown. Cut a 4" x 12" piece of brown construction paper into bat wings. Help each child use craft glue to glue a cut-to-fit piece of tan felt around her tube (excluding the cutout ears). Show her how to flatten the bottom end of the tube; then staple it shut. Help her glue the bat body to the center of the brown paper wings. Then have her glue on two dot eyes punched from black paper. Staple fishing line or yarn to the back of each bat; then display all the bats from your classroom ceiling.

Cheri Anderson—PreK
First Presbyterian Church Day School
DeLand, FL

The Little Old Lady Who Was Not Afraid of Anything

What do you need to help youngsters dramatize *The Little Old Lady Who Was Not Afraid of Anything* by Linda Williams? A few articles of clothing—and a pumpkin, of course! Bring in clothing items that correspond to those in the story, as well as a pumpkin with a face drawn on it. Designate a stage area and invite children to act out the parts of the clothing items and the pumpkin with their distinctive sounds. This repetitive story will be easy for your preschoolers to memorize. If desired, bring in extra clothing items, such as socks or a vest, and invite your preschoolers to think of sounds for these items to make.

Theresa Gibilisco—PreK
Port Monmouth Road School
Keansburg, NJ

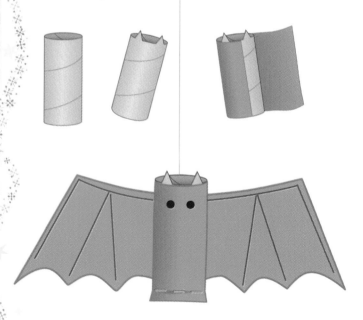

See the corresponding book notes on page 170.

164

The Mitten

Youngsters will ask to perform this musical dramatization of Jan Brett's *The Mitten* again and again! Bring in a big blanket to serve as the mitten. Sing the song below, repeating the verse with the name of each animal that pushes its way into the mitten. Have a child play the part of each animal, snuggling under the blanket when her part is sung. After the mouse snuggles in, have the bear let out a big sneeze. Then have all the animals jump up and toss the blanket high in the air!

(sung to the tune of "The Farmer in the Dell")

The mitten's on the ground; the mitten's on the ground.
Heigh-ho, it's cold outside! The mitten's on the ground.

The [mole] snuggles in; the [mole] snuggles in.
Heigh-ho, it's cold outside! The [mole] snuggles in.

Julie Richter—Preschool Special Education
West Elementary
Emmetsburg, IA

I'm a girl with brown hair and green eyes.

Polar Bear, Polar Bear, What Do You Hear?

After discussing the sounds of the various animals in *Polar Bear, Polar Bear, What Do You Hear?* by Bill Martin Jr., try a listening activity that focuses on the unique sound of each of your students! On a cassette tape, record each child as she says a few sentences about herself. Place the finished tape in a cassette player in your listening center. Have each child who listens to the tape try to identify each speaker. Preschooler, Preschooler, whom do you hear?

Danette Jones—Preschool
Lakewood School
Buchanan, TN

Once Upon a Story...

Jamie O'Rourke and the Big Potato

Your wee ones are sure to enjoy a reading of *Jamie O'Rourke and the Big Potato* by Tomie dePaola as part of your St. Patrick's Day festivities. After sharing it, talk about why potatoes were important to the Irish people. Then encourage each child to make a potato-counting book! To prepare, gather nine sheets of construction paper per child. Label the cover and pages as directed below. Then have a child make a corresponding number of potato prints on each page of his book, with the last page having any number greater than seven. (To make a potato print, a child simply dips the flat side of a potato that's been cut in half into tempera paint, then presses it onto the paper.) Bind the pages in order behind the cover.

Cover: My Potato-Counting Book by _____
Page 1: 1 potato…
Page 2: 2 potatoes…
Page 3: 3 potatoes…
Page 4: 4…
Page 5: 5 potatoes…
Page 6: 6 potatoes…
Page 7: 7 potatoes…
Page 8: MORE!

Peg Bianchi—PreK
Amagansett School
Amagansett, NY

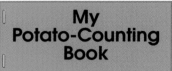

My Potato-Counting Book

by Kenny

Green Eggs and Ham

If you're celebrating Dr. Seuss's birthday in March, try this fresh follow-up to his classic *Green Eggs and Ham*. Make green Jell-O gelatin eggs! Look at your local grocery store for the Jell-O brand egg molds or order them online at www.jello.com. Prepare a batch (or two) of lime Jell-O gelatin and chill it in the molds as directed. Little ones are sure to love these wiggly green treats!

Elizabeth and Anna Tipton—One- to Five-Year-Olds
Jefferson Community College Preschool
Steubenville, OH

1 potato…

2 potatoes…

See the corresponding book notes on page 171.

The Cow That Went Oink

Before sharing *The Cow That Went Oink* by Bernard Most, gather pictures of familiar animals from magazines. Hold up one picture at a time and have your students make the animal's sound. Praise their animal-sound knowledge; then explain that in this story, things are a bit mixed up and the animals aren't making the right sounds! Then read aloud this story of two animals who help one another learn something new.

Ada Goren
Winston-Salem, NC

Chickens Aren't the Only Ones

Chickens and eggs are popular subjects at this time of year. But other animals also hatch from eggs! Explore this idea with the book *Chickens Aren't the Only Ones* by Ruth Heller. Then teach youngsters this "eggs-cellent" song!

(sung to the tune of "Five Little Ducks")

One little egg cracks open wide.
Look, look, look—see what's inside!
What could it be? Oh, what is it?
Swish, swish, swish, it's a baby fish!

One medium egg cracks open wide.
Look, look, look—see what's inside!
What could it be? Oh, what is it?
Peep, peep, peep, it's a baby chick!

One large egg cracks open wide.
Look, look, look—see what's inside!
What could it be? Oh, what is it?
Roar, roar, roar, it's a dinosaur!

Merrilee Walker
Richmond, RI

Once Upon a Story...

The Golden Egg Book

What might be inside an egg? That's what the bunny wonders in *The Golden Egg Book* by Margaret Wise Brown. After sharing this classic tale, give each child a sheet of yellow construction paper with an egg shape outlined on it. Ask her to draw a picture of something she imagines could be inside the egg. Write her dictation below the egg shape too. Cut a hole in a sheet of white paper. Draw a cracked egg around the hole; then program the egg as shown. Personalize each child's cover sheet; then staple it over the construction paper. Display all the projects to keep visitors guessing!

Sarah Booth—Four- and Five-Year-Olds
Messiah Nursery School
South Williamsport, PA

Do You Take a Nap?	
Yes	No
Hannah	Allie
Joseph	Sean
Mark	Jessie
David	

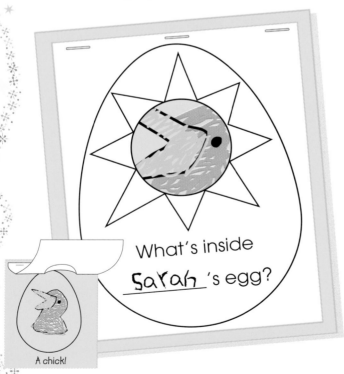

What's inside Sarah 's egg?

A chick!

The Napping House

Before reading aloud Audrey Wood's *The Napping House,* take a poll about naptime. Make a simple two-column graph, labeled as shown. Have each child write her name in either the "Yes" or "No" column to tell whether or not she takes a nap. Then discuss the results and encourage your preschoolers to talk about naptimes—current or former—at their houses. How did they get to sleep? How did they wake up? Then explain that the story you're going to share is about a silly naptime with a silly ending!

Ada Goren
Winston-Salem, NC

See the corresponding book notes on page 172.

The Very Clumsy Click Beetle

Click, click, click. You'll be hearing click beetles all over your room when your little ones make this craft as a follow-up to Eric Carle's *The Very Clumsy Click Beetle*. In advance, collect a class supply of lids from baby food jars. For each child, cut two ovals from thick paper. Glue each pair of ovals together with a jar lid wedged between them. At one end of the beetle, add a small head cutout with two black dot eyes and a pair of cardboard antennae. Use more cardboard pieces for legs and paper scraps for spots. When all the glue is dry, a child can squeeze his beetle, and the safety button on the jar lid inside will produce a clicking sound. Too fun!

Susan Keller—Preschool
Tiro United Methodist Community Preschool
Tiro, OH

Blueberries for Sal

Youngsters will have a "berry" good time when they hunt for blueberries just like Little Sal in *Blueberries for Sal* by Robert McCloskey. To set up your berry hunt, purchase a supply of blue jelly beans from your local candy store. Then create whimsical blueberry bushes by carefully placing the beans (blueberries) on outdoor plants with broad green leaves. (Be sure the plants are not poisonous.) Next, give each child a small tin pail (just like Little Sal's) and invite her to go berry picking. She'll hear the *kerplink, kerplank, kerplunk* as the blueberries hit the bottom of the pail! Instruct the child to not eat her pickings. Have her count how many berries she picked; then provide her with a fresh handful of blue jelly beans as a treat.

Room to Grow
Early Learning Center
Burke, NY

169

Book Notes

After reading each of the books mentioned below and on pages 164 and 165, send home copies of the corresponding note.

I heard a story about a baby bat today! My teacher read ***Stellaluna*** by Janell Cannon.

Let's go to the library and find some more books about bats.

©2002 The Education Center, Inc.

"Clomp, Clomp." That's what the shoes say in ***The Little Old Lady Who Was Not Afraid of Anything*** by Linda Williams.

Name some other pieces of clothing, and I'll tell you what they might say!

©2002 The Education Center, Inc.

In ***Polar Bear, Polar Bear, What Do You Hear?*** by Bill Martin Jr., the polar bear hears a lion roaring in his ear.

I'll make an animal sound. Can you guess which animal I'm pretending to be?

©2002 The Education Center, Inc.

In ***The Mitten*** by Jan Brett, eight different animals crawl inside one mitten!

Let's color the animals on this note together!

©2002 The Education Center, Inc.

Book Notes

After reading each of the books mentioned below and on pages 166 and 167, send home copies of the corresponding note.

Today our story was
Jamie O'Rourke and the Big Potato
by Tomie dePaola.

Let's count and color the potatoes on this note!

Green Eggs and Ham
by Dr. Seuss
is a good story!
Did you know his birthday is March 2?

Let's celebrate by going to the library and finding more books by him!

"Oink!" That's what the cow says in
The Cow That Went Oink
by Bernard Most.

Moo

Oink

Pigs say, "Oink." Cows say, "Moo."
Name another animal and I'll make that sound too!

Today my teacher read
Chickens Aren't the Only Ones
by Ruth Heller.

I learned that chickens aren't the only animals that lay eggs.
Do you want to know some other egg-laying animals?
Ask me to name some for you!

Book Notes

After reading each of the books mentioned below and on pages 168 and 169, send home copies of the corresponding note.

In
The Golden Egg Book
by Margaret Wise Brown,

a little rabbit finds an egg.
Do you want to know
what's inside?
If you ask me, I'll tell you!

The Napping House
by Audrey Wood
is a silly story with funny pictures!

Let's go to the library and find
more books by her!

In
The Very Clumsy Click Beetle
by Eric Carle,
a younger beetle learns to flip
over by watching and copying
an older beetle.

Make some movements.
I'll watch and copy you!

Blueberries for Sal
by Robert McCloskey
is a good book about
picking blueberries.

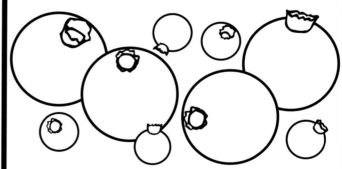

Let's color the blueberries
on this note!
I'll color the little ones!
You color the big ones!

172

OUR READERS WRITE

Our Readers Write

Friend Book

Introduce parents to their children's school friends with a simple-to-make friend book! Take a head-and-shoulders photo of each youngster in your class. Then duplicate each photo on your school copy machine to make a class supply. Bind a set of duplicated photos for each child to take home. Moms and dads can see their children's classmates, and children can keep the book for years to come!

Linda Young—Head Start, STEP INC., Rocky Mount, VA

Comfort in a Pocket

Here's an idea for comforting young ones who are having difficulty transitioning into school. Glue a copy of the poem shown onto a construction paper pocket. Then paint a wooden ice-cream spoon brown. When the paint is dry, use a permanent marker to draw bear features on the spoon. Read the poem on the pocket to your preschooler; then present him with the bear and the pocket. Now, when your tot needs a little tenderness, he has a pair of listening ears at all times.

Sue Fleischmann—Preschool, Holy Cross School, Menomonee Falls, WI

In my pocket is a bear.
He quietly sleeps inside of there.
I take him out when I am sad
And tell him why I feel so bad.
When I feel better, he goes back in
And then goes back to sleep again.

I know my full name!
I know my address!
I know my telephone number!
I know my birthday!

Tyler

All About Me Award

Create these special ribbons to award to your youngsters when they master personal information, such as their full names and addresses. First, die-cut a class supply of award ribbons from construction paper. To create an award, type the desired text and add a photo of the child on white paper; then cut the paper to fit and glue it to the ribbon shape. (Use a computer and scanner if you wish.) Print or have the child print his name on the award. Then laminate the ribbon, punch a hole at the top, and pin it to the child's clothing. Invite your proud preschooler to wear his ribbon home to show off his personal knowledge!

Tracey Bomar, Cottage Grove School, Cottage Grove, TN

The Goody Game

This game makes a great class reward, since it always ends with a sweet surprise for everyone! To prepare, fill a container with a class supply of wrapped candies, stickers, mini erasers, or other small treats. Have students sit in a circle. Play recorded music, and have the children pass the container around the circle. Stop the music and ask the child holding the container to open it and reveal the contents to the group. The child may then take out one treat before you begin the music again. Continue until everyone has had a treat. If desired, vary the container and the contents to reflect each season or holiday.

Cheri Anderson—PreK, First Presbyterian Church Day School, DeLand, FL

Get-to-Know-Me Bag

Invite little ones to introduce themselves with the help of some premade props! During a home visit or meet-your-teacher night, give each child a paper lunch bag. Ask families to use the bag to create a puppet resembling the student. Then have the student stow a few items inside the bag puppet to tell about herself. For example, she might include a wrapper from her favorite candy, something in her favorite color, and a memento from a family vacation. On the first day of class, encourage each young-ster to use the puppet and the items to introduce herself to her classmates.

Gwen Macias—PreK, Silverdale Elementary Head Start, Maysville, NC

Sing 'n' Sit

Call preschoolers to your group area with this fun tune!

(sung to the tune of "Shortnin' Bread")

Everybody, have a seat, have a seat, have a seat.
Everybody, have a seat on the floor.
Not on the ceiling!   *(Point to ceiling.)*
Not on the door!   *(Point to door.)*
Everybody, come and have a seat on the floor.

Jeanne Jackson, Northside Primary, Palestine, TX

Think Ahead!

The beginning of the year is a good time to plan ahead for end-of-the-year gifts that require photos. Start taking pictures now; then save the photos to make a cute booklet for Mother's Day or preschool graduation. For each booklet, cut a front and back cover from craft foam. Add a child's school photo to the front; then invite him to embellish the cover with stickers, stamps, or sequins. Cut a number of white pages to equal the number of photos you wish to include. Write a caption below each picture. Then stack the pages between the covers, punch holes at the top, and bind the booklet with a pretty ribbon. What a cute keepsake!

Peggy Stratton—Four-Year-Olds, First Baptist Church Preschool, Okeechobee, FL

Mother Goose by the Month

Keep your little ones rhyming and reading all year long by focusing on a different nursery rhyme each month. Each month, send home a copy of the rhyme, along with a list of re-lated activities you'll be doing in class. Display the words to the rhyme in a pocket chart or on a wall, and have youngsters recite the rhyme each day. Mother Goose would be proud!

Tammy Wolfe—Special Needs Preschool, LaGrange/Moscow, Moscow, TN

(For nursery rhyme activities, see pages 238–245.)

Birthday Numbers

A birthday is cause for celebration, and it's cause for some math instruction too! Cut out and laminate large numerals to reflect the ages of the preschoolers you teach. Display the numbers on a wall. At the beginning of the year, place a small photo of each child on the number showing her age. When she celebrates her birthday, move her photo (with great fanfare) to the new number. Then extend the lesson by counting how many pictures are on each number.

Pat Smith—PreK, Bells Elementary, Bells, TX

Take Note of This Pizza

After a field trip to a pizzeria, make this crafty pizza to say thank you for the tour! Cut out a large tagboard circle. Use a black marker to divide the circle into eight slices. Next, paint the hands of one child at a time and have her make red handprints anywhere on the circle to represent sauce. Roll strips of brown construction paper into tubes and hot-glue them to the edges of the circle to represent crust. Then squirt glue onto one slice at a time and invite youngsters to sprinkle on oregano and white crinkled paper stuffing (cheese). Hot-glue small brown pom-pom "meatballs" onto the pizza too. Finish by writing a simple message and gluing that over all the toppings. Then make a delivery to the pizzeria!

Desiree Magnani and Toni-Ann Maisano—Directors
Babes in Toyland Preschool
Staten Island, NY

To Our Friends At Elizabeth's Pizza

Ms. Smith's Class

Turkey Tracks

Watch your preschoolers strut their stuff in these fun-to-wear turkey shoes! To make a pair, hot-glue cork strips in the shape of turkey toes (as shown) to the bottom of an old pair of shoes. Then roll out a length of bulletin board paper and prepare a large, shallow container with a thick layer of paper towels in the bottom. Pour in some tempera paint to create a giant-sized stamp pad. One at a time, have a child put on the shoes and step carefully into the container. Then have her step onto the paper and walk its length. Be sure to hold the child's hand as she walks to prevent her from slipping. Look—turkey tracks!

Helen K. Dening

Pumpkin Paint Cups

Add seasonal flair to your easel or art table by using scooped-out mini pumpkins to hold paint! Simply cut off the tops of a few small pumpkins; then clean out the seeds and gooey insides. Fill the pumpkin shells with tempera paint and put in paintbrushes. When the season nears its end, just toss out the empty pumpkins.

Jodi Berscheid—Preschool/Head Start
Oahe Child Development Center, Pierre, SD

From Halloween to St. Patrick's Day

Plan ahead to give each of your youngsters a wonderful surprise from a friendly leprechaun—a miniature pot of gold! Look now for Halloween party favor cups shaped like black pots. Buy a class supply and set them aside until March. Then fill the pots with gold foil–wrapped chocolate coins and hide them in your room for youngsters to find!

Sue Lein, Wauwatosa, WI

That's *My* House!

Teaching preschoolers about their neighborhoods? Make a map that's sure to be a hit in your blocks area. First—with parents' permission—take a photo of each child's house. Also take photos of other interesting places or familiar landmarks in the children's neighborhoods, such as a park, library, mall, or fire station. Construct a giant map by taping together four sheets of black poster board. Lay out the photos of the houses and other landmarks in relation to one another. Use white chalk to add streets and street names. Laminate the map; then make sure little ones have plenty of toy vehicles so they can "visit" one another!

Krista Smith—Head Start, Bessie Weller Elementary, Staunton, VA

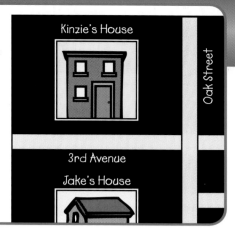

Tattle-Time Telephone

If tattling is an issue in your classroom, try this creative solution! Place an old telephone or play phone on a small table in one corner. Post the number for the "Tattle-Time Telephone Line" next to the phone and invite anyone who needs to tattle to place a call and lodge a complaint. Your little ones will get to tell their stories and practice dialing the phone too!

Sandy Jones—PreK, Home Sweet Home Day Care, Grafton, WI

"Tree-riffic" Work

This cute bulletin board is a great place to display youngsters' work all year long! To begin, cover a bulletin board with light blue background paper. Make two paper trees, one at each end of the board. Staple a length of string between the two trees. Add the title "'Tree-riffic' Work"; then use clothespins to hang children's work from the string line. If desired, change the leaves of the trees for each season of the year.

Carrie Carlisle—Three- and Four-Year-Olds Special Needs
Hilliard City School District Preschool
Hilliard, OH

Printshop Paper

Need a money-saving way to get loads of paper for your classroom? Visit your local printshop and ask for discards! Printshops typically have paper in many different colors, textures, and sizes. And paper boxes are great for storage too!

Michelle Kendall—Preschool Special Education, TCESC/Cornerstone Elementary, Wooster, OH

Thanks, Firefighters!

If your class is visiting a firehouse this fall, say thank you to the firefighters with a special box of goodies! Help the children bake a large batch of cookies, or ask a couple of parents to bake something. Then have youngsters help you cover a cardboard box with red paper. Decorate the box to resemble a fire truck. Simply add black paper wheels and paint a ladder on one side. Draw a windshield or any other details you wish to add. Place the baked goods inside the box along with a note letting the firefighters know how much you and your little ones appreciate them!

Desiree Magnani and Toni-Ann Maisano—Directors, Babes in Toyland Preschool
Staten Island, NY

177

Angel Centerpiece

Invite *your* little angels to make *these* little angels to dress up holiday tables! To make one, stuff a colored paper lunch bag with shredded tissue paper or newspaper strips. Fold over the top and staple the bag shut. Then fold a white paper doily over the top and staple it in place. Glue on a precut four-inch paper circle for the angel's face. Use a crayon to add facial features; then glue on hair made of crinkled gift wrap stuffing, yarn, or floral moss. Bend a sparkly pipe cleaner into a halo and staple it to the top of the bag so it sits atop the angel's head. Perfect!

Tamara L. Sheehy—Four- and Five-Year-Olds, Reeths-Puffer/Pennsylvania Early Childhood Center North Muskegon, MI

Pennies for Presents

Teach your preschoolers about the joy of giving with a penny collection campaign! Begin by making a decorative container for each child to take home. Cut the designs from old wrapping paper and have youngsters glue them onto clean plastic containers. Also make a large classroom container for collecting all the pennies as they're brought in from home. Put all the collected pennies toward holiday gifts for a child in need. (Check with a local social services agency or visit a "giving tree" in your community to get a child's name.) Purchase the gifts; then take the class on a field trip to deliver the gifts to the appropriate agency. Don't forget to sneak in some counting practice as you're collecting the pennies!

Jana Switzer—Preschool, Creative Beginnings Preschool, The Dalles, OR

Dear_____,
Thank you for ___.
It _____.
I _____.
Love,_____

Thank You!

Help parents reinforce the habit of writing thank-you notes by providing a few for your students! On a computer, create a simple "fill-in-the-blank" thank-you note, similar to the one shown. Print a few copies for each child in your class; then send them home, along with a letter to parents asking them to help their child use the notes for a gift received or a kind deed done. Moms and dads are sure to appreciate *your* thoughtfulness!

Sarah Booth—PreK, Messiah Nursery School, South Williamsport, PA

Snowman Kit

If there's a blanket of white snow covering your town, your little ones will love this idea for getting parents involved in learning! Prepare a snowman kit for each child by filling a paper grocery bag with two lumps of charcoal (for eyes), a carrot (for a nose), several stones (for a mouth), a piece of fabric (for a scarf), and two twigs (for arms). Slip in a note asking parents to help their child build a snowman and to add a hat of the child's choice from home. Also ask that they take a photo of the finished snowman to return to school. Display all the snowman photos for *everyone* to enjoy!

Mary Gribble—Three- and Four-Year-Olds, Country Goose Preschool, River Falls/Prescott, WI

'Tis the Season for Supplies!

If you're running low on some supplies at midyear, try this "tree-rific" idea! Mount a large Christmas tree cutout on a wall or bulletin board. Cut a number of ornament shapes from various colors of construction paper. Label each ornament with an item you need for the class, such as tissues, crayons, or cotton balls. Use Sticky-Tac to attach the ornaments to the tree. Invite parents to take an ornament and then send in the requested item. What a great holiday gift for their children!

Stacey Burton—Preschool, Memorial Education Center, Somerset, KY

Pizza Year

Teaching calendar concepts at the start of the new year? Help little ones understand the 12 months of the year by comparing them to 12 slices of pizza! Cut a large circle from poster board. Divide the circle into 12 slices; then label each slice with the name of a month and decorate it with colors and stickers pertaining to that particular month. Assemble the pizza on the floor in front of your group, and have little ones chant the month names as you point to the slices. Explain that a whole year is just like having a whole pizza!

Maria Victoria Delgado—PreK, St. Vincent Ferrer School, Delray Beach, FL

Five Little Snowmen

Here's a "brrrr-illiant" way to fit some rhythm and rhyme into your day! Teach your preschoolers the following chant about five snowmen. To add to the fun, use fabric paint to decorate the fingers and thumb of a white glove to resemble snowmen. Use hot glue to attach a black felt hat to each one.

Five little snowmen watching for the sun,
The first one said, "Let's have some fun!"
The second one said, "Let's race and run!"
The third one said, "Hooray, I've won!"
The fourth one said, "Look out! The sun!"
The fifth one said, "Uh-oh! We're done!"

Sarah Booth—PreK, Messiah Nursery School, South Williamsport, PA

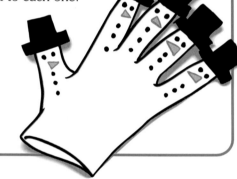

Friendship Chain

As you introduce your little ones to Martin Luther King Jr. and the ideals of peace and kindness to all, try making a friendship chain. Precut a large number of construction paper strips and keep them handy. Each time you see a child demonstrating friendship or kindness to another, roll a paper strip into a link and add it to your friendship chain. Start the chain in one corner of your room and stretch it until it reaches across the wall to the next corner. Reward your little ones with a special treat, such as a field trip to an ice-cream parlor! Then make it a goal to reach across another wall to the next corner and keep the kindness coming!

Trina Hofer—Preschool, Kids World Learning Center, Brookings, SD

Footprints in the Snow

Make tracks to your art area to try this fun *indoor* trek through the snow! To prepare, gather several old pairs of shoes and boots and cut a long length of white bulletin board paper. Have one child at a time choose a pair of shoes to put on. Paint the bottoms of the shoes with blue paint; then invite the child to walk across the paper making footprints in the "snow." Continue until everyone has had a turn to tromp across the paper. Compare the varying designs made by the different shoes and boots. And for extra fun, revisit this activity in the summer by having youngsters make flip-flop footprints in the "sand"!

Rebecca Cassell—Three- and Four-Year-Olds, First Friends Preschool, Kingsport, TN

Our Readers Write

Postcard Graphing

Planning a field trip to your local post office? Mail some postcards while you're there! Before your trip, address a separate postcard to each child's home address; then allow little ones to put on the stamps. While you're visiting the post office, invite each child to drop her postcard into the mail slot. When each child receives the postcard at home, she brings it to school. Create a graph to show how many days it takes for each postcard to arrive at its destination. Neither rain nor sleet nor snow will keep youngsters from learning with this idea!

Jill Bivens—Four- and Five-Year-Olds, Two Rivers Head Start, Aurora, IL

Presidential Puppet

Take note of Presidents' Day with these George Washington masks! To make one, cut the center from a thin white paper plate; then shape the plate to resemble a face as shown. Have a child glue on cotton balls for hair and a section of a white paper doily for a collar. Tape a wide craft stick to the bottom of the plate to serve as a handle. By George, you've got it!

Nancy Goldberg—Three-Year-Olds, B'nai Israel Schilit Nursery School, Rockville, MD

Attractive Valentines

Make good use of old valentines or those you find on sale when the holiday is over. Attach the valentines to self-adhesive magnetic sheets; then cut them apart. Use the magnetic valentines on your chalkboard or at a center on a metal cookie sheet. Have youngsters use the valentines for matching, counting, sorting, or memory games.

Pam Johnson, Tri-County Child and Family Development, Waterloo, IA

Cupcake Caves

Spring is approaching and the bears are coming out of hibernation. Invite your little ones to wake up some friendly bears from their long winter's nap with this cooking project. Have students help you prepare a boxed cake mix according to the package directions for making cupcakes. But before baking, push a Teddy Grahams snack into each cup of batter. Then bake and cool as directed. Frost the cupcake "caves" and pass them out to your youngsters. They'll love finding the bears inside! Wake up, bears!

Carol Breeding—Preschool, New Life Center Daycare, Des Moines, IA

A Pot of Potpourri

Here's a fresh and fragrant idea for a Mother's Day gift! Purchase a class supply of small clay flowerpots at your local discount store. Have each child sponge-paint a pot with bright acrylic paints. When the pots are dry, fill each one with some sweet-smelling potpourri. Then wrap the filled pots with colored plastic wrap and tie each one with a pretty ribbon.

Maria J. Cancelosi—Four-Year-Olds, Pinnacle Learning Center Preschool, Mahwah, NJ

Lollipop Corsages

Moms will be sweetly surprised when they receive these lollipop corsages! To make one, cut a simple flower shape from colorful craft foam. Hot-glue a flat, round lollipop to the center of the flower. Then hot-glue a pin back to the back of the flower. Tie a length of skinny ribbon into a pretty bow around the lollipop stem.

Sarah Booth—PreK, Messiah Nursery School, South Williamsport, PA

I Love You This Much!

These unforgettable Mother's Day cards are sure to become treasured keepsakes! To make one, ask a child to spread her arms wide to show how much she loves her mom. Cut a length of yarn to match the distance between her hands. Then trace both her hands onto construction paper and cut out the shapes. Attach one hand cutout to each end of the yarn. Then add a heart in the center that says, "Mommy, I love you this much!" Fold up the hands and heart and tuck the whole thing into a small manila envelope. Send the cards home for youngsters to present to their moms.

Lisa Toler—Two- and Three-Year-Olds, Stillwater Preschool, Logansport, IN

Colorful Flowers—and Vases Too!

Studying flowers this spring? Show little ones how flowers absorb water by having each child place a freshly cut white carnation into a small soda bottle filled with colored water. They'll be surprised to see the flower petals change color! Add to the fun of this experiment by decorating the bottles to transform them into colorful vases. Help each child tightly wrap aluminum foil around his bottle; then have him use tacky craft glue to add small colored beads all over it. When the glue is dry, invite youngsters to take home their colorful creations!

Monica Saunders—Four-Year-Olds, Hazelwild Educational Foundation, Fredericksburg, VA

A Song for Storytime

Preschoolers will love singing and snapping to this song that helps them prepare for storytime.

(sung to the tune of "The Addams Family Theme Song")

Da, da, da, da!	*Sing five times and snap fingers twice after first, second, and fifth time.*
We fold our legs so neatly.	*Cross legs.*
We fold our hands so sweetly.	*Fold hands in lap.*
We listen so completely.	
It's storytime right now.	
Da, da, da, da!	*Sing five times and snap fingers twice after first, second, and fifth time.*

Gail Mercurio—PreK, Albemarle Road Elementary, Charlotte, NC

Footprints for Fathers

Dads will be glad to receive these cute footprint bookmarks for Father's Day! To make one, have a child press his bare foot onto a large rainbow washable ink pad. Then have him step carefully onto a sheet of light-colored construction paper. Cut out the resulting footprint and laminate it. Punch a hole at the heel and add a short length of knotted ribbon. Send home the bookmarks with the poem shown. What neat feet!

Becky Chaffins—Three-Year-Olds, Marywood Country Dayschool, Rancho Mirage, CA

When you are tired of reading your book,
Mark your place with my little foot!
Happy Father's Day!

Father's Day Festivities

Moms may love tea, but how about root beer and pretzels for dads? Serve up these tasty snacks at a Father's Day get-together. Set out bowls of melted chocolate for dipping the pretzels and consider showing a video or inviting dads and kids to read together for a relaxing party!

Nikki Scheman, Mulberry Child Care and Preschool, Collegeville, PA

Bubble Transportation

It's fun to take bottles of bubbles outdoors at playtime, but it's not so fun if they tip over and spill. Remedy this situation by fitting eight-ounce bottles of bubbles into the compartments of a silverware caddy! Now you can easily carry a bevy of bubbles, and keeping them in the caddy will prevent spills while youngsters are playing.

Janet Pingel—Four-Year-Olds, CESA 11 Rice Lake Head Start, Rice Lake, WI

Playground Pipe

Here's a new angle on playground fun—a PVC pipe roll! To make one, attach a six- to eight-foot length of PVC pipe to a fence on your playground. Attach the pipe at a slight angle, not too far off the ground. Then provide tennis balls and small toy cars for youngsters to roll through the pipe.

Cathy Consford—Director, Buda Primary Early Learning Center, Buda, TX

Under-the-Sea Snack

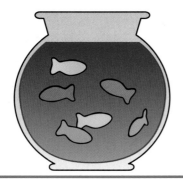

Studying fish, the ocean, or pets? Try this silly snack presentation! Prepare one or two batches of blue gelatin. Pour the gelatin into a new, clean fishbowl. Then put the bowl in the refrigerator until the gelatin is partially set. Push some gummy fish (or other sea creatures) into the gelatin before returning it to the fridge to set completely. Then listen for the gasps and giggles when you serve it to your preschoolers!

Florence Paola—PreK and Kindergarten Special Needs, Jane Ryan Elementary Trumbull, CT

PARTY FEATURES

Let's Have a PUMPKIN Party!

Use this patch of ideas to transform your learning space into a pumpkin-themed party place!

ideas contributed by Lucia Kemp Henry

Pumpkin Patch Decorations

Create a fall feel in your classroom by having each child create a crafty pumpkin decoration. To begin, provide each child with a 9" x 12" sheet of orange construction paper and five pieces of nine-inch-long string. Help the child glue each string vertically onto the sheet of paper. Next, have the child sponge-paint the paper and string with orange paint. When the paint is dry, cut the paper into a pumpkin shape. Trace the child's hand on green paper; then cut on the resulting outline to create a leaf. Twist a quarter of a sheet of green tissue paper to make a vine. Staple the leaf to the vine and the vine to the pumpkin. Then have the child glue a construction paper stem over the end of the vine. To dress up your room for the party, display youngsters' pumpkins on a wall or bulletin board.

Pumpkin Party Toppers

What's better than a party hat? A party crown! Have each child create a pumpkin crown to wear during your pumpkin festivities. To make a crown, cut out three 8" x 5" pumpkins from orange construction paper. Invite the child to color the pumpkins as desired and then glue a 1" x 6" construction paper stem to the top of each one. Next, fold a 3" x 24" strip of green bulletin board paper in half lengthwise. Slip the pumpkins into the folded strip as shown and then staple them in place. Staple the strip to fit a child's head; then staple the tops of the stems together to form the top of the crown. Glue a construction paper leaf to the top of the stems, and the crown is complete!

Scooping Seeds

Carve some fun into your pumpkin party with a lively relay race! In advance, cut out a class supply of craft-foam pumpkin seeds. Place half of the seeds in one plastic pumpkin-shaped container and the other half in another pumpkin-shaped container. Divide your class into two groups; then line up each group a few feet away from a container. Provide the first child in each line with a spoon or spring-type clothespin. At the start signal, the first child in each line walks quickly to the pumpkin and then uses the spoon or clothespin to remove a seed. She returns to the line with the seed, puts it in her hand, and then passes the spoon or clothespin to the next child. The game continues in this manner until each child has scooped a seed.

Pumpkin Picking Time!

Invite your preschoolers to pick a peck of pumpkins at a pretend patch! To prepare, arrange a class supply of miniature pumpkins in your sand table to resemble a patch. Place a stack of number cards near the sand table and then invite a small group of children to the area. Invite each child, in turn, to draw a number card and pick that many pumpkins from the patch. When all of the pumpkins have been picked, have each child count her crop. Then use words such as *more, less,* and *equal* to compare the students' pumpkins. After each child has visited the patch, label each pumpkin with a different child's name and then use it as a place marker on your party table.

Pumpkin Pops

This frozen pumpkin-flavored pop makes the perfect party treat! To make one, place the following ingredients in a three-ounce paper cup: three tablespoons of prepared vanilla pudding, two teaspoons of canned pumpkin, a sprinkle of pumpkin pie spice. Stir the ingredients together with a wooden craft spoon. Stand the spoon in the middle of the cup and then freeze the treat. Peel the paper cup from the frozen pumpkin pop and then eat!

One small package of vanilla pudding mix makes approximately eight pops.

Celebrate the New Year Around the World!

No need for a passport! We've got the perfect multicultural party planned on these four pages! With this collection of festive ideas, you can throw an around-the-world New Year's party without ever leaving the classroom!

ideas contributed by Lucia Kemp Henry

Colombia

Say Goodbye to the Old!

In Colombia, South America, families work together to create a large stuffed doll called Mr. Old Year. The doll symbolizes the past year and any bad luck that may have occurred. When the new year arrives, the family burns the doll (and the bad luck!) to make way for good luck in the new year.

After teaching your preschoolers about this Colombian custom, kick off your New Year's party with a puppet and song that reflect Colombia's tradition of bidding bad luck goodbye! To make a puppet, photocopy the patterns on page 189 and then cut out each one. Have a child color the patterns; then tape a jumbo craft stick to the back of one of them. Glue or staple the patterns back-to-back to create a two-sided puppet. As you sing the first verse of the song shown, have youngsters show the old-year side of the puppet. Then have them flip their puppets to the other side as you begin singing the second verse. Hello, new year!

(sung to the tune of "Are You Sleeping?")

Goodbye, old year. Goodbye, old year.
Ding, ding, dong. Ding, ding, dong.
Take the bad luck with you! Take the bad luck with you!
Ding, ding, dong. Ding, ding, dong.

Hello, new year! Hello, new year!
Ding, ding, dong! Ding, ding, dong!
Let's all give a big cheer! Let's all give a big cheer!
Bad luck's gone! Bad luck's gone!

Bonne Année!

La Multi Ani!

Want to give your New Year's party a truly multicultural feel? Read through the list of translations below; then teach your preschoolers a couple of new ways to say, "Happy New Year!"

Spanish: *Feliz Año Nuevo!*
Russian: *S Novym Godom!*
Italian: *Buon Capo d'Anno!*
French: *Bonne Année!*

Hebrew: *Shanah Tovah!*
Chinese: *Gung Hay Fat Choy!*
Romanian: *La Multi Ani!*

Dragon Parade Headbands

Because the Chinese follow a different calendar, New Year's Day occurs during a different time of year than most other countries. This year, the Chinese New Year begins on February 1. Many celebrations include lots of noisemaking to ward off bad luck and a parade with a festive dragon leading the way. In Chinese culture, the dragon is a symbol of strength and good luck.

Your youngsters will be thrilled to greet the new year with a Chinese custom—a dragon parade! To prepare for the parade, have each child make a dragon headband. First, provide the child with a three-inch-wide strip of red paper long enough to fit around his head. Next, provide the child with a sponge cut into a shape that resembles a segment of a dragon's body. Have the child dip the sponge into green paint and then print a dragon body onto the headband as shown. When the paint is dry, invite the child to use glitter glue and colorful hole reinforcers to decorate the dragon's body.

Provide the child with a copy of the dragon head and tail patterns on page 189. Direct the child to color the patterns and glue them onto the dragon. Write a few New Year's greetings on the strip; then staple it to fit the child's head. Have your youngsters don their dragon headgear. Provide each child with a rhythm instrument or noisemaker and then lead your class on a festive dragon parade to usher in a happy new year!

USA

Cupcake Countdown

In the United States of America, one of the most famous New Year's traditions is watching a large glittering ball drop in Times Square. The ball begins to descend and the people below (and all across the country) begin counting backward from 10 to 1. At the end of the countdown, the people yell, "Happy New Year!"

Is there anything more fun than watching the glittering Times Square ball drop on New Year's Eve? How about dramatizing the countdown with a cookie and a cupcake? Provide each child with a frosted cupcake and a vanilla wafer cookie to use as the ball. Direct the child to hold the cookie above the cupcake; then begin the countdown! At the end of the countdown, prompt each child to drop her cookie onto her cupcake and say, "Happy New Year!" Fill a cup for each child with the punch described in "Gulping Grapes" on page 188 and then invite her to eat, drink, and be merry! Five, four, three, two, one...Happy New Year!

Gulping Grapes

When the clock begins to chime at midnight on New Year's Eve in Spain, people eat grapes to celebrate! Partygoers receive 12 grapes and try to eat one at each chime of the clock to ensure good luck.

In America, many people drink a toast as the clock strikes 12. Why not combine the customs of Spain and the USA by serving grape-flavored punch to drink in 12 sips? Provide each child with a cup of grape-flavored punch. Then tell students that they are going to drink the punch as you *slowly* play a chime 12 times. For each ring of the chime, encourage each child to take an accompanying sip of punch. Can your youngsters empty their cups in exactly 12 sips? Good luck just might be the result!

West Africa

West African Water Relay

In some villages of the West African savannah, the new year is marked by the beginning of the rainy season. People show their thanks for the rain by carrying water-filled gourds to the village.

Invite your youngsters to reenact this water-carrying custom with a relay race. To set up the race, you will need the following: two buckets; two big ladles; a plastic tub filled with dry, blue-tinted macaroni to represent water. Place the tub a short distance away from the two buckets. Divide your class into two teams and line up each team beside a bucket. Provide the first child in each line with a ladle. At the start signal, the first child walks quickly to the tub and fills the ladle with "water." He walks back to his team and pours the "water" into the bucket. Then he hands the ladle to the next child in line. The race continues in this manner until each has had a turn.

Dragon Head and Tail Patterns
Use with "Dragon Parade Headbands" on page 187.

Happy St. Patrick's Day!

It's no blarney! We've planned the perfect St. Patrick's Day party for your wee ones. As luck would have it, this party is not only fun, but it's also filled to the brim with golden learning opportunities!

ideas contributed by Roxanne LaBell Dearman
Western NC Early Intervention Program for Children Who Are Deaf or Hard of Hearing
Charlotte, NC

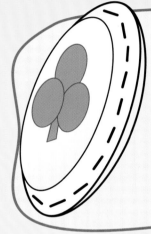

Shamrock Shakers

How do you turn a lesson on positional words into a party game? It's simple! Add shamrock shakers and a lively song! To make a shaker, provide each child with three four-inch green construction paper circles and a green paper stem. (For older students, trace the shapes onto green paper and have them cut out each one.) Provide the child with a paper plate. Then have her glue the circles and stem onto the back of the plate in the shape of a shamrock. Staple another plate to the first one as shown, leaving a small opening at the top. Have the child drop a few dried beans through the opening; then staple it shut. Teach youngsters "St. Patrick's Pokey" below and invite them to shake, shake, shake their shamrocks!
positional words, gross-motor skills

St. Patrick's Pokey
(sung to the tune of "The Hokey-Pokey")

You put your shamrock **in,**
You take your shamrock **out,**
You put your shamrock **in** and you shake it all about.
You do St. Patrick's Pokey and you turn yourself around.
Happy St. Patrick's Day!

You shake your shamrock **high,**
You shake your shamrock **low,**
You shake your shamrock **high;** then you shake it to and fro.
You do St. Patrick's Pokey and you turn yourself around.
Happy St. Patrick's Day!

You shake your shamrock **left,**
You shake your shamrock **right,**
You shake your shamrock **left;** then you shake with all your might.
You do St. Patrick's Pokey and you turn yourself around.
Happy St. Patrick's Day!

Somewhere Over the Rainbow

Finding the end of the rainbow won't be hard for your youngsters with this placemat idea. In advance, photocopy page 192 for each child, plus one copy for yourself. Color your copy in the colors of the rainbow. A few days before the party, display your color copy at a center. Place the uncolored placemats near the colored one. Invite each child to visit the center and color a placemat in the same colors and order as the sample. Have the child write his name on the placemat. Laminate it and then set it aside to use during the party. What about the pot of gold at the end of the rainbow? See the snack idea in "Golden Nuggets" below! *color matching, cognitive development*

Golden Nuggets

What's a leprechaun's favorite pastime? Counting his gold! Have your youngsters play the part of a leprechaun by making a "golden" snack that gets them counting. Provide each child with a silver muffin liner to represent a pot. Then have the child use a tablespoon to scoop the gold (Kellogg's Corn Pops cereal) into the pot. How many tablespoons does it take to fill the pot? Have the child count aloud as she scoops—just like a leprechaun! When the pot is full, direct the child to place it at the end of the rainbow on her placemat. (See "Somewhere Over the Rainbow.") Serve the magically delicious drink described below and then invite youngsters to eat, drink, and be merry! *counting, measurement*

Magically Delicious Drink

This drink isn't really magic, but the magical color change will nurture youngsters' science observation skills. In advance, make a class supply of green ice cubes by adding drops of green food coloring to the water in one or two ice cube trays. If you have shamrock-shaped candy molds, make the ice cubes in the molds for added seasonal fun. Provide each child with a clear cup of lemon-lime soda; then drop a colored cube into the drink. Encourage the child to observe the drink as the ice begins to melt. The soda turns green! Was it magic? No, it's science! *science process skills: observing*

191

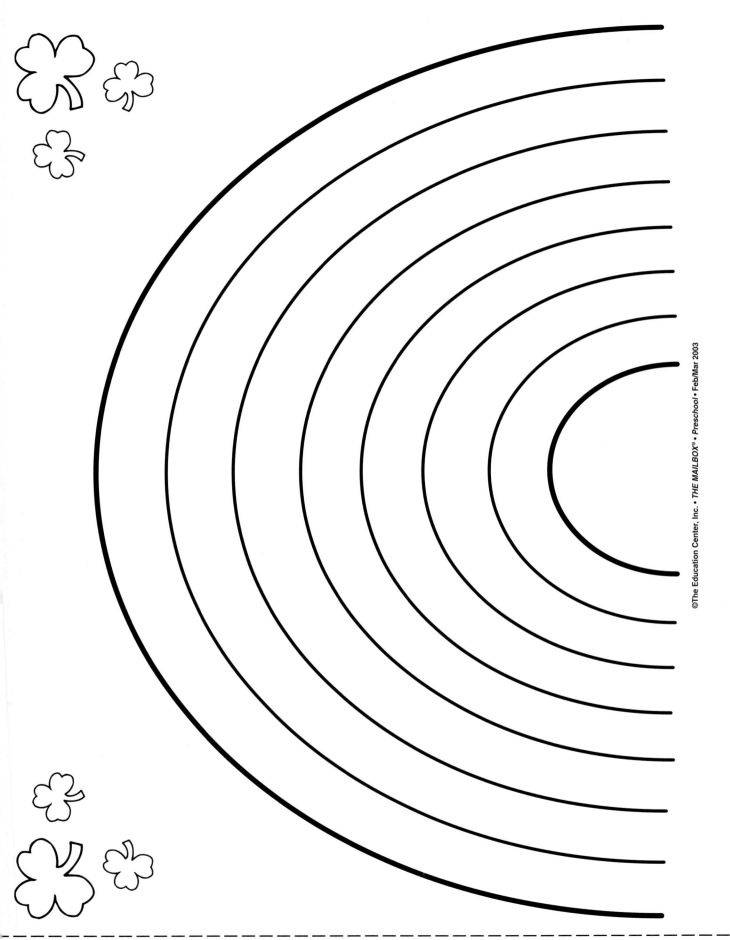

Note to the teacher: Use with "Somewhere Over the Rainbow" on page 191.

A Cinco de Mayo Celebration!

¡Es tiempo de fiesta! It's time for a party! On May 5, use the following ideas to introduce youngsters to a festive Mexican holiday, Cinco de Mayo! The tasty snack, lively activities, and Spanish words will have your preschoolers saying, "¡Muy bien!"

ideas contributed by Danna R. DeMars
St. Charles, MO

snack—el bocado
beans—los frijoles
cheese—el queso

Oh! Burritos!

We don't know which your preschoolers will enjoy more—making these tasty burritos or singing about them! Provide each child with the following: a small flour tortilla, a tablespoon of refried beans, a tablespoon of shredded cheddar cheese, and a small cup of mild salsa for dipping. Demonstrate how to spread the beans on the tortilla, sprinkle the cheese over the beans, and then roll the tortilla into a burrito. Teach youngsters the song shown; then have them sing as they prepare their snacks.

(sung to the tune of "Peanut, Peanut Butter")

First you take the beans and you spread them.
You spread them.
Then you take the cheese and you sprinkle it.
You sprinkle it.
Roll it all together and you eat it.
You eat it!

Burrito, bean burrito!
With salsa!
With salsa!
Burrito, bean burrito!
With salsa!
With salsa!

one—uno
two—dos
three—tres

Uno, Dos, Tres, Toss!

Counting in Spanish gives this sombrero toss an exciting twist! In advance, collect a few sombreros. (Check party stores or ask local Mexican restaurants for donations.) Lay three Hula-Hoop toys on the floor of your group-time area. Label the outside of each hoop with a different numeral from 1 to 3. Teach youngsters the Spanish word for each numeral. Then invite each child, in turn, to toss a sombrero into one of the hoops. Have the child identify the hoop (or closest hoop) by saying its number in Spanish. Continue the activity until the sombreros have all been tossed. Then collect the hats and play the game again! Ready? Uno, dos, tres, toss!

193

Got a Piñata?

A traditional piñata is made from layers of papier-mâché and can be quite elaborate. This simplified piñata is easier to make, but just as much fun! To begin, have your class use a water-glue mixture to cover a large paper grocery bag with tissue paper squares. When the glue is dry, fill the bag with party favors and wrapped treats. Staple the top of the bag shut and wrap duct tape around it as shown. Punch holes in the top of the bag; then tie yarn through the holes to make a hanger. Suspend the piñata from a tree branch or piece of playground equipment. Then blindfold each child, in turn, and have her use a plastic bat to hit the piñata. (Be sure to have the other children stand a safe distance away from the piñata.) When the bag breaks, you won't need to encourage youngsters to scurry and gather up the goodies!

paper—el papél

Fiesta Shakers

With colorful shakers, youngsters won't be able to resist dancing at your celebration! To make a shaker, securely tape a piece of waxed paper over one end of a toilet paper tube. Place a handful of dried beans inside the tube and then cover the other end with another piece of waxed paper. Glue colorful squares of tissue paper over the tube and then add strips of streamers to one end. Now let's dance! (See the activity below.)

to dance—bailar

Let's Dance!

No Cinco de Mayo celebration would be complete without a little dancing! Try this adaptation of the traditional Mexican Hat Dance and get youngsters' feet moving. In advance, check your local library for recordings of traditional Mexican music. Then gather a few sombreros. (Check party stores or ask local Mexican restaurants for donations.)

To begin the activity, place the sombreros on the floor of your group-time area. Then have small groups of students stand around each sombrero. Begin playing the music and have students move to the beat around the sombrero. When students are familiar with the music, give directions such as "Hop around the sombrero," "Tap your foot on the sombrero," or "March away from the sombrero." For more festive fun, have each child use a shaker as he dances. (See "Fiesta Shakers.")

194

SOCIAL DEVELOPMENT FEATURES

Can-Do Lessons With the Little Engine

All aboard! After reading aloud *The Little Engine That Could* by Watty Piper, use the following self-esteem activities to give your youngsters' egos a boost! Choo! Choo! Full-esteem ahead!

ideas by Eva Marie Bareis—Preschool, Cinnamon Hill Preschool, Rapid City, SD

I Think I Can

The phrase "I think I can" has such a nice ring to it! So teach youngsters the following song and encourage them to think "I can."

(sung to the tune of "If You're Happy and You Know It")

I think I can are words I like to use.
They are helpful when I'm trying something new.
If I try with all my might,
In time I'll get it right.
I think I can are words I like to use.

Up the Mountain

Forming a line, walking quietly, sitting in a circle…There are so many things to learn as a new preschooler! Use this class progress chart to give your little engines a visual reminder of just how far they've come in learning some preschool procedures. First, set up a bulletin board scene similar to the one shown. Then use the pattern on page 198 to make a train cutout for each procedure you would like your students to learn. Program each train with a different procedure; then use pushpins to mount the trains at the bottom of the bulletin board. Each time your class successfully demonstrates one of the procedures, move the corresponding train up the mountain. When the trains have reached the top of the mountain, change the title of the display to "We Thought We Could!" Move the trains to the downside of the hill and then celebrate with a special treat!

We Think We Can! We Think We Can!

Line up.

Sit in a circle.

Walk in line quietly.

Loads of Accomplishments

The little engine in the story helps pull a train loaded with treats, from teddy bears to apples to an assortment of candy. Invite each child to create a train car loaded with sweet symbols of her accomplishments. To prepare, photocopy page 199 to make a class supply; then cut out the patterns. Work with each student individually and invite her to choose three patterns. Have her dictate three things that she can do and then write each one on a different pattern. Direct the child to color the patterns and glue them onto a 9" x 6" sheet of construction paper. Then have the child glue on construction paper wheels to create a boxcar. Display each child's car behind a copy of the train pattern on page 198. Wow! Look at what we can do!

I can say my ABCs.

I can dress myself

I can run fast.

Eliza

Movin' Right Along

Let your preschoolers toot their horns with a movement activity that shows off their motor skills! Seat youngsters in a circle; then begin passing a toy train car around the circle. As students pass the train, recite the rhyme below. As you recite the last line, use the name of the student holding the train. Then invite that child to stand and perform an action for the class. After a round of applause, begin passing the train again. Repeat the activity until each child has had a turn.

Clickety, clack!
Clickety, clack!
The train goes round the railroad track.
Chug, chug, choo, choo!
It stops to see what [child's name] can do!

On-the-Right-Track Snack

Wrap up your self-esteem study with a tasty activity that gives literacy skills a lift. To prepare, write the phrase "I think I can" on a tagboard strip. Cut the strip into separate words; then display the phrase on a pocket chart in your circle-time area. After reading the phrase to your youngsters, invite them to count the four words. Then have each child create a four-ingredient snack by mixing equal parts of M&M's Baking Bits, Teddy Graham crackers, chocolate chips, and pretzel sticks. For a tasty home-school connection, have each child prepare a second snack in a resealable plastic bag. Attach a note similar to the one shown; then invite the child to share the snack with his family and show off his can-do know-how!

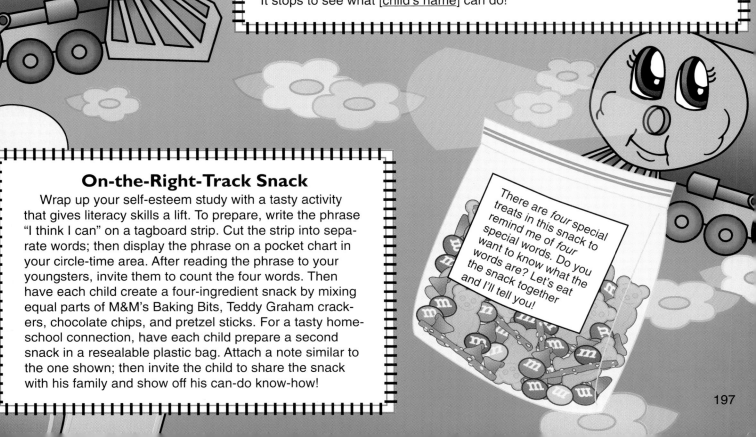

There are four special treats in this snack to remind me of four special words. Do you want to know what the words are? Let's eat the snack together and I'll tell you!

Train Pattern
Use with "Up the Mountain" on page 196 and "Loads of Accomplishments" on page 197.

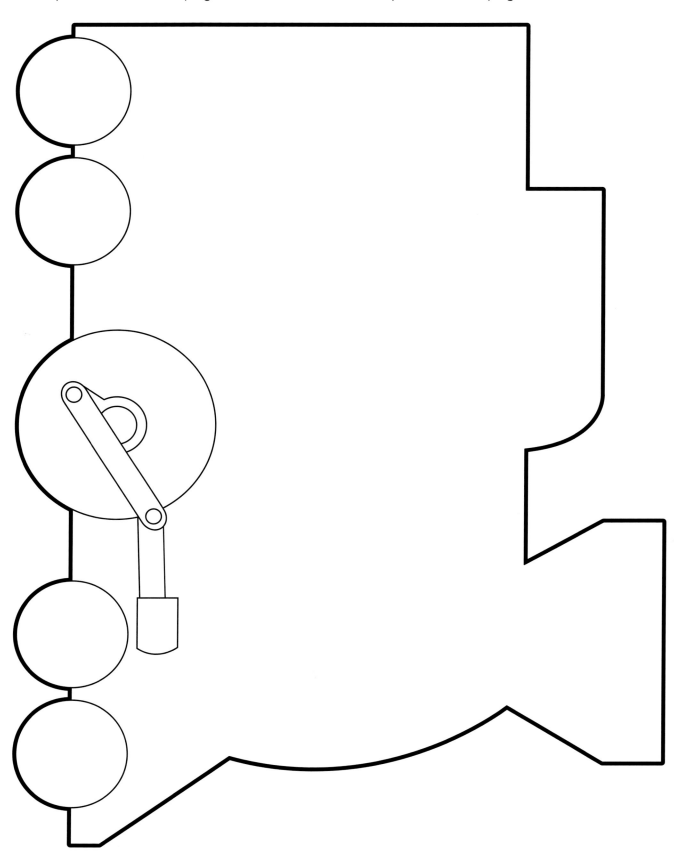

Cooperation Lessons With the Little Red Hen

Who will help you teach your preschoolers about cooperation? The Little Red Hen will! Read your favorite version of *The Little Red Hen* to your youngsters; then invite them to participate in the following cooperation activities. When it comes time for youngsters to cooperate, not one will say, "Not I!"

ideas contributed by Mary Lou Rodriguez, Redwood City, CA

Take a Moment to Talk

After sharing the story with your youngsters, guide them in a discussion about the Little Red Hen and her friends. Revisit the pages where the other animals refuse to help the Little Red Hen by saying, "Not I." Invite youngsters to talk about how the animals' responses may have made the Little Red Hen feel. Then discuss the importance of cooperation and the benefits of working together.

Baking Bread Together

Baking bread together provides the perfect cooperation opportunity. Just ask the Little Red Hen! After hearing her story, your preschoolers will be thrilled to pitch in and help make a batch of the Little Red Hen's banana bread. (See the recipe shown.) If desired, encourage each child's parents to participate by sending in an ingredient for the bread or by lending a hand on the bread-baking day. After gathering the necessary supplies and ingredients, have each child wash his hands and help prepare the bread. Have an adult volunteer supervise small groups of students as they work. Bake the batter according to the recipe shown; then share slices of the cooled bread with your helpers. Ah, if only the Little Red Hen had friends like these!

What should you and your preschoolers do while the bread is baking? Try the activity described in "Who Will Help Me?" on page 201!

The Little Red Hen's Banana Bread
(makes two loaves)

Ingredients:
3 ripe bananas
1 c. sugar
½ c. oil
1 egg
2 c. flour
1 tsp. baking soda
½ tsp. salt

1. Preheat the oven to 350°.
2. Peel the bananas.
3. Mash the bananas with a fork in a small bowl.
4. Mix the sugar, oil, and egg until creamy and light.
5. Blend in the mashed bananas.
6. Add the flour, baking soda, and salt.
7. Stir the mixture until smooth.
8. Spoon the batter into two greased loaf pans.
9. Bake for one hour.

Who Will Help Me?

Even after baking a batch of bread, there are still more cooperation opportunities for your youngsters! Bowls need to be washed, tables need to be cleared, the floor needs to be swept, and the table needs to be set for snacktime. While your bread bakes in the oven, discuss the different cleanup opportunities with your youngsters and make a list on a sheet of chart paper. Review the list; then ask for youngsters' cooperation in cleaning up. For example, you might say, "Who will help me clean the bowls?" Provide each child with any needed supplies, such as a sponge, a broom, paper plates, or napkins. When the room is spick-and-span, treat each of your little chicks to a slice of freshly baked banana bread!

Cooperation on Display

Want to show off your preschoolers' cooperative spirit and their bread-baking skills? Set up this display! In advance, make several large bread-slice cutouts from pieces of poster board. (Make half as many as you have students.) Then cut each slice into two jigsaw puzzle pieces. Provide each child with a puzzle piece and direct her to draw something she did to help bake the bread or clean up after-ward. Have the child dictate a sentence or two about her drawing. Gather youngsters together with their completed drawings. Have each child discuss her drawing. Then instruct students to work together to reassemble the bread slices. Display the slices on a bulletin board and add a title similar to the one shown.

Who Helped Bake the Bread? We Did!

I mashed the bananas. Kaleigh

I dried dishes. Dane

This is me stirring the flour and the sugar. Catherine

I helped set the table so we could eat the bread! A. J.

I swept the floor. Nader

I put the batter in the pan. DeJuan

I wiped the table. Bennett

I washed dishes. Kenyatta

I put the dishes away. Gail

I threw away the trash. Kavi

The Stage Is Set for Cooperation

Use this storytelling activity to further nurture youngsters' understanding of cooperation. In advance, photocopy the patterns on pages 202 and 203. Color the patterns. Cut them out and then attach a piece of self-adhesive felt to the back of each one. Place the patterns near your flannelboard. Invite each child to use the patterns to retell an adapted version of *The Little Red Hen* in which the characters lend the hen a hand. Or have students create new stories that also have the characters working together. The Little Red Hen was right—cooperation is key!

Following Directions ~With~ Peter Rabbit

Oh, the misery that results when Peter Rabbit doesn't listen and follow his mother's directions! Read *The Tale of Peter Rabbit* by Beatrix Potter. Then hop to it and invite youngsters to participate in these activities that encourage listening and following directions.

ideas contributed by Mary Lou Rodriguez, Redwood City, CA

Lessons Learned
language development

What's the most important lesson that Peter learns after his frightening adventure in the garden? Mother knows best! Teach your little ones this simple poem as a reminder to listen to their mothers!

Little Peter Rabbit,
Sometimes he forgot
The lessons that he learned
In Mr. McGregor's plot.

Listen to your mother;
She knows what to do.
Don't be like little Peter,
Or you might lose your shoes!

Jump up and down three times.

Listening to Mother
following one- and two-step directions

After teaching your preschoolers the poem above, discuss what Peter should do the next time his mother gives directions. Afterward, invite each child to don a rabbit ears headband and play the part of an attentive rabbit.

To begin the game, don a pair of rabbit ears yourself and play the part of Peter's mother. Give students one- and two-step directions, such as "Jump up and down three times" or "Wiggle your nose and then hop in a circle." After a few rounds, invite a child to stand in front of the class. Then repeat the activity with the child giving directions to the group.

Inside Mr. McGregor's Garden
following verbal directions, positional words

While being chased around Mr. McGregor's garden, Peter goes under a gate, hides inside a watering can, and climbs on a wheelbarrow! Reenact Peter's adventure with this activity that reinforces listening skills and positional words. To prepare, photocopy the map of Mr. McGregor's garden on page 206. Color the map. Then glue a piece of gray construction paper over the bucket of the watering can to create a pocket (see illustration). Photocopy the rabbit pattern on page 207. Color the rabbit. Laminate it and then cut it out.

To begin the activity, invite a child to join you at a center. Then give the child verbal directions and have her move the rabbit according to your directions. For example, you might say, "Make Peter hop four times and then hide him *inside* the watering can." Continue giving the child directions; then present her with a copy of the badge on page 207. Peter would be proud!

Escape From Mr. McGregor's Garden
following three- and four-step directions, gross-motor development

Escaping from Mr. McGregor's garden sure is a challenge! Invite your students to take on this challenge by setting up a classroom obstacle course based on Mr. McGregor's garden. For example, have students tiptoe around a pond cutout, walk on a straight line behind black-currant bush cutouts, and then crawl under the gate (a chair). Explain to students the sequence and steps of the course. Then invite each child, in turn, to go through the course without having any of the directions repeated. When students master the three-step course, add a fourth step and have them go again!

Blackberry Treats
following pictorial directions

After following their mother's directions, Flopsy, Mopsy, and Cotton-tail are treated to a supper of blackberries, bread, and milk. Your preschoolers will enjoy a similar treat at the conclusion of this activity! To begin, photocopy the step-by-step recipe cards on page 207. Color the cards. Laminate them and then cut them out. Display the cards in sequence at a center; then place the needed ingredients and utensils near the cards. Invite each child, in turn, to the area and have him follow the directions on the recipe cards to create a tasty treat.

205

Safety With Little Red Riding Hood

Everyone knows the story of Little Red Riding Hood and her encounter with the Big Bad Wolf. If only Little Red had taken note of a few pointers on safety! Luckily, her tale has a happy ending, and she's still around to give your preschoolers some tips on staying safe!

by Ada Goren

Just Walk Away

Of course, Little Red Riding Hood's biggest mistake is talking to a stranger, who happens to be a big wolf! Give each of your students a chance to ignore a stranger, with some encouragement from the class! In advance, prepare a few stranger masks by cutting out large, close-up faces from magazines. Mount each of these on tagboard and add a craft stick handle. Next, seat a child in front of the group and ask her to play the part of Little Red Riding Hood. Teach the class the chant below. Then hold one of the masks in front of your face and approach Little Red Riding Hood. Try to engage the child in conversation by saying something such as, "Hi. Could you help me find my lost dog?" or "Would you like some candy?" Have students chant the directions to Little Red Riding Hood; then praise the child for getting up and walking away without speaking to you, the stranger. Continue until every child has had a chance to play Little Red Riding Hood and ignore a stranger.

Don't do it, Little Red.
Don't do it, we say!
Don't talk to that stranger!
Just walk away!

Who's There?

Little Red Riding Hood isn't the only one who makes a safety mistake in this story. Grandma really should have been more careful about opening her door to the wolf. Teach your little ones to be cautious about opening the door with this dramatization. Ask one child to go outside your classroom door. Have another child stand inside the door with you; play the part of this child's parent. Have the child outside knock. Direct the child inside to ask, "Who is it?" and listen for the reply. Then have the child turn to you and ask, "Is it okay to open the door?" before letting in the child waiting outside. If your classroom door has a window in it or next to it, add a step to the drama by having both the child and parent look outside to check on the caller's identity before letting her in. Repeat the process until every child has practiced asking permission before opening the door.

Stick Together

Perhaps Little Red Riding Hood shouldn't have been wandering in the forest alone in the first place! Remind your students that it's always best to venture out with a grown-up and that it's safest to stick close together in public places, such as a shopping mall or a grocery store. To help youngsters practice staying with mom or dad, create a two-person obstacle course. Use tape lines and a few pieces of furniture to create a course that zigzags, circles around objects, passes under a table, and perhaps requires climbing over something (such as a beanbag chair). Divide your class into pairs and designate one child in each pair the child and one the parent. Have them hold hands and go through the course together. Then have them switch roles and repeat the course. Whatever you do, don't let go!

Learning Good Manners With Goldilocks!

After a scare with the three bears, Goldilocks learns a lesson: Good manners are important! Read *Goldilocks and the Three Bears* to your youngsters. Then let that fair-haired heroine teach your tots all about etiquette. Her pointers on politeness are "just right"!

Goldilocks Gets an Invitation

What is Goldilocks' first faux pas? She enters the home of the three bears without being invited! Use this activity to help familiarize youngsters with invitation etiquette and telephone manners. To prepare, place two toy telephones in your circle-time area. After demonstrating a polite telephone conversation, invite two children to participate in a role-playing activity. Have one child pretend to be Goldilocks and another child pretend to be one of the three bears. (For added fun, encourage the child to talk in the appropriate bear voice.) Direct the bear to call Goldilocks and use his best telephone manners to invite her to visit his home. Then have Goldilocks respond politely to his invitation. Have the two students hang up the telephones; then repeat the activity with a new pair of children. Somebody's been invited to my house!

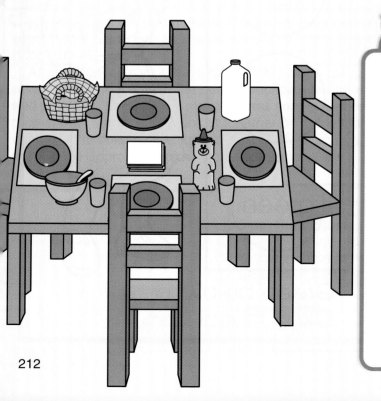

Let's Talk About Table Manners

Now that an invitation has been extended, it's time for some tips on table manners! Set up this game and you're sure to hear youngsters politely saying, "Pass the porridge, please!" To prepare for this activity, set a table for four in your dramatic-play area. Then gather items similar to those shown on page 214. Place each one near a different place setting at the table. Next, make several copies of the game cards on page 214. Color the cards. Laminate them and then cut out each one. Stack the cards facedown and then place them at the table.

To play the game, the first player takes the top card from the deck and then politely asks the child sitting near the item to pass it. The first player says, "Thank you" and then lays the card faceup in front of her. The players continue the game in this manner until all of the cards have been drawn. "Pass the porridge, please!"

Fingers, Forks, or Spoons?

Although Goldilocks demonstrates poor manners by helping herself to the bears' porridge, she did politely eat the porridge with a spoon and not with her fingers. Use this activity to help your little folks remember which foods are for fingers, which ones are for forks, and which ones are for spoons. To prepare, cut out magazine pictures of different foods and then make sorting mats similar to the ones shown. Invite a small group of children to an area and discuss the polite way to eat each food. Then have the children help you sort the foods onto the appropriate mat. Afterward, provide each child with a spoon and a small bowl of oatmeal; then invite him to snack politely on the "porridge."

My Apologies!

Sometimes accidents happen. But after accidentally breaking Baby Bear's chair, Goldilocks never apologizes! Teach youngsters the word *apology* and then discuss the importance of apologizing. Afterward, have students sing the following song to help them remember the importance of saying, "I'm sorry."

(sung to the tune of "I'm Bringing Home a Baby Bumblebee")

I'm learning how to make an apology.
Won't my mommy be so proud of me?
I'm learning how to make an apology.
Say, "I'm sorry!"

Dear Bear Family,
   Thank you for sharing your porridge with me. Thank you for letting me use your chairs and your beds. I'm sorry I broke Baby Bear's chair. Your house is pretty.

Love,
Goldilocks

A Thank-You for the Three Bears

After an afternoon at the home of the three bears, Goldilocks owes them a great big thank-you! Invite your youngsters to help Goldilocks write a note of thanks to her trio of hosts. During your group time, review *Goldilocks and the Three Bears*. Discuss the different things that Goldilocks does at the bears' home. Then have youngsters dictate a note thanking the bears for these things. Write their response on a sheet of chart paper and display it near your writing area. Place a supply of inexpensive thank-you cards in the area; then invite each child to visit the center and write additional notes of thanks. Goldilocks would be proud!

SONGS & SUCH

Welcome!

This song may be simple, but it sure is catchy! After singing it a few times, your youngsters just might want to join in! So invite your class to sing along to the tune of "Shoo Fly." Welcome, preschoolers!

Welcome to school today!
Welcome to school today!
Welcome to school today!
We have come to learn and play!

Eva Bareis—Preschool, Cinnamon Hill Preschool, Rapid City, SD

So Glad You're Here!

Looking for a song that will help your youngsters learn each child's name? Invite students to sing this jazzy jingle to each child! This tune is not only great for the first days of school, it's also a wonderful way to welcome new students who arrive later in the year.

(sung to the tune of "If You're Happy and You Know It")

We're so glad to have you in our preschool class!
   (Shout child's name.)
We're so glad to have you in our preschool class!
   (Shout child's name.)
We're so glad you're here today! We will sing and learn and play!
We're so glad to have you in our preschool class!
   (Shout child's name.)

Ada Goren, Winston-Salem, NC

What Did You Do in Preschool?

Here's a simple song that will help your youngsters remember their first day in preschool. Invite students to name different activities from the day, such as playing, singing, and dancing. Then incorporate their answers in the song below. Now, when students' parents ask what they did in school, your youngsters can respond in song!

(sung to the tune of "Johnny Works With One Hammer")

Today I [played] with new friends,
New friends, new friends.
Today I [played] with new friends.
We had lots of fun!

Eva Bareis—Preschool, Cinnamon Hill Preschool, Rapid City, SD

Eyes, Ears, Nose, and Mouth

Help youngsters tune in to body parts with this song!

(sung to the tune of "Row, Row, Row Your Boat")

Eyes, ears, nose, and mouth.
These are parts of me!
Arms and legs and elbows too!
And don't forget my knee!

Deborah Garmon, Groton, CT

Apples Up on Top

How can you pick apples that are high in a tree?
Sing this song to discover a clever solution!

(sung to the tune of "Up on the Housetop")

Up in the treetop, way up high.
Three red apples for my pie.
How will I get them to the ground?
I'll shake that tree 'til they fall down!
Shake, shake, shake!
Watch them fall!
Shake, shake, shake,
I'll catch them all!
Oh, into my basket,
One, two, three!
No more apples in the tree.

Eva Bareis—Preschool, Cinnamon Hill Preschool
Rapid City, SD

Another Apple Anthem

(sung to the tune of "Twinkle, Twinkle, Little Star")

Shiny, shiny, apple red,
Hanging high above my head.
On my tiptoes, reaching high.
One last stretch, it's worth a try.
Shiny, shiny, apple red,
Grabbed it, ate it, now I'm fed!

Jana Sanderson—Four-Year-Olds
Rainbow School
Stockton, CA

SONGS & SUCH

Sing a Song of Snowmen

Have each child play the part of a frosty snowman with this song and snowman mask. To make one mask, cut out two eyeholes from a white paper plate. Add a black construction paper hat and an orange paper nose. Use a black marker to draw a dotted mouth and then tape a jumbo craft stick to the back. Have each child hold her mask and sing the following song. Frosty would be so pleased!

(sung to the tune of "I'm a Little Teapot")

I'm a little snowman,
Round and fat,
With an orange nose
And a big black hat.
I like to be outside
On a snowy day
Until the sun
Melts me away!

Sarah Booth—PreK
Messiah Nursery School
South Williamsport, PA

Penguin Action

Set to music, this penguin poem becomes a miniature musical! Invite five of your preschoolers to waddle up to the front of the class and pretend to be penguins. Then play a lively instrumental recording as you recite the poem. Direct each little penguin to play his part as directed in the poem. Repeat the activity until each child has had a chance to play the part of a penguin. With this Antarctic activity, your youngsters will soon be ready for "Brr-oadway"!

Five little penguins standing on the shore.   *Stand like penguins.*
One dove in and then there were four.   *One swims away.*
Four little penguins sliding down, "Whee!"   *Wiggle hands above head.*
One went too far and then there were three.   *One "slides" back to seat.*
Three little penguins don't know what to do.   *Shrug shoulders; look at each other.*

One waddled off and then there were two.   *One waddles back to seat.*
Two little penguins having lots of fun.   *Clap hands and cheer.*
One went home and then there was one.   *One waddles away and waves good-bye.*

One little penguin sitting in the sun.   *Sit down.*
He/She went to sleep.   *Pretend to fall asleep.*
Now the penguin song is done!

Cathy Seibel—PreK, Head Start
Greensburg, PA

Twinkle, Twinkle

'Tis the season for holiday lights! Kwanzaa kinaras, Hanukkah menorahs, and Christmas tree lights are all around! Use the following song as you teach youngsters about any of these well-lit holidays.

(sung to the tune of "Twinkle, Twinkle, Little Star")

Twinkle, twinkle, candlelight,
Shining on this holiday night.
Shining bright for us to see
Just how special this time can be.
Twinkle, twinkle, candlelight,
Shining on this holiday night.

LeeAnn Collins, Sunshine House Preschool, Lansing, MI

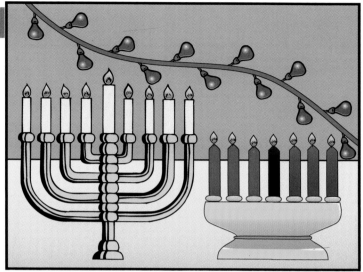

It's Freezing, It's Snowing

What happens after a long, cold night of snow? You wake up to a world all aglow!

(sung to the tune of "A Tisket, a Tasket")

It's freezing. It's snowing.
The old wind is blowing.
I went to bed, laid down my head,
All the time not knowing,
Not knowing, not knowing,
The wind and snow kept going.
I woke up from a dark cold night
To see the world a-glowing!

Rebecca Fisch—PreK, Yeshiva Rabbi Hirsch, Brooklyn, NY

Snowflakes Falling

(sung to the tune of "Kookaburra")

Snowflakes falling, falling to the ground,
Making a white blanket all around.
Snow on the house!
Snow on the tree!
Snow even on me!

LeeAnn Collins

SONGS & SUCH

Will You Be Mine?

This simple song will have youngsters asking, "Will you be my valentine?"

(sung to the tune of "Clementine")

February, February, time to make a valentine.
Will you send one, give a friend one?
I will be yours if you'll be mine!

Nancy Cropper—Preschool
James E. Moss Elementary
Murray, UT

Good Morning, Groundhog!

Use this song to serenade that sleepy groundhog on Groundhog Day (February 2)! For more movement fun, encourage your preschoolers to dramatize the song as they sing.

(sung to the tune of "Are You Sleeping?")

Little groundhog, little groundhog,
Underground, underground.
Now it's time to wake up!
Now it's time to wake up!
Yawn and stretch.
Yawn and stretch.

Little groundhog, little groundhog,
Underground, underground.
Climb out of your burrow.
Climb out of your burrow.
Look around.
Look around.

Little groundhog, little groundhog,
Underground, underground.
Do you see your shadow?
Do you see your shadow?
Down you run!
Down you run!

Ann Schuft—Four-Year-Olds
Roudenbush Pre-school
Westford, MA

Circus Song

Ladies and gentlemen! It's the greatest song on earth! If you're planning a trip to the big top, teach your tots this tune to prepare them for some circus sights. Lions, elephants, and clowns! Oh, my!

(sung to the tune of "Frosty the Snowman")

Lions in the circus
Are as wild as can be.
With their manes so long
And their roars so loud,
They'll do tricks for you and me!

Elephants in the circus
Are as big as they can be.
With their ears so wide
And their trunks so long,
They'll amaze both you and me!

Clowns in the circus
Are as funny as can be.
With their big red noses
And their floppy shoes.
They're a silly sight to see!

Tabitha Bohannon
The Growing Tree Learning Center
Putnam, TN

A Tasteful Tune

Teaching about nutrition? Teach youngsters this song! Before singing, discuss different healthful foods with your students. Then incorporate each food into the song below. What will youngsters think of this catchy nutrition tune? Oh, they'll eat it up!

(sung to the tune of "Boom! Boom! Ain't It Great to Be Crazy?")

Yum! Yum! Don't you love to eat [green beans]?
Yum! Yum! Don't you love to eat [green beans]?
They're delicious and good for you!
Yum! Yum! Don't you love to eat [green beans]?

Repeat the verse as many times as desired, substituting other healthful foods for the underlined words.

Ada Goren
Winston-Salem, NC

SONGS & SUCH

Earth Day Hooray!

Herald in Earth Day (April 22) with this toe-tapping tune.

(sung to the tune of "The Ants Go Marching")

Soon it's gonna be Earth Day. Hooray! Hooray!
Soon it's gonna be Earth Day. Hooray! Hooray!
We'll do our part. We'll do our share
To clean up the earth everywhere.
That's what Earth Day's all about.
Give a shout! Say, "Hooray!" for Earth Day.

Ada Goren
Winston-Salem, NC

Rain and Thunder

(sung to the tune of "Are You Sleeping?")

Rain and thunder.
Rain and thunder.
Boom! Boom! Boom!
Boom! Boom! Boom!
See the flash of lightning.
Oh, my gosh, it's frightening!
Boom! Boom! Boom!
Boom! Boom! Boom!

Marisa Ellin—Child Development Specialist
An Even Start in Newport
Newport, RI

Let's Hear It for Frogs!

Sing this lively springtime song and invite youngsters to perform the froggy actions as directed. Now hop to it! Ribbit!

(sung to the tune of "Do You Know the Muffin Man?")

Oh, look! I see some [hopping] frogs,
Some [hopping] frogs, some [hopping] frogs!
Oh, look! I see some [hopping] frogs,
[Hopping] around the pond!

Sing additional verses replacing the underlined word with other action words, such as *dancing, croaking,* and *sleeping.*

I'm a Little Umbrella

During those April showers, there's nothing more satisfying than popping open a big umbrella. Invite your youngsters to sing the following song in honor of the umbrella!

(sung to the tune of "I'm a Little Teapot")

I'm an umbrella.	*Point to self.*
I keep you dry	*Point to "you."*
When the rain falls from the sky!	*Raise arms up; then wiggle fingers downward.*
I have a sturdy handle	*Pretend to hold umbrella handle.*
And a curvy top.	*Circle arms overhead.*
Keep me up 'til the rain has stopped!	*Maintain previous position; then put one palm out to gesture "stop."*

Ada Goren
Winston-Salem, NC

Preschool Pomp and Circumstance

When youngsters sing this song at your end-of-the-year program, parents will want to stand and cheer! In advance, have each child paint a picture for the program. As she sings the first three lines of the song, the child holds the painting behind her back. She holds up the painting as she sings the fourth line in the song and then brings it back down to sing the rest of the song.

(sung to the tune of "Take Me Out to the Ballgame")

We like [your school's name] Preschool!
Here we made lots of friends.
We learned our letters and numbers too.
Look! I painted a picture for you.
Let us root, root, root for our preschool.
Every day is so cool.
So, let's tell our moms and our dads
That we love preschool!

Cindy Quigley—Preschool (K4)
Little Lambs Preschool
Corning, NY

Shout Hooray for the USA

Celebrate the Fourth of July by teaching youngsters this lively song.

(sung to the tune of "If You're Happy and You Know It")

If you love the USA, [clap your hands].
If you love the USA, [clap your hands].
If you love the USA, [clap your hands] and say, "Hooray!"
If you love the USA, [clap your hands]!

Sing additional verses, replacing the underlined words with the following phrases: *stomp your feet, slap your knees,* and *do all three.*

Sarah Booth—PreK
Messiah Nursery School
South Williamsport, PA

Great Grasshoppers!

(sung to the tune of "Jingle Bells")

Grasshoppers, grasshoppers!
They don't have a care.
Their strong legs push off the ground
And lift them in the air!

Grasshoppers, grasshoppers!
They can jump so high.
I love to watch them as they go
Leaping toward the sky!

Cynthia Holcomb
San Angelo, CA

Thematic Units

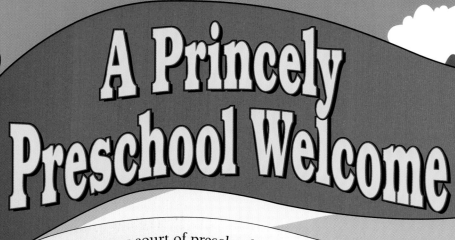

A Princely Preschool Welcome

Give your new court of preschoolers the royal treatment with this majestic collection of welcome-to-school ideas.

ideas by LeeAnn Collins–Director
Sunshine House Preschool, Lansing, MI

Come Into My Castle!

Here's a way to stir up some royal excitement even before the school year begins! Send your prospective preschoolers an invitation to your classroom castle. Photocopy page 230 to make a class supply. Cut the castle door on each pattern as shown; then glue a photograph of yourself behind each opening.

Next, make one copy of the open newsletter on page 231. On the copy, write a note introducing yourself to your preschoolers; then duplicate the note to make a class supply. Send each child a note and a castle invitation. If desired, send along a copy of page 232 and a personalized resealable plastic bag. Invite each child to complete the activity, place it in the bag, and then bring it to school on the first day (see "Jewels in Your Crown" below).

Jewels in Your Crown

How will your preschoolers become acquainted? By the jewels in their crowns! Before school begins, send each child a personalized resealable plastic bag and a copy of page 232. On the first day of school, provide the child with a personalized paper crown. (For a quick-and-easy crown, staple a length of bulletin board border to fit a child's head.) Invite the child to glue her jewels onto the crown and then add foil star stickers. Have students wear their completed crowns to your circle-time area. Introduce each child by reading the information on her crown and then singing the song shown. Hail, hail, royal preschoolers!

(sung to the tune of "The Farmer in the Dell")

Princess/Prince [child's name] is here!
Princess/Prince [child's name] is here!
Welcome to [your name]'s kingdom.
Let's give a royal cheer!

Lower the Drawbridge!

Transform your classroom into a castle with this door decor idea. Obtain a large rectangular piece of cardboard, such as the side of a refrigerator box. Then paint the cardboard or cover it with woodgrain-patterned Con-Tact paper to resemble a drawbridge. Place the drawbridge on the floor in front of your classroom door. Then use black electrical tape to add construction paper chains as shown. For a final touch, cut out gray construction paper stones and tape them around the door to resemble a stone wall. Now, your castle is ready for some kings and queens!

Precious Gems

Every castle contains a stash of royal gems! So use this nametag idea to create your castle's treasure. To begin, mask the text on the jewel patterns on page 232. Then photocopy them onto colored paper to make a class supply plus a few extra. Laminate the patterns. Cut them out and then punch a hole in the top of each one. Use a pushpin to display the patterns on a bulletin board titled "Precious Gems in [your name]'s Class."

On the first day of school, invite each of your little princes and princesses to choose a jewel from the display. Use a permanent marker to write each child's name on the jewel and then pin it to his clothing. At the end of the day, return the jewels to the board. Add a photograph of each child beside his gem and you've got a priceless display!

Precious Gems in Mrs. Shaughnessy's Class

Timmy
Tricia
Ursula
Kevin
Harry
Sandra

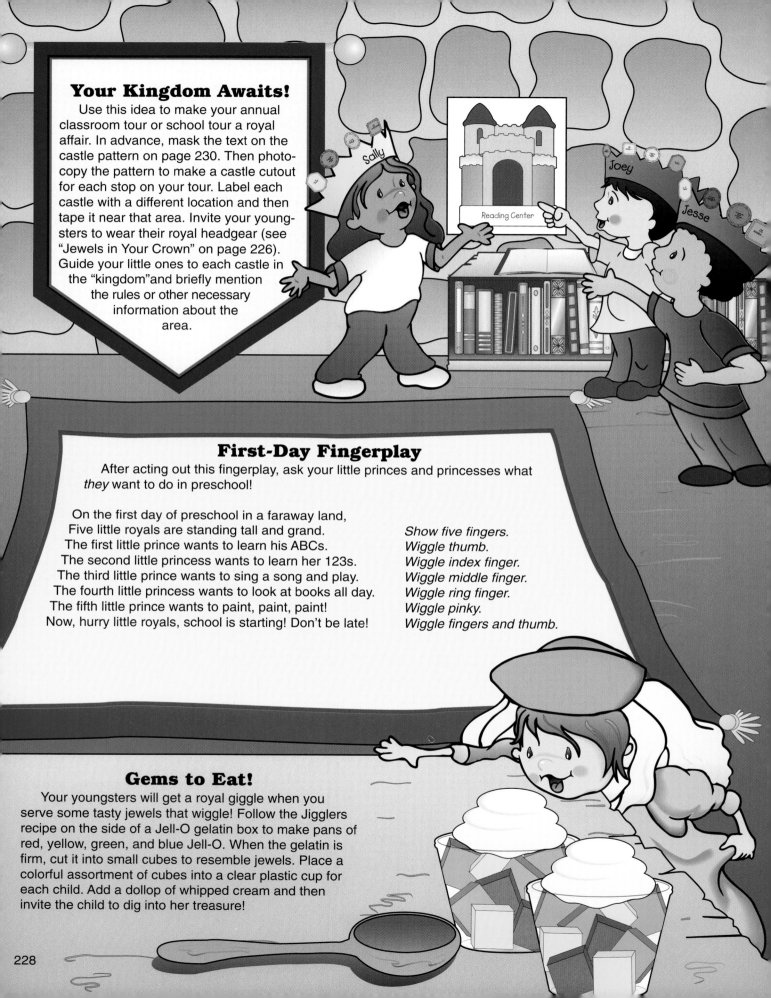

Your Kingdom Awaits!

Use this idea to make your annual classroom tour or school tour a royal affair. In advance, mask the text on the castle pattern on page 230. Then photocopy the pattern to make a castle cutout for each stop on your tour. Label each castle with a different location and then tape it near that area. Invite your youngsters to wear their royal headgear (see "Jewels in Your Crown" on page 226). Guide your little ones to each castle in the "kingdom" and briefly mention the rules or other necessary information about the area.

First-Day Fingerplay

After acting out this fingerplay, ask your little princes and princesses what *they* want to do in preschool!

On the first day of preschool in a faraway land,
Five little royals are standing tall and grand.
The first little prince wants to learn his ABCs.
The second little princess wants to learn her 123s.
The third little prince wants to sing a song and play.
The fourth little princess wants to look at books all day.
The fifth little prince wants to paint, paint, paint!
Now, hurry little royals, school is starting! Don't be late!

Show five fingers.
Wiggle thumb.
Wiggle index finger.
Wiggle middle finger.
Wiggle ring finger.
Wiggle pinky.
Wiggle fingers and thumb.

Gems to Eat!

Your youngsters will get a royal giggle when you serve some tasty jewels that wiggle! Follow the Jigglers recipe on the side of a Jell-O gelatin box to make pans of red, yellow, green, and blue Jell-O. When the gelatin is firm, cut it into small cubes to resemble jewels. Place a colorful assortment of cubes into a clear plastic cup for each child. Add a dollop of whipped cream and then invite the child to dig into her treasure!

Heigh-ho, the Dairy-o!

Gather your preschoolers in a circle; then get them moving and mingling as they act out this royal adaptation of "The Farmer in the Dell."

(sung to the tune of "The Farmer in the Dell")

[The king is in the castle].
[The king is in the castle].
Heigh-ho, the dairy-o!
[The king is in the castle].

Sing additional verses, replacing the underlined phrase with the following phrases in turn: "The king takes a queen," "The queen takes a prince," and "The prince takes a princess." Then sing the final verse below and have the remaining students bow down.

The royal court bows down.
The royal court bows down.
Heigh-ho, the dairy-o!
The royal court bows down.

Prince and Princess Puppets

With this craft idea your preschoolers will be able to take home a royal pal! In advance, cut out a class supply of tagboard child shapes. Then cut out paper crowns and clothing to fit the shapes. Direct each student to glue a crown and some clothing onto a shape. Then have her use crayons, glitter glue, and other craft items to add some finishing touches. Glue a jumbo craft stick to the back of the shape and your preschooler has a noble puppet!

By Royal Proclamation

As the day winds down in your preschool kingdom, officially declare each of your youngsters a prince or princess! For each boy and girl in your class, duplicate the appropriate award pattern on page 233. Write the child's name on the line and then sign and date the award. As each child leaves your kingdom, hand him an award, bow, and then bid him a royal good-bye. "Farewell, your highness! Until we meet again!"

Hear ye, hear ye!
The royal courts declare that

Samuel
(child's name)
was a prince in
preschool today!

Mrs. Pridgen
teacher signature
Sept. 23, 2002
date

Sippin' on Science
Easy Experiments With Milk

Your preschoolers are sure to find these experiments with milk fascinating and fun! Just be sure to check for milk allergies before you begin. Ready, set, *slurp!*

by Ada Goren

Taste Test

Begin your exploration of milk by inviting little ones to do a taste test. To prepare, duplicate the recording sheet on page 237 to make a class supply. Then purchase one quart each of whole milk, reduced-fat milk (2%), and skim milk. To begin, pour a small amount of whole milk into a cup for each child and have her taste it. If she likes it, have her draw a happy face in the box above the first cup. If she doesn't like it, have her draw a sad face. Continue the tasting and recording procedure with the reduced-fat milk and then with the skim milk. Discuss the results. How many children liked each type of milk? Did anyone like all three types? Vote on the class's favorite type.
comparing, communicating

That's Milk?

Stir in some learning about scientific changes when you invite your little ones to examine a secret powder—dehydrated milk! Out of students' view, pour some powdered milk into a plastic container. Pass the container to each child and invite him to observe, touch, and smell the powder. Next, invite youngsters to predict what will happen when you mix the powder with water. Write students' responses on a chart. Then mix a new batch of powdered milk with water and invite students to observe the changes. Have students guess what the liquid is; then give each child a taste on an individual spoon. Afterward, discuss students' predictions and reveal the identity of the powder. That's milk!
predicting, observing, hypothesizing, communicating

Milk Taste Test ☺ or ☹.
Which types of milk do you like? Draw ☺ or ☹.

whole milk reduced-fat milk skim milk

Powders and Predictions

Here's another powder investigation that will add a little more flavor to your milk study! Provide each child with a plastic spoon, a small cup of milk, and a tablespoon of NesQuik chocolate drink mix in a snack-sized resealable plastic bag. Invite youngsters to closely examine the powdered mix and smell it. Ask them to predict what will happen when they add the powder to the milk. Then have each child use her spoon to stir in the powder. Direct youngsters to observe the changes in the milk and discuss them. Then invite each child to drink up!

The following day, repeat the activity using *strawberry-flavored* NesQuik mix. As students are drinking the strawberry milk, discuss their predictions for each investigation. Was it easier to make a prediction with the second powder? Why or why not? ***predicting, observing, comparing***

No Stirring Required

Now your little ones have seen what can happen when things are stirred into milk, but what if you add something and don't stir at all? Pour 1/4 cup of milk into a clear plastic cup; then allow the cup to sit still for a minute or two. Squeeze in a drop of food coloring close to the side of the cup. Ask youngsters to watch what happens, but don't stir in the coloring. They'll notice thin lines of color begin to develop down the side of the cup. Observe the cup of milk after ten minutes, a half hour, and an hour. What is happening? It will take about an hour and a half for the food coloring to completely *diffuse* into the milk. The result will be a colorful cup of milk—no stirring required! ***observing***

*The **diffusion** occurs because the molecules in the milk and food coloring are moving, even if we can't see them. The molecules move from the more crowded area (the food coloring, a highly concentrated substance) to the less crowded area (the milk).*

235

Lemons and Milk Don't Mix!

Caution: This experiment is sure to turn sour! But that's what it's meant to do! Show your youngsters a lemon slice and a cup of milk. Ask students to predict what will happen if you squeeze some lemon juice into the milk. Write students' predictions on a sheet of chart paper. Then squeeze the juice from the lemon slice into the milk. Stir in the juice and wait a minute. Then stir the milk again. Invite youngsters to look at the milk. Have them dictate the outcome of the experiment for you to write on the chart paper. Then explain that the acid in the lemon juice caused the milk to *curdle,* or become thick and lumpy. Better save the lemons for lemonade!

predicting, observing, communicating

What will happen if we add lemon juice to milk?

We predict...
— it will turn yellow
— we'll have lemon milk
— it will make lemonade

What happened?
— it got lumpy
— it stayed white
— it looks yucky
— it isn't lemonade

Pam Crane

Easy Ice Milk

Don't end your science explorations on a sour note! Wrap up your study by making a sweet treat—ice milk! To begin, have each child stir together 1/3 cup whole milk, one teaspoon sugar, and a small dash of vanilla in a paper cup. (To ensure success, chill all the ingredients well.) Pour the concoction into a zippered sandwich bag and seal it well. Have each child and a partner place their bags inside a large zippered plastic bag filled with ice and 1/4 cup salt. Have them sit across from one another on the floor, with a sheet of newspaper spread out between them. Invite them to toss the bag back and forth, flipping it over onto the newspaper each time, as they sing the following song. Set a timer for three minutes. When the timer goes off, open the bag of ice and remove the two sandwich bags. Wipe off the bags; then have the children open them and observe the contents inside. Provide each child with a spoon and invite him to dig in. Wow! The milk changed from a drink to a dessert! Yum! ***observing***

(sung to the tune of "Row, Row, Row Your Boat")

Pass, pass, pass your bag.
Pass your bag of ice.
Pass your bag and soon you'll see…
We're making something nice!

Milk Taste Test

Which types of milk do you like? Draw 😊 or ☹ .

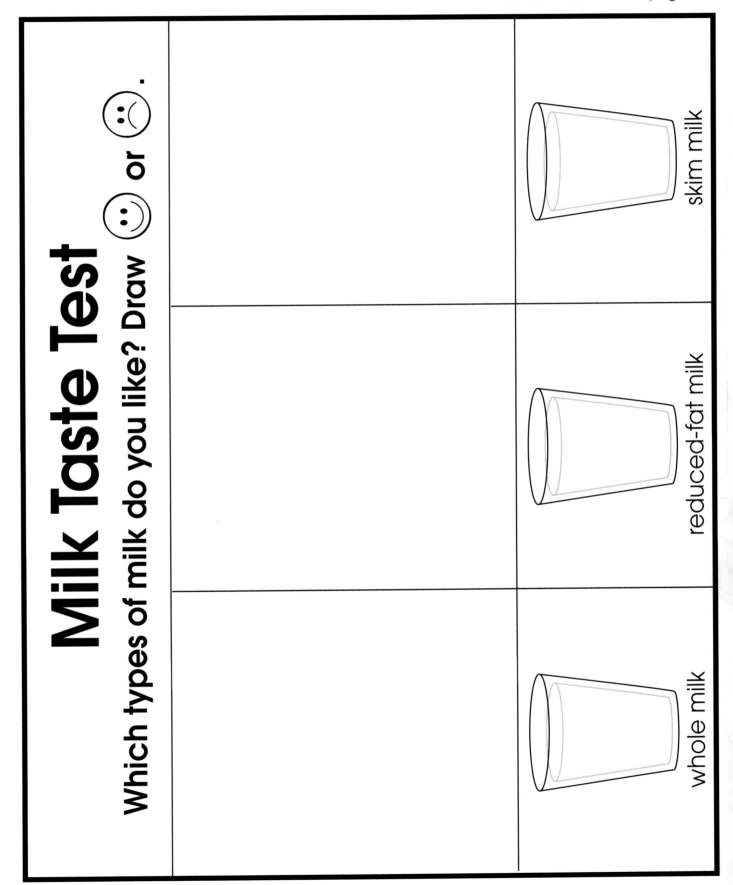

skim milk

reduced-fat milk

whole milk

It's Nursery Rhyme Time!

That's right—it's time for your preschoolers to meet Mother Goose and her cast of characters. Let Little Miss Muffett, Humpty Dumpty, and that contrary Mary teach your little ones some lilting language; then use these activities to add to the fun!

by Ada Goren

What an Accomplishment!

Learning several nursery rhymes is quite an accomplishment! Get ready to celebrate by duplicating the certificate on page 244 on white construction paper for each child. Personalize each child's copy. Then, as your youngsters learn each rhyme and complete the accompanying activity, invite them to color the corresponding icon on their certificates. Or add even more pizzazz with the decorating options below. When the certificates are complete, send them home so that little ones can share their nursery rhyme knowledge with their families.

heart—Color the large heart; then add mini heart stickers next to it.
mitten—Use markers to draw a design on the mitten.
crown—Color it; then glue on tiny plastic jewels or sequins.
cake—Glue on "candles" made from short pieces of yarn; write your initial on the side.
star—Add glue and glitter or color with a glitter crayon.
spider—Glue a large pom-pom to the spider body.
pail—Glue on a cut-to-size piece of aluminum foil.
candlestick—Add glue and glitter to the flame or color it with a glitter crayon.
egg—Glue on wiggle eyes and draw a smile.
flower—Color the petals; then add an ink fingerprint to the center.

238

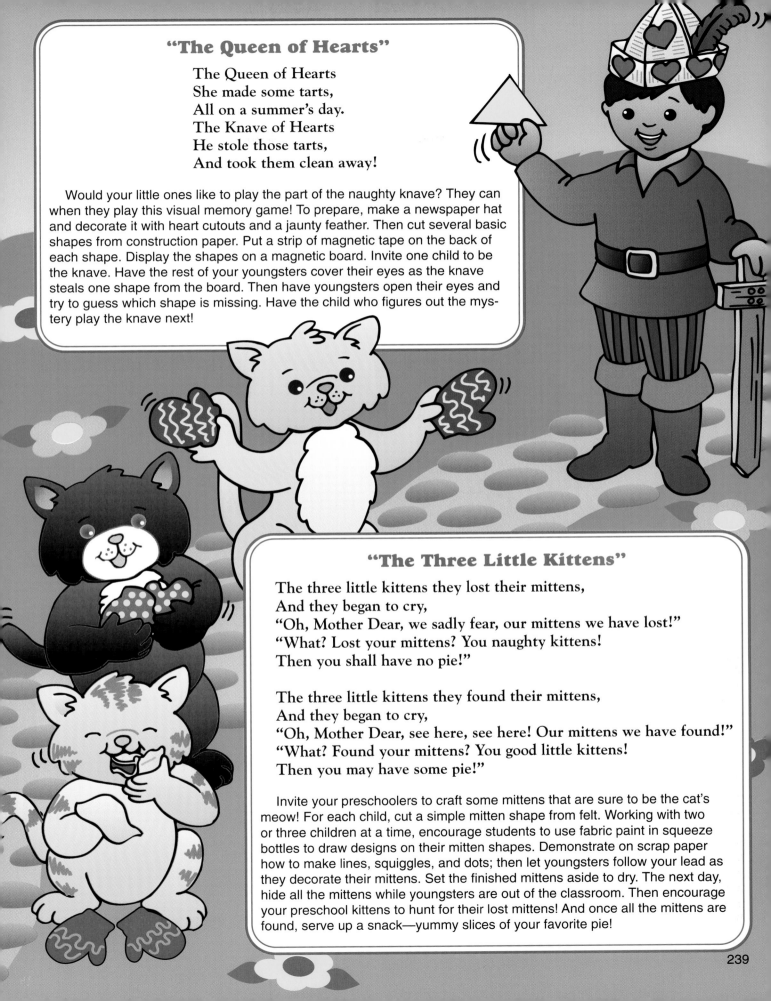

"The Queen of Hearts"

The Queen of Hearts
She made some tarts,
All on a summer's day.
The Knave of Hearts
He stole those tarts,
And took them clean away!

Would your little ones like to play the part of the naughty knave? They can when they play this visual memory game! To prepare, make a newspaper hat and decorate it with heart cutouts and a jaunty feather. Then cut several basic shapes from construction paper. Put a strip of magnetic tape on the back of each shape. Display the shapes on a magnetic board. Invite one child to be the knave. Have the rest of your youngsters cover their eyes as the knave steals one shape from the board. Then have youngsters open their eyes and try to guess which shape is missing. Have the child who figures out the mystery play the knave next!

"The Three Little Kittens"

The three little kittens they lost their mittens,
And they began to cry,
"Oh, Mother Dear, we sadly fear, our mittens we have lost!"
"What? Lost your mittens? You naughty kittens!
Then you shall have no pie!"

The three little kittens they found their mittens,
And they began to cry,
"Oh, Mother Dear, see here, see here! Our mittens we have found!"
"What? Found your mittens? You good little kittens!
Then you may have some pie!"

Invite your preschoolers to craft some mittens that are sure to be the cat's meow! For each child, cut a simple mitten shape from felt. Working with two or three children at a time, encourage students to use fabric paint in squeeze bottles to draw designs on their mitten shapes. Demonstrate on scrap paper how to make lines, squiggles, and dots; then let youngsters follow your lead as they decorate their mittens. Set the finished mittens aside to dry. The next day, hide all the mittens while youngsters are out of the classroom. Then encourage your preschool kittens to hunt for their lost mittens! And once all the mittens are found, serve up a snack—yummy slices of your favorite pie!

"Old King Cole"

Old King Cole was a merry old soul,
And a merry old soul was he.
He called for his pipe, and he called for his bowl,
And he called for his fiddlers three.

Old King Cole was merry—but what if he had been sad, angry, or frightened? Use this rhyme and the reproducible on page 245 to help your little ones explore emotions. First, talk about the meaning of the word *merry.* Show youngsters the picture of the happy king from the reproducible. Then show youngsters the picture of the sad king. Ask how they think the king is feeling. Then recite the rhyme again, but replace the word *merry* with the word *sad.* Encourage your preschoolers to say the rhyme with you, using sad voices and faces. Talk about reasons why someone might be sad. Then repeat the process with the other two pictures, using the words *angry* and *frightened.* Then finish the activity on an upbeat note by revisiting the picture of the merry King Cole and reciting the original rhyme.

"Pat-a-Cake"

Pat-a-cake, pat-a-cake, baker's man,
Bake me a cake as fast as you can.
Pat it and prick it, and mark it with a B,
And put it in the oven for baby and me!

Cook up some letter recognition with this activity! To prepare, use a photocopier to enlarge the cake pattern on page 244. Color the enlarged cake and then cut it out. Tape the cake to a magnetic board. Then gather a supply of magnetic letters that you want youngsters to recognize—including the letter *B.* Set the letters near the magnetic board.

Begin the activity by reciting the nursery rhyme and placing the letter *B* on the cake. Then replace the *B* with a different letter, and ask if anyone can identify it. When a child correctly identifies the letter, allow him to choose the next letter to put on the cake. Keep going until your little bakers are done!

"Twinkle, Twinkle, Little Star"

Twinkle, twinkle, little star.
How I wonder what you are!
Up above the world so high,
Like a diamond in the sky!
Twinkle, twinkle, little star.
How I wonder what you are!

These twinkling stars will look beautiful *and* give your preschoolers practice with their fine-motor skills. For each child, cut a star shape from heavy blue paper. Use a hole puncher to punch several holes around the star's perimeter. Then give each child her star cutout and a 36-inch length of silver ribbon, knotted at one end. Demonstrate how to lace the ribbon in and out of the holes to create a shiny border around the star shape. When the child has laced the ribbon through all the holes, tape the ribbon securely to the back and cut off any excess length. Use silver glitter glue or a silver glitter crayon to write the child's name on her star. Display the finished stars around a copy of the nursery rhyme.

Little Miss Carolyn, sat on her tuffet.
Eating her curds and whey.
Along came a spider and sat down beside her.
And this is what he had to say

Hi!
don't be scared of
me. I'm nice!

"Little Miss Muffett"

Little Miss Muffett sat on a tuffet,
Eating her curds and whey.
Along came a spider and sat down beside her,
And frightened Miss Muffett away!

What might have happened if Miss Muffett hadn't run away? Encourage your little ones to speculate with a class book that will inspire creative thinking! To prepare, write the adapted verse two times on separate sheets of paper, as shown in the illustration. Make a version for the girls in your room (with the word *her* in the appropriate places) and a version for the boys (with the words *his* and *him*). Duplicate the poems (along with a blank speech bubble as shown) to make the correct number of copies of each version for your class. Then snap a photo of each of your youngsters holding a bowl and spoon. To make a class book page, personalize the verse with the child's name. Then have the child glue her photo to one side of the page, below the verse. Have her draw a spider next to her photo, below the speech bubble. Then have her dictate what the spider said to her when he came along. Assemble the finished pages behind a construction paper cover with the title "Along Came a Spider." Share the book with your students before placing it in your reading center for everyone to enjoy.

"Jack and Jill"

Jack and Jill went up the hill,
To fetch a pail of water.
Jack fell down and broke his crown,
And Jill came tumbling after.

Jack and Jill went in only two directions—up and down—but your little ones can expand on the pair's adventures with this activity, which focuses on positional words and movement. In advance, fill a pail with water and place it outdoors near your playground equipment. Explain to students that, just like Jack and Jill, they need to fetch a pail of water. Then lead your group on a path through the playground, narrating your route as you go. For example, you might take your group *up* the ladder, *down* the slide, *over* the balance beam, *under* a tree, *through* the tunnel, *next to* the sandbox, and *across* the sidewalk to reach the pail. Once your preschoolers have gone over, under, up, and down without a single broken crown, ask them what they think Jack and Jill wanted to do with the pail of water. Then reveal how your class is going to use the water! Hand out clean paintbrushes and invite the children to water-paint on a wall, a fence, or the playground equipment. It'll be good, clean fun!

"Jack Be Nimble"

Jack be nimble!
Jack be quick!
Jack jump over the candlestick!

Get your youngsters jumping just like Jack with this nursery rhyme twist on the game of hopscotch! To prepare, sew a simple felt beanbag. Cut the shapes for a candle, a flame, and a candlestick from other colors of felt and hot-glue or sew them to one side of the beanbag. When your candlestick beanbag is ready, use chalk to draw a hopscotch grid on your sidewalk. Show little ones how to toss the beanbag onto a numbered square and then jump through the grid, avoiding the square with the beanbag. Leave the hopscotch game available for your preschoolers to use during outdoor time. And remember—jump over that candlestick!

"Humpty Dumpty"

Humpty Dumpty sat on a wall.
Humpty Dumpty had a great fall.
All the king's horses and all the king's men
Couldn't put Humpty together again.

Give each of your students his own Humpty Dumpty so he can act out the great fall. Then use the cracked eggs to make a yummy snack! For each child, hard-boil an egg; then put all the eggs in the refrigerator to cool. At snacktime, give each child an egg and invite him to use crayons to draw a face on it to resemble Humpty Dumpty. Then have him hold the egg atop a brick wall (a cardboard brick block). Recite the rhyme together, letting all the Humpty Dumptys fall to the table at the appropriate point. Then demonstrate how to peel off the cracked eggshell. Have each child put his peeled egg in a disposable bowl and mash it with a plastic fork. Give each child a small spoonful of mayonnaise to mix with his egg. With a little shake of salt and pepper, your preschoolers will have made egg salad! Pass out crackers and invite youngsters to enjoy the healthy snack they've created.

How Our Garden Grows

First, we put dirt in a pot.

We put seeds in the dirt.

"Mary, Mary, Quite Contrary"

Mary, Mary, quite contrary,
How does your garden grow?
With silver bells and cockle shells,
And pretty maids all in a row.

Just how *does* a garden grow? Encourage your students to answer this question by planting some seeds themselves! Bring in a flowerpot, some potting soil, and some fast-growing seeds, such as marigolds. Have your preschoolers help you fill the pot with soil, plant the seeds, and water them. Help little ones tend to the flowers for a few days until you see sprouts. Then ask youngsters to write a class experience story, explaining the steps it took to grow the flowers. Ask students to list everything you did; then guide the class to put the steps in the correct order. Write each step on a separate sheet of chart paper; then ask students to help you draw illustrations for each page. Post all the pages on a wall or bulletin board, with a title similar to the one shown. Add additional pages as your flowers grow and bloom. Glue a picture of the flowers to the final page.

243

Pat-a-Cake

Twinkle, Twinkle, Little Star

Jack and Jill

Old King Cole

Little Miss Muffett

The Three Little Kittens

Nursery rhymes are lots of fun!
Pick a picture and let's say one…

Congratulations,

_____
(child's name)

for learning so many rhymes!

Jack Be Nimble

The Queen of Hearts

Mary, Mary,
Quite Contrary

Humpty Dumpty

244

Note to the teacher: Use this page with "What an Accomplishment!" on page 238 and the cake pattern with "Pat-a-Cake" on page 240.

Scarecrows Are Super!

This collection of scarecrow ideas is stuffed with lots of learning fun!

ideas contributed by LeeAnn Collins—Director
Sunshine House Preschool
Lansing, MI

Storytime

Begin With a Book

Start your scarecrow unit with a story! Share one of the titles shown with your youngsters. Then place the book and other scarecrow stories in your reading area. To add a fall feel to the center, set up a corn-field display and watch those scarecrow stories come to life!

The Little Scarecrow Boy
Written by Margaret Wise Brown

Nothing At All
Written by Denys Cazet

Jeb Scarecrow's Pumpkin Patch
Written by Jana Dillon

The Little Old Lady Who Was Not Afraid of Anything
Written by Linda Williams

Music/Movement

Shoo, You Silly Crows!

Just how does a scarecrow keep those pesky birds from eating all the corn? Invite your preschoolers to brainstorm different scare tactics that a scarecrow might use. Write their responses on a sheet of chart paper; then incorporate them in the song shown. Encourage your preschoolers to act out the tune, and your classroom is sure to be crow-free!

(sung to the tune of "The Farmer in the Dell")

The scarecrow [waves his/her arms].
The scarecrow [waves his/her arms].
This is how he/she scares the crows
To keep them from the corn!

Sing additional verses, replacing the underlined phrase with student suggestions.

Be on the Lookout for Crows!

To prepare for this small-group activity, gather a few old flannel shirts. Next, cut out a supply of crows from construction paper. Program each crow with a different letter, number, or shape that you wish to reinforce. Then hang the crows around your classroom at children's level. Have each child in a small group wear a flannel shirt as a scarecrow costume. Name a symbol or show a card with the symbol; then direct one of the little scarecrows to find that crow and bring it to you. Continue the activity in this manner until each little scarecrow has done his duty!

Small-Group Activity

Head to Toe With a Scarecrow

This scarecrow chant is perfect for reinforcing body parts. To prepare, make a felt scarecrow and crow for your flannelboard. During circle time, display the scarecrow on the board. Place the crow on the scarecrow's knee and begin reciting the first verse of the chant below. Pause before saying the bold-faced word and have youngsters name the appropriate body part. Move the crow to the next body part and continue chanting the rhyme.

Scarecrow, scarecrow,
Can't you see?
A big black crow is sitting on your **knee!**

Scarecrow, scarecrow,
Don't you care?
A big black crow is tangled in your **hair!**

Scarecrow, scarecrow,
Don't you know?
A big black crow is sitting on your **toe!**

Scarecrow, scarecrow,
Be a little bolder!
Scare that crow that's on your **shoulder!** 247

Calling All Crows—and Scarecrows!

Here's a lively song and movement activity that allows youngsters to dramatize being crows and scarecrows. In advance, make a construction paper scarecrow mask similar to the one shown. Have youngsters stand in a circle. Choose four or five children to play the part of crows and have them stand in the middle of the circle. Direct the remaining children to hold their hands behind their backs. Have the students close their eyes. Then walk behind the children and secretly place the scarecrow mask in the hands of a child.

To begin the activity, direct the "crows" to fly around the middle of the circle as youngsters sing the song below. After singing the last line, have the child with the scarecrow mask hold it up to his face and scare those crows away!

(sung to the tune of "Skip to My Lou")

Crows in the cornfield,
Shoo, crows, shoo!
Crows in the cornfield,
Shoo, crows, shoo!
Crows in the cornfield,
Shoo, crows, shoo!
What we need is a scarecrow!

Group Activity

Colorful Crows

Even though crows are black, a scarecrow still must know all of the basic colors! Have your little scarecrows brush up on their color-recognition skills with this idea. To prepare, cut out simple crow shapes from different colors of felt; then place the crows on your flannelboard. Have a child stand up and pretend to be a scarecrow. Recite a chant similar to the one shown; then direct the child to remove the crow mentioned in the chant. Repeat the activity with different students until all of the colored crows have been collected!

Scarecrow [child's name],
Standing all alone,
Shoo that [black] crow back to its home!

248

Math Center

Counting Buttons

You can count on this scarecrow idea to reinforce youngsters' early math skills. To prepare, use the pattern on page 251 to make a scarecrow cutout for each number you wish to reinforce. Then program the hat of each scarecrow with a different number. Place the scarecrows in your math center along with a supply of large plastic button counters. To use the center, a child identifies the number on each hat and then places that many buttons on the scarecrow's clothing. What well-dressed scarecrows!

Snack Activity

Snackin' on Scarecrows

Your preschoolers will like this snack as much as crows like corn! In advance, tint a batch of shredded coconut with yellow food coloring. Then provide each child with the following ingredients: a Ritz cracker, one teaspoon of cream cheese, a pinch of yellow coconut, one Bugles snack, and a few shelled sunflower seeds. To make a scarecrow snack, a child uses a craft stick to spread the cream cheese on the cracker and then uses the sunflower seeds to create a scarecrow face. She adds yellow coconut hair and a Bugles snack hat. Mmm, scarecrow snack!

Literacy Activity

Cornfield Literacy

Use this literacy idea to reinforce letter-matching skills. To prepare, duplicate the pattern on page 251 to make a scarecrow for each letter you wish to reinforce. Program the hat of each scarecrow with a different letter. Then make two or three construction paper corn cutouts for each scarecrow. Program each corn cutout with a letter that matches one of the scarecrows. Invite students to match the scarecrows with the corn according to letter. For more advanced students, glue magazine pictures onto the corn cutouts. Then have students match the scarecrows and corn according to letter-sound association.

249

This is my family.
Let's count and see
How many people there are
And who they could be!

brother Kyle   Daddy   Mommy   Me

Me and My Family!

What are your youngsters' family ties? Find out with activities that explore the makings of a family!

ideas contributed by Mary Lou Rodriguez, Redwood City, CA

Family Fingerplay

Have youngsters follow your lead as you perform this family fingerplay; then guide students in a discussion about the different members in their families. Afterward, program a sheet of paper similar to the one shown above and then photocopy it for each child. Have the child draw a picture of her family and herself on the paper; then invite her to dictate the name and relation of each member.

This is a family.
Let's count and see
How many people there are
And who they could be!

Show all ten fingers.

This is the mother,
And this is the father.
This is the sister,
And this is the brother.
Here is a grandpa
And a grandma too!
An aunt,
An uncle,
And cousins who

Wiggle index finger.
Wiggle middle finger.
Wiggle ring finger.
Wiggle pinkie.
Wiggle thumb.
Wiggle other thumb.
Wiggle other index finger.
Wiggle other middle finger.
Wiggle other ring finger and pinkie.

Make up a family for me and you!

Point to self and then others.

The Martin Family

This is my mom, Judy. She likes to read.

This is my grandpa. I don't know his name. It's just Grandpa.

This is me, Aaron. I like to play with my cat, Buster.

This is my cat, Buster. He likes to rip things up.

Family Trees

Find out a little more about each child's family with this activity. To prepare, count the number of family members on each child's drawing from "Family Fingerplay." Then provide the child with that many leaf cutouts. (Be sure the cutouts are large enough for the child to draw on.) Invite the child to draw each family member and himself on a separate leaf. Then have the child glue each leaf onto a large construction paper tree cutout. Encourage the child to dictate a sentence or two describing each family member. Write his response near the leaf; then label the top of the tree with the child's family name. Display each child's creation in your classroom and you'll have a forest of informative family trees!

Create a Coat of Arms

In medieval times, coats of arms were used by knights as a means of identification. Today, a coat of arms is a family design and a symbol of heritage. Invite your youngsters and their families to have a little fun creating their own coats of arms. To prepare, make a tagboard shield cutout for each child's family. Divide each shield into four sections as shown. Next, photocopy the parent note on page 255 for each child. Send home a shield and note inviting each child's family to create a coat of arms. As each child returns her coat of arms, invite her to show it to the class and discuss the different symbols on it.

Campbells!

We are the Campbells!

Ya Ha Ha Ha! Ya Ha Ha Ha!

Family Actions

Does Daddy have a distinctive laugh? Does Mommy have a memorable mannerism? Invite your students to brainstorm the endearing qualities of different family members. Incorporate their responses into the song shown and then, if possible, have youngsters act it out!

(sung to the tune of "The Wheels on the Bus")

The **fathers** in the house go [student response],
[Student response], [student response].
The **fathers** in the house go [student response],
All around the house!

Sing additional verses, replacing the boldfaced word, in turn, with other family-member words, such as *mothers, sisters, brothers, babies,* and *grannies.*

Around-the-House Objects

Car keys, a pacifier, a tube of lipstick… Sometimes different members of families use different things and sometimes they don't! Use this engaging activity to help youngsters explore this concept. In advance, collect a variety of common objects, such as a set of car keys, a toothbrush, a tube of lipstick, a cleaning glove, a cooking utensil, and a pacifier. Place the objects in a large paper bag and invite a small group of students to join you at a center. Pull out each item, in turn, and have each child tell you which of her family members uses it. Use the objects to prompt discussions about each child's family and the roles of different members.

My mom cooks with this.

My baby brother has one of these.

253

Dinnertime!

For many families, meals are a way to spend quality time together. Invite your preschoolers to have a mock family meal with this lively adaptation of "The Farmer in the Dell." Set up a small table and chairs in your circle-time area. Lead students in a discussion about meal times with their families. Then choose one child to be the mother (or other family member, depending on the needs of your students). Have the child stand at the table as you sing the song shown. Then direct her to choose another family member to join her at the table. When all of the chairs have been filled, sing the final verse and invite the family to have a seat!

(sung to the tune of "The Farmer in the Dell")

Dinnertime is here!
Dinnertime is here!
Heigh-ho! It's time to eat.
Dinnertime is here!

The [mother] calls the [father].
The [mother] calls the [father].
Heigh-ho! It's time to eat.
The [mother] calls the [father].

Sing additional verses, replacing the underlined words with other family-member words, such as *brother, granny,* and *grandpa.*

The family all sits down.
The family all sits down.
Heigh-ho! It's time to eat!
The family all sits down.

A Family Toast!

What's the best way to wrap up your family studies? Have a family toast! Use a house-shaped cookie cutter to cut a slice of bread for each child. Toast the bread; then have the child spread peanut butter on it. (For students with peanut allergies, use soy nut butter or almond butter.) Have each child count the number of people in her immediate family. Then provide her with that many teddy bear–shaped graham crackers. Direct the child to place the crackers on the house and then eat!

Scavenger Hunt Show-and-Tell

Here's a fun way to get families involved in your family unit! Have a family scavenger hunt; then have each of your preschoolers show off his family finds! To prepare, photocopy the parent note on page 255 for each child. Then staple each note to a brown paper grocery bag. As each child brings his items from home, invite him to show them to the class and talk about each treasure.

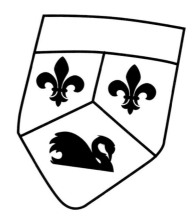

Dear Family,

We are learning all about families and would like your help in creating a family design on a coat of arms! Please read through the following directions. Have your family work together to create a coat of arms; then send the completed project to school with your child. Thank you for your help!

1. Write your family name in the top section.
2. Draw a family portrait in another section.
3. Draw or glue a picture of a favorite family food.
4. Draw or glue a picture of a favorite family pastime.

©The Education Center, Inc. • THE MAILBOX® • Preschool • Oct/Nov 2002

Dear Family,

We would like to invite you to join our family scavenger hunt! Below you will find a list of categories. Help your child find an inexpensive item from each category that he or she can bring to school. Place the items in this bag. Your child will show the items to the class and then bring them home. Have fun searching!

• a baby item from a family member
• a hat from a family member
• junk mail with your family name on it
• a shoe from a family member
• a family photo

©The Education Center, Inc. • THE MAILBOX® • Preschool • Oct/Nov 2002

Tinkering Around With Tools!

Does everyone know what time it is? It's tool time! Use this collection of tool-themed ideas and watch your preschoolers' knowledge build and build and build!

ideas contributed by Sue Fleischmann—Preschool Holy Cross School, Menomonee Falls, WI

supplies needed

Setting Up Shop

Before beginning your tool time, read through the supply list below. Then enlist the help of parents, friends, and coworkers in gathering the tools and equipment needed for this unit. Also, visit your local home improvement store to ask for donations of items such as empty paint cans, paint sticks, and a scrap of wood.

Supply List

- gardening tools and a large plastic flowerpot *("Tools of the Trade" page 257)*
- cooking utensils and a stockpot *("Tools of the Trade" page 257)*
- painting tools small enough to fit inside a clean gallon-sized paint can *("Tools of the Trade" page 257)*
- clean gallon-sized paint can *("Tools of the Trade" page 257)*
- tools small enough to fit inside a toolbox *("Tools of the Trade" page 257)*
- empty toolbox *("Tools of the Trade" page 257 and "Nuts About Bolts" page 258)*
- architectural blueprints *("Blueprint Special" page 257)*
- large nuts, bolts, and flat-bottomed screws *(activities on page 258)*
- slotted and Phillips screwdrivers *("That Screwy Screwdriver" page 258)*
- wooden plank or board *("That Screwy Screwdriver" page 258)*
- rulers, yardsticks, and measuring tapes *("Lines, Angles, and Squares! Oh, My!" page 259)*
- framing squares and combination squares *("Lines, Angles, and Squares! Oh, My!" page 259)*
- level *("Are You on the Level?" page 259)*

storytime

Talking About Tools

Who uses tools? Pose this question to your preschoolers to prompt a discussion about tools; then read *Tools* by Ann Morris. After sharing the book, resume your tool talk. Invite students to recall the different tools mentioned in the story. Then write their responses and observations on a sheet of chart paper. Display the chart throughout your study and continue adding youngsters' observations to it.

Tools of the Trade

Use this classification activity to familiarize your youngsters with different types of tools. In advance, gather the first six bulleted items on the supply list on page 256. Place the flowerpot, stockpot, paint can, and toolbox in front of your class at circle time. Then invite your youngsters to help you sort the different tools into the appropriate containers. As you sort the items, guide students in a discussion about the use of each tool. Afterward, place the tools in a center and invite each child to sort them independently.

Blueprint Special

Blueprints may not look like conventional tools, but they're an essential tool in any building project! Introduce your preschoolers to this cool tool and then follow up with an activity that builds prewriting skills. In advance, obtain a blueprint sample from a local architect. Show youngsters the blueprint and explain that builders use it as a tool to help them construct a building. Afterward, provide each child with a sheet of blue paper and a white crayon. Then let your little architects design building plans of their own!

This Is the Way We Build a House

In addition to blueprints, builders need a wide variety of other tools! Use this activity and song to familiarize your youngsters with the different tools of the trade. To prepare, make a supply of tool cutouts by enlarging the following patterns on page 260: measuring tape, saw, sanding block, hammer, paintbrush. Show youngsters each tool. Explain what it is used for; then have students follow your lead as you pantomime using the tool. Next, teach youngsters the song shown and invite them to act out building a house.

(sung to the tune of "Here We Go Round the Mulberry Bush")

This is the way we [measure] the board,
[Measure] the board, [measure] the board.
This is the way we [measure] the board
When we build a house!

Sing additional verses, replacing the underlined word, in turn, with *saw, sand, hammer,* and *paint.*

257

Nuts About Bolts

Why does a toolbox have all those compartments? For sorting screws, nuts, and bolts! Invite your preschoolers to do just that with this portable center idea. Place a supply of large bolts, nuts, and screws in the main compartment of a toolbox. Then invite each child to sort the items into the smaller compartments of the box. When the child has finished sorting, have him return the items to the main compartment and close the toolbox. Now the box is ready for the next round of sorting!

That Screwy Screwdriver

Here's a great visual-discrimination activity involving a common household tool, the screwdriver! To prepare for this activity, drive a variety of slotted screws and Phillips head screws halfway into a wooden plank or board. (Be sure to thoroughly sand any rough areas on the wood.) Then collect a variety of screwdrivers to fit the different screws. Invite a small group of children to join you at a table. Show the board to the group and have youngsters find the differences in the screws. Next, have students examine the screwdrivers and then find the screws that fit each one. When your class is familiar with this activity, set the board and screwdrivers at a center for youngsters to explore.

Toolbox Bingo

What are the benefits of playing Toolbox Bingo? You'll be building youngsters' listening skills, developing their vocabulary, and fine-tuning their ability to follow directions! Plus, it's just plain fun! Photocopy the toolbox pattern (page 261) several times onto red paper. Next, make several copies of the tool patterns on page 260. Cut apart the patterns; then set aside one of each to use as a calling card for the game. Glue five or six of the remaining patterns onto each toolbox to create different bingo cards. Laminate the cards for durability. Provide large bolts or nuts as bingo markers; then get ready for a rousing game of Toolbox Bingo!

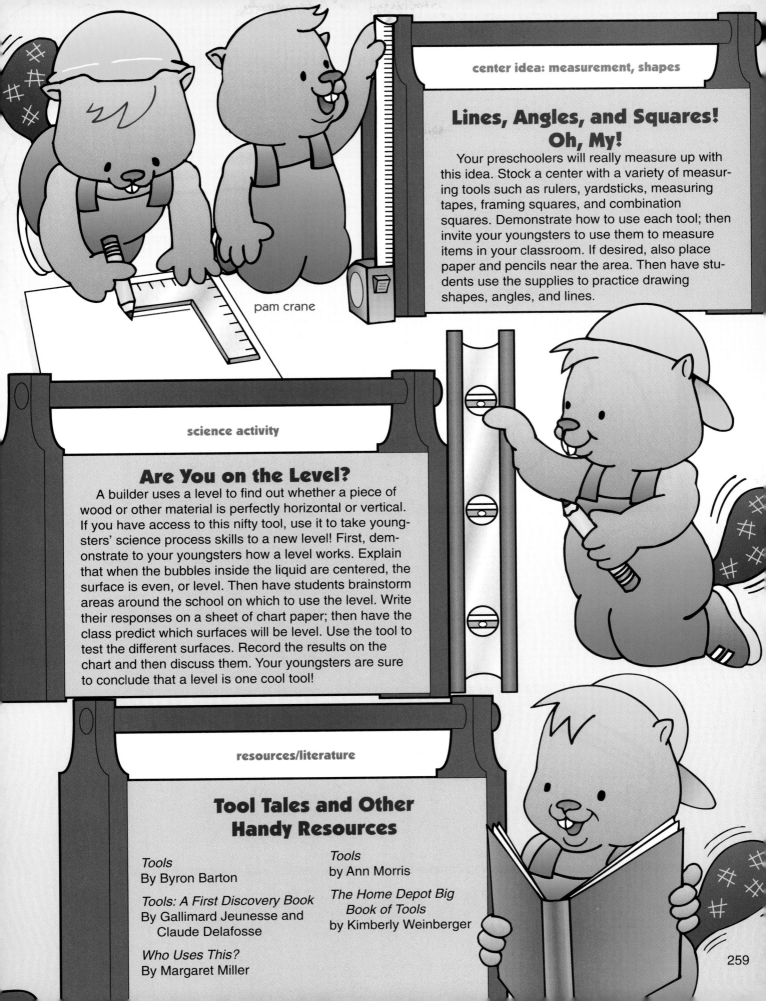

Lines, Angles, and Squares! Oh, My!

Your preschoolers will really measure up with this idea. Stock a center with a variety of measuring tools such as rulers, yardsticks, measuring tapes, framing squares, and combination squares. Demonstrate how to use each tool; then invite your youngsters to use them to measure items in your classroom. If desired, also place paper and pencils near the area. Then have students use the supplies to practice drawing shapes, angles, and lines.

pam crane

science activity

Are You on the Level?

A builder uses a level to find out whether a piece of wood or other material is perfectly horizontal or vertical. If you have access to this nifty tool, use it to take youngsters' science process skills to a new level! First, demonstrate to your youngsters how a level works. Explain that when the bubbles inside the liquid are centered, the surface is even, or level. Then have students brainstorm areas around the school on which to use the level. Write their responses on a sheet of chart paper; then have the class predict which surfaces will be level. Use the tool to test the different surfaces. Record the results on the chart and then discuss them. Your youngsters are sure to conclude that a level is one cool tool!

resources/literature

Tool Tales and Other Handy Resources

Tools
By Byron Barton

Tools: A First Discovery Book
By Gallimard Jeunesse and Claude Delafosse

Who Uses This?
By Margaret Miller

Tools
by Ann Morris

The Home Depot Big Book of Tools
by Kimberly Weinberger

259

Tool Patterns

Use with "Overalls Organization" on page 120, "This Is the Way We Build a House" on page 257, and "Toolbox Bingo" on page 258.

Stirring Up Senses in the Kitchen

The kitchen isn't just a place for tasting—it has all kinds of things to stimulate each of the five senses. So step into our kitchen and check out the "sense-ational" activities that we've cooked up for your preschoolers!

ideas contributed by Roxanne LaBell Dearman
Western NC Early Intervention Program for Children Who Are Deaf or Hard of Hearing, Charlotte, NC

Sense of Touch

Scrub-a-dub-dub

Dish out some hands-on fun with an activity that invites each child to explore his sense of touch. To prepare, gather unused dish sponges and scrubbers with a variety of textures. Set a bottle of mild dish soap near your water table; then invite a small group of children to join you at the table. Have students examine the different sponges and scrubbers, and describe their textures using words such as *smooth, soft, rough,* and *prickly.* Next, invite your youngsters to immerse the sponges and scrubbers in the water. Encourage students to discuss any changes in the textures of the wet sponges and scrubbers. Then add a few drops of the dish soap to the water and discuss the feel of the soapy sponges and scrubbers. Rub-a-dub-dub! There's lots to feel as we scrub!

Sense of Touch

Not-So-Hot Potato

How do you transform a typical relay race into an exciting lesson on the sense of touch? Add oven mitts! To prepare for the race, gather a class supply of potatoes and two oven mitts. Place half of the potatoes in one basket and the other half in another basket. Divide your class into two teams. Line up each team a short distance away from a large stockpot and then place a basket of potatoes beside the first child in each line.

At the start signal, the first child in each line dons an oven mitt, picks up a potato with the mitt, and then carries it to the pot. She drops the potato in the pot, returns to the line, and then hands the next child the oven mitt. The game continues in this manner until each child has had a turn. When the race is over, repeat the activity without the mitts; then have youngsters discuss how the oven mitt affected their sense of touch during the race.

Set Your Sights on This!

What will happen when you blindfold youngsters for this tossing game? Try it and see! Place a plastic dish tub a short distance away from a small group of students. Blindfold each child in turn; then have him try tossing a sponge into the pan. Repeat the activity without the blindfold. Then lead youngsters in a discussion about how their sense of sight helped them toss the sponge into the pan.

Sense of Sight

Can You Find the Can?

Here's a literacy activity that will also help youngsters appreciate their sense of sight. To prepare, gather a few unopened canned goods that are similar in size. Set the cans at a center and then invite a small group of children to join you in the area. Identify each can and then point out important words on it. For example, show youngsters the word *peaches* on a can of peaches. After identifying the different cans, name one of them. Then have a child find it and hand it to you. Repeat this activity several times, giving each student a turn. Next, blindfold each child in turn. Mix up the cans. Then name a can and ask the child to hand it to you. Remove the blindfold and let the child see which can he chose. After this activity, your youngsters will agree that the eyes have it!

Sense of Smell

Teatime!

Ah, the aroma of tea! Your youngsters will be steeped in exploration fun with this discovery center idea. In advance, collect a supply of tea bags in different flavors. Set the tea bags in your discovery center; then invite youngsters to use their sense of smell to explore the different teas. Encourage students to discuss their observations and describe the different scents. For added exploration, throw in a few single-serving coffee bags and invite students to compare the smell of the coffee and the tea.

Something's Missing Lemonade
(makes eight one-cup servings)
1½ c. freshly squeezed lemon juice (6 lemons)
6 c. water
ice

Mix the juice, water, and ice together in a pitcher.

Sense of Taste

From Sour to Sweet

Something's missing in this activity, and youngsters' taste buds will be able to tell! Follow the recipe above to make a batch of sugarless lemonade with your students, but keep the missing ingredient a secret! Provide each child with a cup of the lemonade and have her take a *small* sip. Discuss why the lemonade is *sour* and guide students to realize that the sugar is missing. Stir a spoonful or two of sugar into each child's cup and then invite her to taste the lemonade again. As students sip on the sweetened drink, discuss how the sugar changed the taste of the lemonade. Wrap up the activity with the chant below, "Who Forgot the Sugar in the Lemonade?"

Sugar

Who Forgot the Sugar in the Lemonade?

Follow up the activity described in "From Sour to Sweet" with this adaptation of "Who Took the Cookies From the Cookie Jar?"

Teacher: Who forgot the sugar in the lemonade? [Child's name] forgot the sugar in the lemonade!
Named child: Who, me?
Students: Yes, you!
Named child: Couldn't be!
Students: Then who?
Named child: [Child's name] forgot the sugar in the lemonade!

Continue the chant until each child has been named. The last child names the teacher.

Named child: [Teacher's name] forgot the sugar in the lemonade!
Teacher: Who, me?
Students: Yes, you!
Teacher: Oh, no! What should I do!
Students: Add sugar!

Sense of Hearing

Clanging Around in the Kitchen

The kitchen has all kinds of quirky noises. So invite students to perk up their ears with an activity that focuses on the sense of hearing. In advance, gather several kitchen items and small appliances that make distinctive noises. For example, you might use a blender, toaster, handheld mixer, and coffee mug and spoon. Before students arrive in the morning, set up a screen, such as a puppet stage. Then place the items behind it. During group time, use each item behind the screen and have students try to identify it. When all of the items have been used, remove the screen and show students your kitchen collection. Then conclude the activity with the following song.

(sung to the tune of "The Wheels on the Bus")

The blender on the counter says, "Whirr! Whirr! Whirr!
Whirr! Whirr! Whirr!
Whirr! Whirr! Whirr!"
The blender on the counter says, "Whirr! Whirr! Whirr!"
In the busy kitchen.

Sing additional verses using other phrases such as the following:
The bread in the toaster says, "Pop! Pop! Pop!"
The mixer in the bowl says, "Bzzz! Bzzz! Bzzz!"
The spoon in the cup says, "Clink! Clink! Clink!"

Sense of Hearing

Find the Timer

When the timer in the kitchen rings, something's cooking! When the timer rings in your classroom, youngsters will be learning! To begin, invite a small group of students to the play kitchen in your classroom. Set a timer for one minute. Direct students to cover their eyes as you hide the timer in the area. Then have them uncover their eyes and wait quietly. When the timer rings, have students find it by using their sense of hearing. Set the timer again for one minute and repeat the activity. After a few rounds, invite each child to take a turn hiding the timer for other students to find.

MATH GIFTS

Use this collection of gift-themed activities, and your youngsters will be gifted in math!

ideas contributed by Roxanne LaBell Dearman
Western N.C. Early Intervention Program for Children Who Are Deaf or Hard of Hearing
Charlotte, NC

Gift number [one] wrapped with a bow! [Child's name] unwrapped it, and what do you know?

It's a doll!

OPEN IT UP! WHAT IS IT?

Youngsters' imaginations will be wrapped up in this number recognition activity! To prepare, label five gift bags each with a different number from 1 to 5. Place a piece of colorful tissue paper inside each bag and then add a bow to the bag. To begin the activity, provide five children each with a different bag. Have each child identify the number on her bag; then have the students stand in sequence in front of the class. Begin reciting the chant shown. After saying the last line, invite the child with bag number one to peek inside. Have her imagine what's in the bag and then tell the class. Continue the activity in this manner with the remaining bags. Oh, what fun it is to open imaginary presents!

BOWS IN ROWS

What's the result of this one-to-one correspondence activity? An arrangement of bows that looks like a holiday tree! To prepare, gather 15 medium-size gift bows. Then cut out 15 construction paper circles. Glue the circles and a construction paper tree trunk onto a piece of poster board as shown. Invite each child to place one bow on each circle to create a tree. For added learning fun, encourage the child to count the total number of bows on the tree, count the number of bows in each row, or compare the different number of bows in the rows. Wrap up the activity by having students use words such as *more, less, most,* and *least* to compare the rows of bows.

WRAPPING PAPER PATTERNS

It's true! Holiday wrapping paper can help your preschoolers practice patterning skills! Find holiday wrapping paper with an AB pattern. Cut a length of paper with the pattern on it. Glue the paper onto a piece of tagboard; then laminate it for durability. Next, cut out a supply of shapes from a piece of the wrapping paper. Set the shapes near the tagboard strip. Invite each child to use the shapes to extend the pattern on the tagboard.

THE LONG AND SHORT OF IT

You don't need to go to great lengths to introduce your preschoolers to measurement! Simply cut a few pieces of gift-wrapping ribbon for students to use as measuring tools. If desired, attach small self-adhesive bows to each end of the ribbons to help little fingers hold them. Invite students to measure items around the classroom against the different lengths of ribbon.

If you have access to a large supply of ribbon, cut lengths equal to the height of each child. Display the ribbons on a wall and then label each one with the child's name. After removing the display, use each child's ribbon to gift wrap a present for her parents. Then attach a note similar to the one shown. Now *that's* a wrap!

This ribbon is very special, you see. Untie it, and it's the same size as me!

TAKE A PEEK!

At this center, peeking into presents reinforces number recognition! To prepare, collect a supply of gift boxes with lids. Wrap each box and lid separately; then attach a different number of bows to each lid. Inside each box, write the numeral that corresponds with the number of bows on its lid. Place the boxes at a center. To use the center, a child counts the number of bows on a box and then opens it to read the numeral inside.

267

Gingerbread Jamboree

Gingerbread shapes and gingerbread books.
Gingerbread counting and gingerbread cooks!
See how much fun learning can be
With a Gingerbread Jamboree!

by Sue Fleischmann—Preschool, Holy Cross School, Menomonee Falls, WI

And Now for the Weather...

A gingerbread boy to dress will add some seasonal fun to your circle-time weather report! In advance, use a photocopier to make enlarged copies of the patterns on pages 272 and 273. Color the enlarged patterns. Laminate them and then cut out each one. Place strips of self-adhesive Velcro on the patterns so the clothing can be attached to the gingerbread boy. Display the clothing and the gingerbread boy in your circle-time area. Begin your morning weather report by chanting, "Gingerbread kids, all together, can you tell me what's the weather?" Discuss the day's weather with your youngsters; then choose a child to dress the gingerbread boy appropriately. *science, thinking skills*

Guess Who?

Chances are, your youngsters will have no problem guessing the mystery character in this action poem. But they'll still have fun acting it out! *body part recognition, motor-skills development*

I have big raisin eyes,	*Point to eyes.*
And a red hot candy nose.	*Point to nose.*
I have yummy white frosting	
From my head down to my toes!	*Point to head and toes.*
I can run, run, run	
Just as fast as I can.	*Run in place.*
Can you guess who?	
I'm the Gingerbread Man!	

The sunlight caused the colored paper to fade. The cardboard candy shapes blocked the sunlight so the paper beneath them retained the original, darker color.

Gingerbread Science

We all know what the sun can do to a snowman. But what will the sun do to a gingerbread man? Invite your youngsters to find out with this simple science investigation. In advance, cut out a class supply of gingerbread people from brown construction paper. (For best results, use thin, inexpensive construction paper.) Next, cut out a supply of candy shapes from heavy cardboard. Provide each child with a gingerbread cutout and a few cardboard candy cutouts. Have the child set her gingerbread shape in a sunny window and place the candy cutouts on top of it. Explain that the gingerbread shape will stay in the sunny window for a few days; then invite the child to predict what might happen. After a few days, remove the candy cutouts from the gingerbread shape. Your youngster will be thrilled to discover candy prints on the paper! After discussing the child's predictions and observations, explain how the sun helped decorate her gingerbread man. *science process skills*

Look! Look! I'm a Gingerbread Kid!

These large-as-life cookie cutouts are lovely to look at *and* loaded with learning fun! Have each child lie down on a large sheet of brown bulletin board paper. Trace around his body with a pencil; then cut on the resulting outline. Have the child use markers, crayons, and construction paper scraps to decorate his gingerbread cutout. Display the gingerbread kids on a wall in your classroom. Then invite each child to measure himself against each cutout. If desired, challenge youngsters to use problem-solving skills to find out whose gingerbread cutout is whose. *early measurement, problem-solving skills, creativity*

Let's Count!

Mini erasers in holiday shapes make the perfect manipulative for this center! Purchase a supply of candy-shaped or gingerbread boy–shaped erasers at a party supply store. Then make ten gingerbread house cutouts. Program each house with a different number from 1 to 10. For younger students, also add a corresponding number of dots to each house. Place the houses and erasers at a center; then invite each child to place the correct number of erasers on each house. *number recognition, counting objects, one-to-one correspondence, creating sets to match numerals*

Gingerbread Play Dough

Follow the recipe shown to make a batch of gingerbread-scented dough. Set the dough in a center; then add a variety of gingerbread boy and girl cookie cutters for students to use. Encourage each child to sort the play dough shapes, seriate them by size, or create a pattern with them. Or, for fine-motor fun, place pairs of child-safe scissors in the area. Encourage youngsters to roll out small balls of dough; then have them practice their scissor skills by cutting the scented dough into strips. *sorting, size seriation, patterning, fine-motor skills*

Gingerbread Play Dough

Ingredients
2 c. flour
1 c. salt
1 tbsp. ground cloves
1 tbsp. ground allspice

1 tbsp. ground ginger
1 tbsp. ground cinnamon
2 tbsp. vegetable oil
1 c. water

Combine ingredients in a large bowl. Mix together well and knead them until smooth. Store the dough in an airtight container and refrigerate until ready to use.

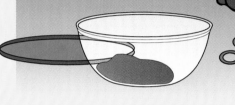

Sizing Up Shapes

To prepare for this center, gather gingerbread cookie cutters in a variety of sizes. Trace the cutters onto brown construction paper. Laminate the paper and then cut out the gingerbread shapes. Tape the shapes onto a cookie sheet. Next, follow the recipe above to make a batch of gingerbread play dough. Set the dough in a sealed container near the cookie sheet and the gingerbread cookie cutters. Invite each child to cut out play dough gingerbread shapes and then match the play dough shapes with the shapes on the cookie sheet. *fine-motor skills, visual discrimination*

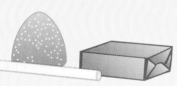

Gingerbread Books

Add these gingerbread books to your reading area, and it will quickly become the sweet spot in your classroom!

Maisy Makes Gingerbread
by Lucy Cousins

The Gingerbread Baby
by Jan Brett

The Gingerbread Boy
by Paul Galdone

The Gingerbread Man
by Eric Kimmel

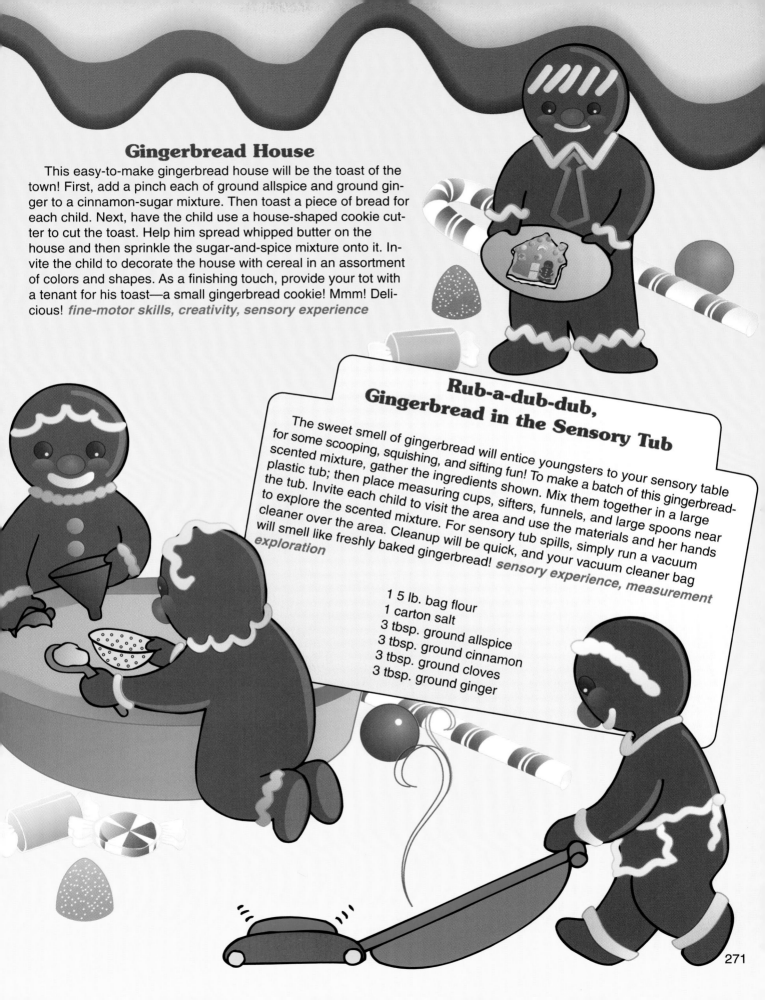

Gingerbread House

This easy-to-make gingerbread house will be the toast of the town! First, add a pinch each of ground allspice and ground ginger to a cinnamon-sugar mixture. Then toast a piece of bread for each child. Next, have the child use a house-shaped cookie cutter to cut the toast. Help him spread whipped butter on the house and then sprinkle the sugar-and-spice mixture onto it. Invite the child to decorate the house with cereal in an assortment of colors and shapes. As a finishing touch, provide your tot with a tenant for his toast—a small gingerbread cookie! Mmm! Delicious! *fine-motor skills, creativity, sensory experience*

Rub-a-dub-dub, Gingerbread in the Sensory Tub

The sweet smell of gingerbread will entice youngsters to your sensory table for some scooping, squishing, and sifting fun! To make a batch of this gingerbread-scented mixture, gather the ingredients shown. Mix them together in a large plastic tub; then place measuring cups, sifters, funnels, and large spoons near the tub. Invite each child to visit the area and use the materials and her hands to explore the scented mixture. For sensory tub spills, simply run a vacuum cleaner over the area. Cleanup will be quick, and your vacuum cleaner bag will smell like freshly baked gingerbread! *sensory experience, measurement, exploration*

1 5 lb. bag flour
1 carton salt
3 tbsp. ground allspice
3 tbsp. ground cinnamon
3 tbsp. ground cloves
3 tbsp. ground ginger

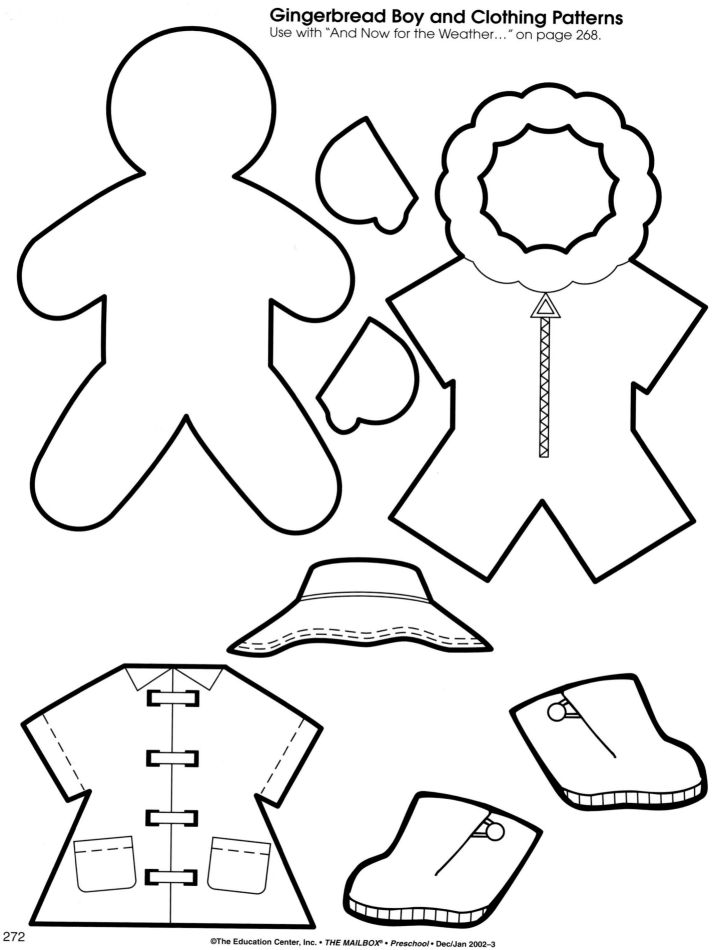

GET HEART HAPPY!

Hearts are everywhere at this time of year, so go ahead—bring them into your classroom too! Heart shapes will be a "love-ly" way for your preschoolers to learn about math, science, music, and more!

by Ada Goren

CRAFT DISPLAY

A "HEART-Y" WELCOME

Let everyone know about the heart hoopla in your class with this door decoration idea! Mount the title shown on or near your classroom door. Then encourage your preschoolers to create hearts at your art center to add to the display. Set out precut construction paper hearts, heart-shaped paper doilies, heart stickers, craft foam hearts, and a variety of papers, markers, glue, crayons, and other craft materials. Invite youngsters to freely design hearts each day during your center time; then display their original creations around your door. Keep the heart art going throughout your unit, and keep adding students' creations to the door display. Little ones will be so proud!

We Welcome You With All Our Hearts!

SONG

LITTLE RED HEARTS

Teach youngsters this simple song and invite them to play along with the help of their ten fingers! Before singing, affix a red heart sticker to each of a child's ten fingertips. Or use a washable marker to draw a red heart on each one. Then have each student hold up one finger at a time as the song progresses. At the end, have children wiggle those little red hearts!

(sung to the tune of "Ten Little Indians")

One little, two little, three little red hearts,
Four little, five little, six little red hearts,
Seven little, eight little, nine little red hearts,
Ten little wiggling red hearts!

THIS IS SORT OF FUN

Big or little, red or pink, lacy or ruffled—
hearts can be just about any size, color, or design! Use the heart patterns on page 280 to sharpen
your preschoolers' sorting skills. Duplicate the patterns
on three different colors of paper. Then cut out all the
hearts and laminate them for durability. Store the hearts in
a zippered plastic bag (or a heart-shaped candy box) and
put it at your math center. Have a child at this center
take the hearts out of the bag and sort them as she
wishes—by color, by size, or by design.

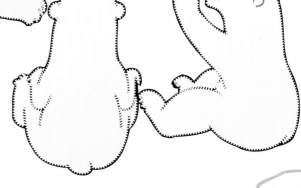

VISUAL MEMORY

MISSING!

Use the same reproducible
hearts created for "This Is Sort of
Fun" at your flannelboard to improve
little ones' visual memory. Use masking
tape to place three to five of the heart cutouts on your flannelboard. Ask youngsters
to look at them for about 30 seconds. Then
have students close their eyes as you remove one of the hearts and put it out of
sight. Have youngsters open their eyes
and try to determine which heart is missing from the flannelboard. Invite the student who correctly identifies the
missing heart to remove another
heart from the board in the
next round.

GET THOSE HEARTS PUMPING!

Get your preschoolers' real hearts pumping with the help of a heart shape outlined on your classroom floor. Use masking tape to outline a large heart shape on the floor. (Make it large enough for your whole group to stand inside it.) Then teach little ones the song shown and have them move as you direct in the second line of each verse. Substitute various gross-motor movements—such as *walk, sidestep, hop,* or *twist*—for the underlined action words.

(sung to the tune of "The Farmer in the Dell")

Inside the heart, inside the heart,
[Tiptoe, tiptoe],
Inside the heart!

Outside the heart, outside the heart,
[Jump, jump, jump, jump],
Outside the heart!

HEALTH/ NUTRITION

HEALTHY HEARTS

Explain to your students that moving and exercising (as they did in "Get Those Hearts Pumping!") is very good for their real hearts. Duplicate the chart on page 281 and post it in your classroom. Each day for a week, lead your students in an exercise routine that'll get their little hearts working! When the session is complete, stick a heart-shaped sticker in the box for that day. When the week is over and all the boxes are filled with heart stickers, reward each child with a badge duplicated from page 281. Then invite the whole class to enjoy a heart-healthy snack, such as graham crackers or air-popped popcorn!

Keep Those Hearts Healthy!

Monday	Tuesday	Wednesday	Thursday	Friday

I Keep My Heart Healthy!
Ask Me How!

A Heart Marks the Spot

These peekaboo page keepers are perfect for your preschool readers! For each child, cut two 6" x 2½" rectangles from construction paper and a slightly smaller rectangle from colored cellophane. Stack the two construction paper rectangles and use a large heart punch to punch out a heart shape near the top. (Or simply use scissors to cut a heart shape through both thicknesses of paper.) Help a child glue the cellophane rectangle on top of one paper rectangle and then glue the remaining paper rectangle on top so that the cellophane is sandwiched between the paper and shows through the heart-shaped opening. Invite the child to use stickers, crayons, or markers to complete the bookmark. Laminate the bookmarks, if desired, and keep them in a basket in your reading area. Invite students to use the heart-shaped windows in the bookmarks to frame letters or words in the books.

Broken Hearts

It can be a puzzle for a preschooler to spell her name—so give yours plenty of practice with these heart-shaped name puzzles! To make one, cut a large heart from construction paper. Use a black marker to print a child's name across the heart. Laminate the heart, if desired. Then cut the heart shape into three to five puzzle pieces. Try to cut *between* letters or clusters of letters, avoiding cutting *through* any letters. Place each child's puzzle pieces in a zippered plastic bag labeled with her name. Store the puzzles at your literacy center. Invite a child to find her puzzle and assemble it. If necessary, have her use the label on the bag as a guide to help her spell her name and put the broken heart back together!

HIDDEN HEARTS

"I found one!" That's what you'll hear as youngsters discover the craft foam heart shapes hidden in your sensory table. Simply cut a supply of heart shapes from various colors of craft foam. Scatter them in your sensory table; then cover them with red and pink crinkled gift wrap stuffing or pink and purple Easter grass. Invite children at this center to uncover the hidden hearts. For an added challenge, create a stack of number cards to keep near your sensory table. Have a child draw a card and then try to find a corresponding number of hearts.

CENTER IDEAS

CANDY BOX CHAOS

Collect heart-shaped candy boxes to add a "heart-y" touch to your classroom centers!

Manipulatives Area: Provide the tops and bottoms of candy boxes in various sizes and designs. Have youngsters match the tops to the bottoms.
Blocks Center: Encourage youngsters to add heart-shaped boxes to their building fun!
Play Dough Center: Have youngsters create play dough confections to fill a box. Or use smaller boxes as cutters for creating heart-shaped cookies and cakes.
Literacy Area: Gather a collection of small objects or pictures, some that begin with the letter *H* and some that do not. Put a heart-shaped box in the center and ask youngsters to fill it with items that begin with *H*, like *heart.*
Painting Easel: Use the top and bottom of a large heart-shaped box as printers to make both heart outlines and solid hearts.

LOVELY LOCKETS

Craft these construction paper lockets for youngsters to give as Valentine's Day gifts! For each child, fold a 3" x 6" piece of red construction paper into a 3" x 3" square. Cut a heart shape on the fold. In advance, have students bring in small pictures of loved ones, or gather a small picture of each child.

To make a locket, tie the ends of a 24-inch length of red yarn to make a necklace. Tape the center of the necklace to the back of the heart cutout. Next, have a child glue her photo inside the locket. When the glue is dry, invite her to use glitter glue to decorate the front of her locket; then allow the glitter glue to dry thoroughly. Finally, to keep the locket closed, put a tiny bit of Sticky-Tac adhesive inside the locket. The locket will stay closed when being worn and can be easily pulled open to reveal the photo inside.

A SHAPELY SNACK

Think pink to prepare this heart-shaped snack little ones will love! For each child, toast a slice of bread. Have the child use a large heart-shaped cookie cutter to cut a heart shape from the toast. Then have him spread strawberry cream cheese over the toast before sprinkling on some heart-shaped sprinkles! And what better to accompany this toasty heart snack than a pink drink? Prepare a cup of milk mixed with strawberry Nesquik drink mix for each snacker. Make the sipping special by attaching a craft foam heart shape to each child's drinking straw (as shown).

Mmm…these hearts are sure to make 'em happy!

279

Heart Patterns

Use with "This Is Sort of Fun" and "Missing!" on page 275.

Keep Those Hearts Healthy!

©The Education Center, Inc. • *THE MAILBOX®* • *Preschool* • Feb/Mar 2003

Monday	Tuesday	Wednesday	Thursday	Friday

Shedding Light on Shadows

On Groundhog Day (February 2), Punxsutawney Phil will make his annual search for his shadow! Get your youngsters geared up for this day with the following shadow-related explorations. What does the groundhog predict for this unit? Lots of learning fun for your preschoolers!

ideas contributed by Julie Koczur, Great Falls, MT

science discovery
Step Outside

What makes a shadow? Invite your youngsters to find out with this shadow exploration. On a sunny day, bundle up your youngsters (if needed) and head outside. Guide your little ones to notice their shadows. After a few minutes of exploration, return to the classroom. Dim the lights and shine a light source, such as a flashlight or slide projector, toward a screen or other light-colored surface. Have each child, in turn, use his hand to cast a shadow on the screen. Lead your little ones to discover that a shadow is formed when an object is placed in front of a source of light. Explain that when an object, person, or animal blocks the light from the sun, a shadow is created outside. So that's how the groundhog gets a shadow!

movement, dramatic play
Great Groundhogs!

This lively action song will have each of your youngsters searching for her shadow, just like a groundhog! To prepare, make a groundhog-ears headband. Then set up a screen and light source. Invite a child to don the headband and play the part of the groundhog. Have the child crouch below the light source, facing the screen so the light is not in her eyes. As the class sings the song shown, invite the little groundhog to pop up so her shadow is cast on the screen. Then have her act out the part as directed in the song.

(sung to the tune of "The Hokey-Pokey")

The little groundhog peeks from beneath the ground.
[She] rubs [her] sleepy eyes, and [she] starts to look around.
[She] sees [her] little shadow, and [she] quickly runs away.
Happy Groundhog Day! Hey!

science discovery

Shades of Shadows

It's true! Shadows come in different shades! Introduce your preschoolers to the shady side of shadows with this investigation. To prepare, cut out groundhog shapes from the following materials: black construction paper, white copier paper, red tissue paper, and a clear overhead transparency. Set up a light source and a screen. Hold up the groundhogs in front of the light and have students compare the different shadows. As an extension, cut out additional groundhog shapes from different materials and have students predict whether the shadows will be light or dark.

Need a groundhog tracer? Use a photocopier to enlarge a groundhog pattern on page 285. Cut out the enlarged pattern. Trace it onto a piece of tagboard. Cut out the tagboard shape and then use it as a tracer to make a perfect groundhog!

science discovery

Big Groundhog, Little Groundhog

What will your preschoolers discover with this exploration idea? The size and shape of a shadow can change depending on how close an object is to the source of light. To prepare for this activity, cut out a groundhog shape from black construction paper. Tape a jumbo craft stick to the back of the groundhog; then set up a light source and a screen. Gather your youngsters near the screen and direct them to watch the screen. Hold the groundhog in front of the light. As you gradually move the groundhog away from the light, have your youngsters observe the shadow. *(It gets smaller.)* Direct students to continue watching the shadow as you move the groundhog toward the light. *(The shadow gets bigger.)* Invite each child to take a turn moving the groundhog in front of the light. Then guide students in a discussion about what causes the shadow size to change.

A, B, C, D, Easter!

Spring into this alphabet unit that doubles as an Easter extravaganza. From bunnies to chicks to ducks—learning about letters is a basketful of fun.

by Angie Kutzer, Garrett Elementary, Mebane, NC

Basket Fillers
letter identification, fine-motor skills

Look to the news to provide your little ones with a way to fill their baskets. Give each child a colored-paper copy of the basket pattern on page 290, a section of the newspaper, scissors, and glue. Write a different letter on each child's basket (or use the same letter if you do letter-of-the-week studies). Then have him search through the paper to find that specific letter. Encourage him to cut out as many examples of the letter as he can find and glue them in his basket. If desired, extend the learning during group time by counting the contents of each child's basket and comparing students' totals. Then display the baskets on a bulletin board titled "A Basketful of Learning!"

Scrambled Letters
letter recognition, visual discrimination

Reinforce letter recognition and visual discrimination with this mixed-up letter activity. Use a permanent marker to write a different uppercase letter on each of several plastic Easter eggs. Write each letter so that its top half is on the upper portion of the egg and its bottom half is on the lower portion as shown. Take apart the eggs. Place the tops and bottoms in a basket and then mix them up. Encourage pairs of students to put the eggs back together. Vary the difficulty by the number of eggs you use. Depending on which letters are represented, your youngsters may discover that some egg halves are interchangeable. After completing this activity, your youngsters will agree—scrambled eggs are the best!

286

Hop to It!

letter identification, gross-motor development

Gather your little cottontails together for this alphabetical bunny hop. In advance, cut 26 large shapes from Con-Tact paper. Label each shape with a different letter; then adhere the shapes to the floor, forming a mazelike path as shown. Invite each of your youngsters to act like a bunny and hop through the path, naming each letter as he lands on it. Or, for a greater challenge, mix up the order of the letters, and have each child try to hop from *A* to *Z* in sequence.

Here an Egg, There an Egg

uppercase-lowercase matching, gross-motor development

Now that your bunnies have had a chance to practice hoppin' down the bunny trail, send them out to deliver these Easter eggs. In advance, prepare a path of letters (uppercase) as described in "Hop to It!" on this page. If space is an issue, create a path with only those letters you wish to reinforce. Next, cut out an egg shape for each letter on the path. Label each egg with a different lowercase letter; then store the eggs in a basket. To complete the activity, a child takes the basket of eggs. She hops to each shape on the path and leaves the matching lowercase letter egg on the shape. Hippity, hoppity, learning's on the way!

287

What's It Made Of?

letter identification, writing awareness, graphing

Invite your youngsters to take a closer look at letters with this graphing idea. Prepare a three-column grid with the labels "curvy," "straight," and "both." Program 26 egg cutouts, each with a different uppercase letter; then place the cutouts in a basket. During group time, have each child take an egg from the basket. Ask the child to name her letter and describe how the letter is formed—with curvy lines, straight lines, or both. Then have the child tape her egg in the corresponding column on the graph. Continue the activity in this manner until all of the letters have been placed on the graph. If desired, make another graph using lowercase letters; then compare the two graphs. Letters are great, both curvy and straight!

curvy	straight	both
	A	J
	I	B
S	M	P

pam crane

Chicky Chow

letter formation, fine-motor skills

Use yellow pom-pom chicks to help your youngsters practice letter formation. In advance, glue corn kernel cutouts onto a tagboard sheet in the shape of a letter of your choice. When the glue is dry, clip a piece of tracing paper (available at art supply stores) over the tagboard as shown. Set the tagboard near a shallow pan of yellow tempera paint and several large yellow pom-poms (chicks).

Invite a child to dip a pom-pom chick into the paint and then press the chick over the lines of corn. After she "feeds" the chick, help the child remove the sheet of tracing paper and identify the letter she painted. When the paint is dry, provide seasonal stickers for the child to place around the letter. Then ready the center for another student by clipping on a new piece of tracing paper. Here chicky, chicky!

288

The Jelly Bean Scene
letter formation, cooperation

This cooperative game gets little ones racing to form the alphabet. To prepare, photocopy the jelly bean patterns on page 291 onto colored paper to make a large supply. Laminate the jelly beans and then cut them out. Divide your students into four or five groups and give each group some of the jelly beans.

To play the game, call out a letter of the alphabet and show it to your students. Then give youngsters a signal and have the groups race to form the letter with their jelly beans. When the letters are complete, treat each child to a few real jelly beans. Then get ready to play another round. Ready, set, go!

Just Ducky!
letter-sound association, gross-motor development

Preschoolers will go quackers over this idea! Provide a Hula-Hoop ring for each pair of students. Explain that they are ducks and the hoop is their pond. Name a letter of the alphabet and review its sound. Then call out various words. If a word begins with the targeted letter sound, encourage the ducks to jump into their ponds and quack. If the word doesn't match, have them stay put. These little ducks will be all ears just waiting to take the plunge!

Easter Basket Pattern

Use with "Basket Fillers" on page 286.

When I Grow Up, I Want to Be...

What do your youngsters want to be when they grow up? You just might find out when you use the activities in this community helpers unit! Heigh-ho, heigh-ho, it's off to work we go!

ideas contributed by Dena Warner—PreK, Kendall-Whittier Elementary, Tulsa, OK

Who Am I?

Start your unit with a group activity that introduces your youngsters to different community helpers. In advance, gather pictures of community helpers. Then collect tools that represent the different occupations. (See box for suggestions.) Put the tools in a cloth bag or a pillowcase.

To begin the activity, display the different pictures and discuss the helpers on each one. Next, invite a child to pull an item from the bag. Identify the item. Discuss its use and then have the child match the tool with its helper. Continue the activity in this manner until all of the tools have been matched. *classification, language development*

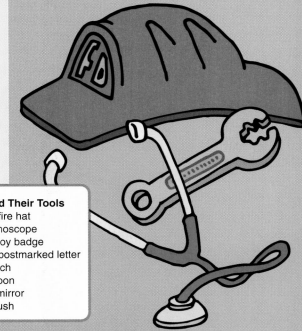

Helpers and Their Tools
Firefighter: toy fire hat
Doctor: toy stethoscope
Police Officer: toy badge
Postal Carrier: postmarked letter
Mechanic: wrench
Chef: mixing spoon
Dentist: dental mirror
Painter: paintbrush

Singing About Community Helpers

There's no better way to reinforce a concept than with a song! After discussing different types of community helpers and their tools, invite your preschoolers to join you in singing about them.

(sung to the tune of "Oscar Mayer Weiner Song")

Oh, I wish I were a helper like a [doctor]!
That is what I'd truly like to be.
'Cause if I were a helper like a [doctor],
I'd use a [stethoscope] so happily!

Sing additional verses, replacing the underlined words with other occupations and corresponding tools.

292

Job in a Box

Nurture youngsters' imaginations by putting together several career prop boxes. Read through the suggestions below. Gather the needed supplies and then place each set of community helper items in a separate box labeled with the name of the career. Encourage your preschoolers to dress up in the outfits and use the props to dramatize the profession. For added learning fun, see "Skilled Professionals" for suggestions on incorporating basic preschool skills into each prop box. ***dramatic play***

Career Boxes
Veterinarian: white button-down shirt (lab coat), stuffed dogs and cats, toy stethoscope, gauze, assortment of dog biscuits
Chef: apron, rolling pin, plastic mixing bowl, mixing spoon, muffin pans, muffin liners
Mechanic: overalls; tools and tool belt; toolbox; large bolts, nuts, and screws; toy cars and trucks
Eye Doctor: white button-down shirt (lab coat), empty bottles of eyedrops, eye chart, variety of plastic glasses frames without lenses

Skilled Professionals

Pack a little curriculum punch into your prop boxes with these skill-building suggestions!
Veterinarian: Have students sort the dog biscuits by size or color. ***sorting***
Chef: Encourage youngsters to use the muffin liners to create rows of patterns in the muffin pans. ***patterning***
Mechanic: Direct students to sort the bolts, nuts, and screws in the toolbox. Or have students seriate the tools by size. ***sorting, seriating by size***
Eye Doctor: Invite pairs of students to use the prop box. Have one child play the part of the patient and the other child pretend to be the doctor. Encourage the patient to identify the letters on the eye chart as the doctor points to them. ***letter identification***

Dressing the Part

Here's a display idea that shows off your preschoolers as professionals! Take a photo of each child dressed in the community helper outfit of his choice. (If desired, use the outfits and props from the career boxes described on page 293.) Glue each developed photo to a piece of colorful construction paper; then program each piece of paper with the name of the child's chosen career. Display the photos on a bulletin board; then add a title similar to the one shown. After looking at the display, everyone will agree—your preschoolers are dressed for success! *dramatic play*

"Look at me! Look at me! When I grow up, I want to be..."

a police officer   a businessperson   a doctor   a firefighter

a nurse   a ballerina   a chef   a sailor

Community Helpers Around the School

You don't need to travel far to find community helpers. There are several right inside the school building! Gather your youngsters together; then go on a community helper hunt around your school. For example, you might visit the custodian, media specialist, cafeteria manager, secretary, and director. Talk with each helper about his job and invite students to ask questions. Take a photograph of each helper; then compile the developed photos into a community helper class book. Set the book in your reading area for youngsters to enjoy independently. *language development, literacy*

Business As Usual!

Invite your preschoolers to explore the wonderful world of business with this idea! Set up a pretend office in your dramatic-play area by stocking it with items such as the following: briefcases, file boxes with hanging files, memo pads, toy telephones, child-size desks, sticky notes, and pencils. Add some "work clothes" such as clip-on ties, dress shirts, sports coats, and dresses. Invite each child to visit the area and get down to business! *dramatic play*

To the Zoo!

We've combined interesting animal facts with exciting cross-curricular activities to create one wild unit about the zoo—just for you!

ideas contributed by Roxanne LaBell Dearman
Western NC Early Intervention Program for Children Who
Are Deaf or Hard of Hearing
Charlotte, NC

Meet the Zookeeper
visual awareness

Who will guide your preschoolers through the zoo? The zookeeper! Make an enlarged color copy of the zookeeper pattern on page 301. Cut out the pattern and then laminate it. Before students arrive, use a dry-erase marker to copy "The Zookeeper's Tidbit" onto the zookeeper pattern. Then display the zookeeper in the appropriate area or center. Introduce each lesson by singing the song shown and directing students to find the zookeeper.

(sung to the tune of "Do You Know the Muffin Man?")

Oh, do you see the zookeeper,
The zookeeper, the zookeeper?
Oh, do you see the zookeeper?
Let's find out where he is!

Zoo Review
assessment

Your youngsters will learn a lot about animals with this unit. Help them remember all that animal information with a reproducible tracking sheet. Make a copy of page 300 for each child. After she completes each activity, invite her to color the corresponding animal on the sheet. When all of the animals are colored, recite the poem on the sheet and review each interesting animal tidbit!

The Zookeeper's Tidbit
An elephant uses its trunk to pick up things, break branches from trees, and put branches in its mouth. It also drinks by sucking water through its trunk and then squirting it into its mouth.

Imitating Elephants
dramatic play, movement

After showing students pictures of elephants and discussing "The Zookeeper's Tidbit" (above), encourage youngsters to act like elephants with the following song. As students sing each verse, have them use their arms as an elephant would use its trunk.

(sung to the tune of "The Mulberry Bush")

This is the way we [lift our trunks],
[Lift our trunks, lift our trunks].
This is the way we [lift our trunks]
Like elephants in the zoo!

Sing additional verses, replacing the underlined phrase with other actions, such as *take a drink, break a branch,* and *pick up things.*

The Zookeeper's Tidbit
Squirrel monkeys spend almost their entire lives living in trees. They rarely come down to the ground.

Fallen Monkeys
fine-motor development, counting

These little squirrel monkeys need help getting back to their trees! Obtain a set of monkeys from a Barrel of Monkeys game. Hide the monkeys in your sand table; then place two or three Easter egg trees near the table. (Or place bare tree branches in containers of play dough to use as trees.) Invite students to find the monkeys and hang them back on the trees. Then have youngsters count the monkeys in the trees before burying them in the sand for the next visitor to the center.

The Zookeeper's Tidbit
Kangaroo babies are called joeys. After a tiny joey is born, it lives in the mother's pouch for eight months.

Out of Pocket
letter-sound association or letter matching

These little joeys are lost! Invite youngsters to use their literacy skills to reunite the joeys with their mamas. In advance, gather a few child-size aprons with pockets. Then label each apron with a different letter you wish to reinforce. Next, create a class supply of joey cutouts by enlarging the kangaroo on page 300 and then photocopying it several times onto colored paper. Cut out the patterns and then program each one with a picture of an item that begins with a letter on an apron. Or, for younger students, program the joeys with letters that match those on the aprons.

To begin the activity, provide a few children with aprons to wear. Have them hop to the front of the class and pretend to be mama kangaroos. Next, provide the remaining children each with a joey. Have each child, in turn, hop to the matching kangaroo and place the joey in the pocket. Then encourage the mama kangaroos to confirm whether or not the joeys belong in their pockets.

The Zookeeper's Tidbit
Giraffes have excellent eyesight. Because their heads are up so high, they can see great distances.

Keep Your Eyes Peeled!
visual memory, cognitive development

Your little ones will need to use their eyesight in this activity—just like a giraffe! In advance, gather several different plastic animal figurines. Next, make a simple giraffe headband for each child in a small group. Have students wear the headbands and pretend to be giraffes. Display the plastic animals on a tray or table. Then direct your little giraffes to use their keen eyesight to observe the animals. Shield the tray or table from students' view and remove one of the figurines. Reveal the animals again and invite a child to identify the missing one. When students are familiar with this activity, set the materials in a center for pairs of youngsters to use independently.

Alligators and Crocodiles on the Loose!

visual discrimination, shape recognition, sorting

Searching for escaped alligators and crocodiles makes this shape activity all the more exciting! In advance, make a class supply of construction paper alligator and crocodile faces similar to the ones shown. While students are away, hide the faces around the room. Gather youngsters together and share "The Zookeeper's Tidbit" (above). Review rectangles and triangles with students. Then explain that the alligators and crocodiles have escaped from the zoo. Place two Hula-Hoop toys on the floor—one for alligators and one for crocodiles. Direct each child to find a missing reptile, identify it by the shape of its snout, and then place it in the appropriate hoop. Are you reptile hunters ready? Let the hunt begin!

Can You Spot the Snow Leopard?

The Zookeeper's Tidbit
Snow leopards have light-colored fur with dark spots. Their unique markings help them hide in the rock-covered mountainside as they sneak up on their prey.

Putting Spots on the Snow Leopard

creativity, fine-motor skills

There's no hiding it—making these snow leopards will bring out students' creativity! To begin, use a photocopier to enlarge the leopard on page 300. Cut out the enlarged leopard and then trace it onto a class supply of tan construction paper. Place the paper at your art center. Then add a variety of materials for making leopard spots, such as black construction paper, black paint, circular sponges, and black washable ink pads for fingerprints. Have each child use the medium of her choice to cover a leopard pattern with spots. When the spots are dry, help the child cut out the leopard pattern. Have her add construction paper eyes and a nose; then direct her to draw on a mouth and whiskers. Camouflage students' leopards on a bulletin board mountain scene and then add a title similar to the one shown.

Going to a Rock Hop
number identification, counting, gross-motor skills

Give students a jump on number identification and counting skills by having them do what a rockhopper penguin does best—hop on rocks! In advance, cut out ten construction paper rock shapes. Then use clear Con-Tact paper to adhere the rocks to the floor in a straight line. Program ten index cards, each with a different number from 1 to 10.

To begin the activity, have a child draw a card and identify the number. Then direct him to hop across that many rocks. As the little penguin hops, encourage the other children to count along. Continue the activity until each child has had a chance to hop like a penguin. One, two, three, four! Let's count as we hop across the floor!

Giving Patterns a Shake
patterning

Shaking and rattling will get youngsters' patterning skills on a roll! To prepare, cut out a long construction paper snake and a supply of diamond shapes in various colors. Then gather several shaker-type instruments. Set the materials at a center and invite a small group of students to join you. Review "The Zookeeper's Tidbit" (above) with them and then provide each child with a shaker. Have students observe carefully as you use the diamonds to create a pattern on the snake. If a diamond that does not belong on the pattern is placed, direct your preschoolers to shake a warning with their rattles—just like the eastern diamondback rattlesnake! Repeat the activity a few times; then invite a child to create a pattern as the other students observe and stand ready to rattle.

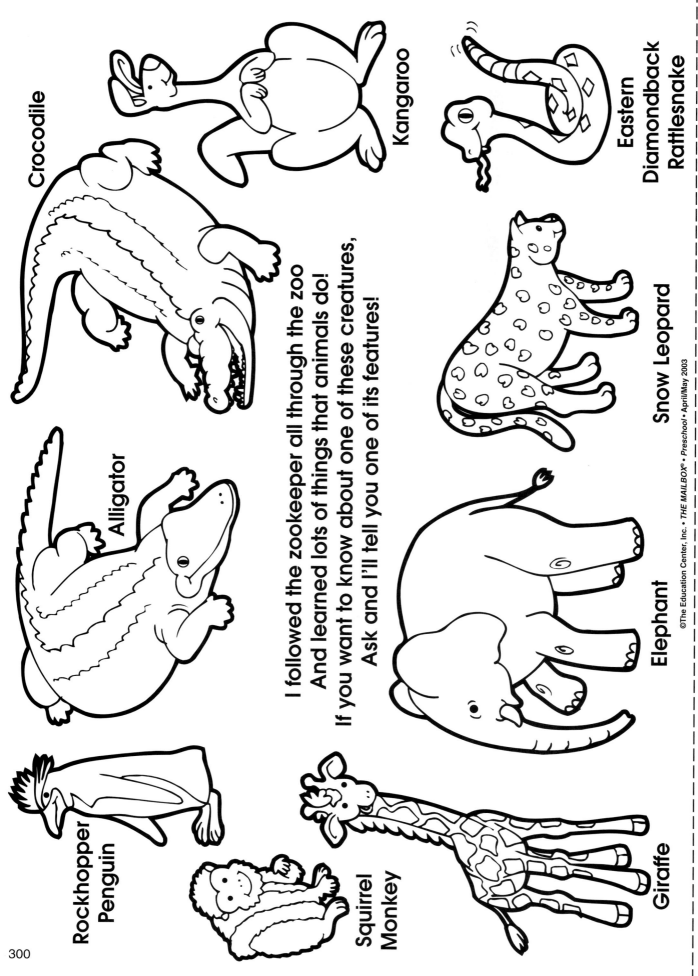

Crocodile

Kangaroo

Eastern Diamondback Rattlesnake

Snow Leopard

Alligator

I followed the zookeeper all through the zoo
And learned lots of things that animals do!
If you want to know about one of these creatures,
Ask and I'll tell you one of its features!

Elephant

Rockhopper Penguin

Squirrel Monkey

Giraffe

©The Education Center, Inc. • THE MAILBOX® • Preschool • April/May 2003

300

Note to the teacher: Use with "Zoo Review" on page 295 and with the activities on pages 296–298.

Night-Night!

Starlight, star bright, need ideas about the night? Your wish has been granted! The following night-themed activities will have your youngsters starry eyed about learning!

ideas contributed by Roxanne LaBell Dearman
Western NC Early Intervention Program for Children Who Are Deaf or Hard of Hearing
Charlotte, NC

Night

I like to look at the stars.   Luke

It's dark! Cecil

My dog barks a lot at night.   Eliza

Guess What!
thinking, classification, language development

Introduce the topic of nighttime with a group activity that gets youngsters guessing and discussing. In advance, pack a pillowcase with items related to night, such as a pair of pajamas, a night-light, die-cut stars, and a picture of the moon. As you remove each item from the pillowcase, invite students to identify it. Then have students guess what the items have in common. Introduce your nighttime theme and then lead students in a discussion about the night. If desired, use a white crayon to record students' comments on a black sheet of construction paper. Display the sheet in your classroom throughout your nighttime unit.

Before Bedtime
self-concept, language development

Reading a story, brushing teeth, good-night kisses—what are your youngsters' bedtime rituals? Find out with this simple song! Ask each child, in turn, to tell the class one thing she does before turning in for the night. Then incorporate her response into the song below.

(sung to the tune of "If You're Happy and You Know It")

Before I go to bed, I [brush my teeth]!
Before I go to bed, I [brush my teeth]!
Before I go to bed and lay down my sleepy head,
Before I go to bed, I [brush my teeth]!

Let's Count Sheep!
number identification, rote counting

Did you know that a little insomnia can do wonders for youngsters' math skills? Have each child dramatize a sleepless night; then prescribe that old remedy—counting sheep! In advance, make a page of sheep, as shown, for each number you wish to reinforce. Place the pages in a pillowcase. Gather a small group of students together and invite a child to pretend to wrestle with sleeplessness. Invite the remaining students to join you in saying the chant shown. After saying the chant, have the child pull a page out of the pillowcase and identify the number on it. Direct the child to make another attempt at sleeping while the group counts the sheep aloud. By the time students are finished counting, your little one should be fast asleep! Continue the activity in this manner until each child has had a chance to count sheep and fall asleep. That old remedy works every time!

Little [child's name] just can't sleep!
What should [she/he] do?
Let's count sheep!

Good-Night Mobile
literacy, rhyming words

Put a twinkle in youngsters' eyes with a moon mobile that reinforces rhyming words! Read *Goodnight Moon* by Margaret Wise Brown; then discuss the different rhyming words in the story. Next, work with one child at a time to create a mobile. First, provide the child with a tagboard moon cutout and two or three construction paper stars. Have the child name a pair of rhyming words for each star; then have her illustrate the words on the stars as shown. Tie the stars to the moon. Punch a hole in the top of the moon and thread a length of yarn through it to complete the mobile. Display the mobiles over your naptime area or have each child take her mobile home to hang over her bed. Encourage students to watch the spinning stars and bid each item good night. Before long, your preschoolers will be sound asleep—and familiar with rhyming words! Good night, bear! Good night, chair!

The Write Light
writing

Watching the light of fireflies is a popular night-time pastime. This friendly firefly won't light up the night, but it will light up youngsters' interest in writing. Make a supply of the writing strips on page 306. Program each strip with a different child's name or with a simple word. Photocopy each programmed strip to make a supply for your writing center. Next, tape a firefly cutout to the end of a yellow highlighter. Have youngsters light up the words by tracing over the words with the highlighter. To encourage creative writing, place blank pieces of paper and crayons at the center. Have students use the crayons to draw a picture and then use the highlighter to write about it.

It's Not All Bunk!
cognitive development, matching

Bunk beds are fun, but did you know that they can also help build a variety of preschool skills? Use this bunk bed adaptation of Concentration and embed some learning fun into your curriculum! To prepare, use the patterns on page 307 to make pairs of beds that have been programmed with the skills of your choice. Place the beds facedown on a table. Have students use the cards to play a game of Concentration. When a child finds a match, he sets the cards to the side and creates a bunk bed by placing one card over the other.

Pairing Up PJ's
visual discrimination, fine-motor skills

Put your preschoolers' visual discrimination skills to the test with this pajama matching activity. In advance, collect old pairs of pajama tops and bottoms; then place them in a pillowcase. Set the pillowcase near an empty laundry basket. Invite each child to match the tops with the bottoms, fold the pajamas, and then put them in the laundry basket. After the pj's have been paired up, direct the child to mix them up and then place them back in the pillowcase for the next child to use.

Oh, My Stars!

*letter, number,
or shape identification*

When your preschoolers look at the sky at night, what do they see? Stars! Create a starry night in your classroom and stargazing will not only be fun, it will sparkle with learning opportunities too! In advance, use a star-shaped hole punch to make letters, shapes, or numbers on pieces of black construction paper. Or use a yellow overhead marker to draw stars on overhead transparencies. Set up an overhead projector so it projects onto the ceiling of your classroom. Dim the lights and invite your preschoolers to participate in some stargazing. Place the paper or transparencies on the overhead projector, one at a time, and have students identify the letter, number, or shape created by the stars.

Many Moons

science knowledge, fine-motor development

In addition to stars, your preschoolers might also see the moon in the sky at night. Sometimes it's full. Sometimes it's crescent shaped. And sometimes it's not visible at all! Explain to your youngsters that the moon appears to change its shape in the sky and then show them reference book pictures of different phases of the moon. Next, make a simple chart showing the moon in three different phases: full, half, and crescent. Place the chart in your play dough area; then add several laminated mats with stars. Have students use the chart as a guide in making play dough moons in different phases. Then have youngsters place each moon on a starry mat. One small step for preschoolers, one giant leap into learning!

Writing Strips

Use with "The Write Light" on page 304.

307

From Trains to Planes!

Use the following transportation activities to drive, fly, and float into a fleet of learning fun!

ideas contributed by Sue Fleischmann
—Child and Family Specialist
Waukesha County Project Head Start, Waukesha, WI

Talking About Transportation
language development, graphing

Transportation is a big word for your little preschoolers. So begin your unit with an activity to help youngsters understand the concept of transportation. In advance, prepare a graph similar to the one shown. During your group time, have each child place his name on the graph to show how he came to school that day. Discuss the graph and explain that *transportation* is how we get from place to place. Next, sing the following song and then ask a child which is his favorite form of transportation. Continue singing the song until each child has had a chance to discuss his favorite way to get from here to there.

(sung to the tune of "Alouette")

Verse 1
Transportation!
What a fascination!
Transportation
Gets us from here to there!

Verse 2
Would you like to take a plane?
Would you like to take a train?
Ride a bike? Take a hike?
Go by car? There you are!
Oh!

Repeat Verse 1

Verse 3
Would you like to take a plane?
Would you like to take a train?
Ride a bike? Take a hike?
Go by boat? What's your vote?
Oh!

Repeat Verse 1

How did you get to school today?

	Sara	Cody		
	Twana	Lane		
Kyle	David	Shanti		
Sean	Tina	Bart		
walk	car	bus	bike	train

I Think I'll Ride...an Egg?
thinking, language development

What is and isn't transportation? Help little ones find out with this group activity that gets them giggling. In advance, cut out a variety of magazine pictures of different modes of transportation. Then cut out several pictures of objects that are not modes of transportation. Glue each picture onto a separate index card; then stack the cards in a pile. During your group time, begin saying the chant shown. As you say the last line, hold up a card from the stack. Then have students complete the sentence by naming the object in the picture. Discuss whether the named object would be a suitable mode of transportation; then continue the chant. As you make your way through the stack of cards, be prepared for giggles as your youngsters come across some silly suggestions for transportation!

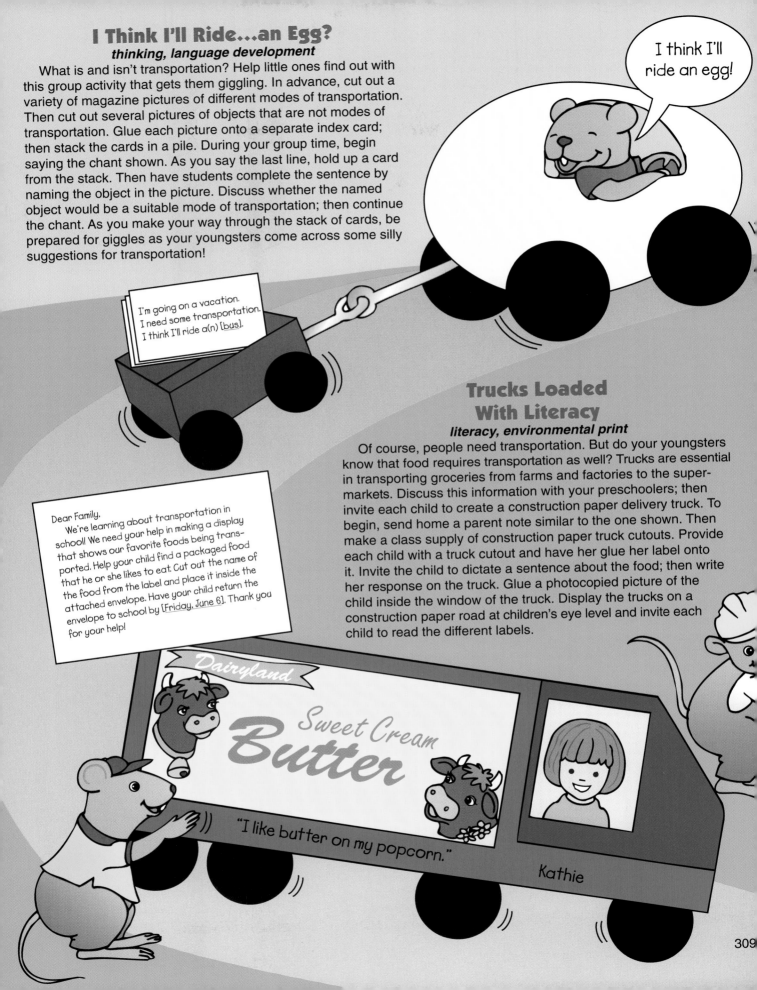

I think I'll ride an egg!

I'm going on a vacation.
I need some transportation.
I think I'll ride a(n) [bus].

Dear Family,
We're learning about transportation in school! We need your help in making a display that shows our favorite foods being transported. Help your child find a packaged food that he or she likes to eat. Cut out the name of the food from the label and place it inside the attached envelope. Have your child return the envelope to school by [Friday, June 6]. Thank you for your help!

Trucks Loaded With Literacy
literacy, environmental print

Of course, people need transportation. But do your youngsters know that food requires transportation as well? Trucks are essential in transporting groceries from farms and factories to the supermarkets. Discuss this information with your preschoolers; then invite each child to create a construction paper delivery truck. To begin, send home a parent note similar to the one shown. Then make a class supply of construction paper truck cutouts. Provide each child with a truck cutout and have her glue her label onto it. Invite the child to dictate a sentence about the food; then write her response on the truck. Glue a photocopied picture of the child inside the window of the truck. Display the trucks on a construction paper road at children's eye level and invite each child to read the different labels.

Dairyland

Sweet Cream **Butter**

"I like butter on my popcorn."

Kathie

Load, Load, Load the Boat
dramatic play, counting, spatial reasoning

Boats are a popular means of transportation for people and for things! So set up a pretend port at your water table and get ready for a flood of learning. To prepare, unsnap the tops from a variety of plastic toy boats. Place the bottom of each boat in your water table. Then set manipulatives, such as counting blocks and bears, near the table for students to use as cargo and passengers. Invite youngsters to load the boats and then transport the blocks and bears from one side of the water table to the other. As students load and unload the boats, encourage them to count the cargo or passengers on each boat. Toot! Toot! All ashore who's going ashore!

Transporting Treats
social development

Here's a snacktime idea that will give youngsters a real taste of transportation and also encourage cooperation. In advance, follow the recipe shown to make a batch of Peanut Butter Boulders. (Check with parents for student peanut allergies. If necessary, substitute soy nut butter for peanut butter.) Place the boulders in a large toy dump truck. During snacktime, seat youngsters at a table; then set the truck on the table. To serve the snack, push the truck toward a child. Have the child take a serving and then push the truck toward the next child. Encourage students to continue transporting the snack to one another until each child has been served.

Peanut Butter Boulders
(makes approximately 20 treats)

Ingredients:
¾ c. peanut butter
½ c. light corn syrup
¼ c. sugar

2½ c. Kellogg's Rice Krispies cereal
½ c. chocolate chips

Put the peanut butter in a large bowl. In a saucepan, mix the sugar and the corn syrup over medium heat. Bring to a boil; then remove from heat and pour over the peanut butter. Mix together well; then stir in the cereal and chocolate chips. Roll the mixture into small balls and place them on a sheet of waxed paper. When the balls have set, wrap each one in plastic wrap.

Go Ahead and Half It!

letter, number, or shape matching; positional words; language development

Is there any use for only half of a vehicle? There is in this group activity! To prepare, die-cut construction paper vehicles for half the number of students in your class. Cut each vehicle in half. Then program the halves of each vehicle with matching numbers, letters, or shapes. During your group time, provide each child with half of a vehicle. Instruct students to find their partners by matching the symbols programmed on each half. When the matches have been made, direct partners to sit together. Then invite each pair of students to identify their vehicle and the symbols on it. If desired, add more curriculum punch to the activity by discussing the front and back of a vehicle. Then have each child tell the class where she might go in her vehicle. Wow! Matching, positional words, and language opportunities. That's a lot of learning packed into half a vehicle!

Walk/Don't Walk

movement, literacy, safety

Don't overlook one of the most common modes of transportation—walking with your own two feet! This movement activity doubles as a safety lesson and helps youngsters remember that walking is a form of transportation. To prepare, make a Walk-Don't Walk sign similar to the one shown or similar to those seen in your area. Then head to the playground with your preschoolers. Discuss walking as a means of transportation and the importance of the Walk-Don't Walk sign. Then give youngsters an opportunity to practice reading the sign. Stand a short distance away from students so the sign can be easily seen. When the sign reads "Walk," have students quickly walk toward you. When the sign reads "Don't Walk," have students stand still. Keep flipping the sign between "Walk" and "Don't Walk" until the students reach you. Then invite a child to take a turn holding the sign and have the class repeat the activity. On your mark...get set...walk!

All Aboard!

dramatic play, writing

An airplane, a bus, and a train in your dramatic-play area? Sure! Just set up two rows of chairs and let little imaginations do the rest! To encourage early writing, place crayons, pencils, and strips of paper near the area and then invite students to make tickets. Add a puppet stand for a ticket booth and the transportation station is ready for business!

Vehicle Variety

Make color copies of the patterns on pages 313 and 314. Cut out the patterns. Laminate them and then use them to set up these simple learning opportunities! Youngsters' skills will soar from here to there!

- Attach a self-adhesive magnetic strip to the back of each pattern. Place several identical cars on a magnetic board and then add one car that is different. Have students identify the one that is different. *same and different*
- Place the vehicles at your math center. Invite each child to copy, continue, or create patterns with the vehicles. *patterning*
- Place pairs of vehicles in a stack. Invite students to use them to play a game of Concentration. *visual discrimination, taking turns*
- Place the vehicles in a center and invite each child to sort them by color or type. *sorting, classification*

Nice Wheels!

creativity, shape awareness, literacy

Conclude your transportation unit with an activity that stimulates preschoolers' creativity! Review the different modes of transportation covered in your unit; then invite each child to create an imaginary vehicle. To begin, stock your art center with construction paper shapes and small craft items. Provide each child with a large sheet of construction paper. Then invite her to create a vehicle by gluing the shapes and craft items onto the paper. Encourage the child to dictate a sentence or two about her creation; then write her response on her paper. Display students' vehicles on a wall and compliments are sure to come rolling in!

Marty's Car

"This is a bird car. It flies and drives."

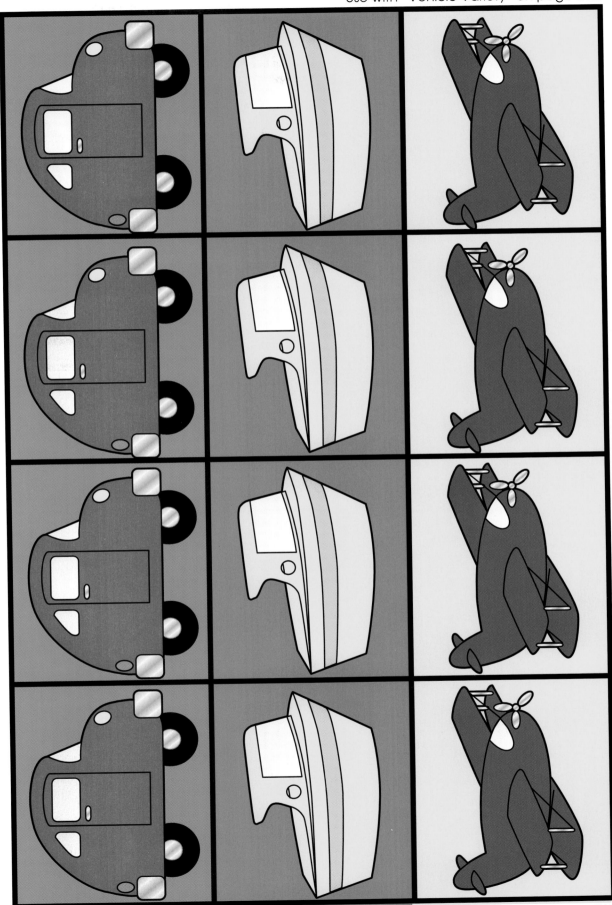

Vehicle Patterns

Use with "Vehicle Variety" on page 312.

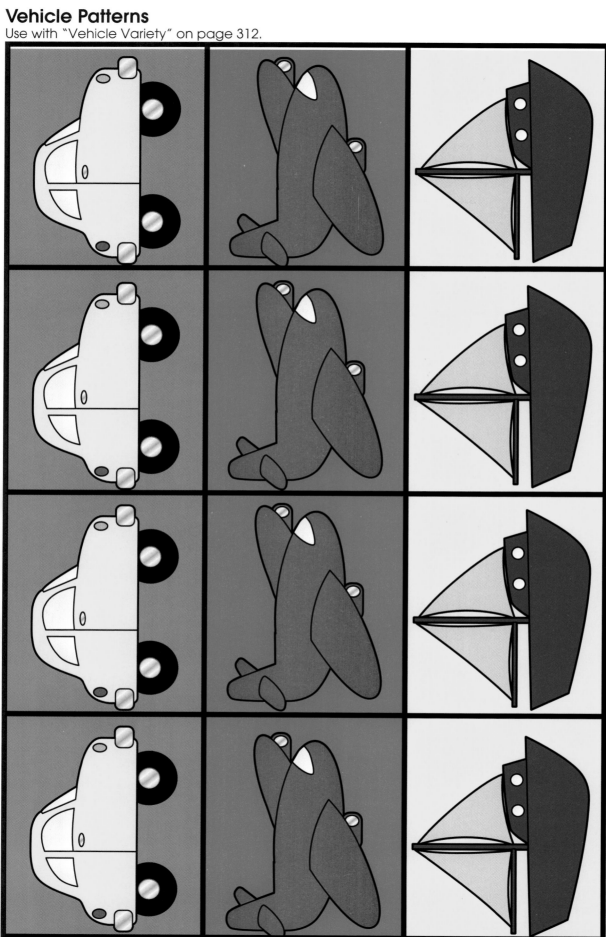